BEER LOVER'S the CAROLINAS

Best Breweries, Brewpubs & Beer Bars

★ DANIEL HARTIS ★

First Edition

gPP

Guilford, Connecticut

*To Airen, without whose patience this book
would not have been possible.*

All the information in this guidebook is subject to change. We
recommend that you call ahead to obtain current information
before traveling.

Copyright © 2014 Morris Book Publishing, LLC

All photos by Eric Gaddy unless otherwise noted.

Editor: Tracee Williams
Project Editor: Staci Zacharski
Layout Artist: Casey Shain
Text Design: Sheryl P. Kober
Maps: Alena Joy Pearce © Morris Book Publishing, LLC

ISBN 978-0-7627-7997-0

Printed in the United States of America
10 9 8 7 6 5 4 3 2 1

Contents

About the Author

Daniel Hartis was born and raised in the small town of Waxhaw, NC, just south of Charlotte. He didn't truly experience good beer, however, until he moved to Asheville to go to school. While working for the school paper, he was asked to write about the many microbreweries that called the city home.

After graduating, Daniel returned to Charlotte with a newfound interest in craft beer. In the years to come, Charlotte would see brewery after brewery pop up, and in 2011 Daniel founded CharlotteBeer.com, a site devoted to Charlotte's breweries, beer bars, and events. While that site is devoted to Charlotte's current craft beer climate, Daniel has also extensively researched the history of the city's brewing scene, and in 2013 he wrote *Charlotte Beer: A History of Brewing in the Queen City.*

When he is not drinking or writing about craft beer, he enjoys spending time with his wife, son, and daughter.

Acknowledgments

When you tell most people that you're writing a book about beer, they act as if you have hit the lottery. I can understand the sentiment. Who wouldn't want to be paid to visit breweries? Make no mistake: It *is* a dream job, but it's work just the same. And, of course, I'm not the only one who put in the work needed to see this book to completion.

First and foremost I have to thank my wife, Airen. During the time I spent chasing beers and brewery owners, photos, and other information, she was chasing around our two toddlers. It takes a special woman to afford a man so much time at bars and breweries, even if it is "work." If a glass be raised to anyone, it should be to her for allowing me the time to write this book in the first place. I have to thank our wonderful kids, Grayson and Claire, who also let daddy write when he could have been playing instead. One day many, many years from now, perhaps I'll buy you both a beer to make up for it.

I am grateful for all the brewers and owners who so graciously shared with me their stories, or made time for me when they had little for themselves. The logistics of planning so many visits under a tight deadline made for lots of quick visits, often on busy weekends. I visited many breweries for the first time, but it certainly won't be the last! I appreciate every person who took the time to speak with me or allow us in to take photos.

Speaking of photos, a huge debt of gratitude goes to Eric Gaddy, whose photos appear throughout the book. Eric accompanied me on most of my travels, serving not only as a photographer but also as a friend and frequent supplier of conversation, jokes, water, and oft-needed antacid. Eric helped make memorable the time on the road, and often we had just as much fun on the way to the breweries as we did at the breweries themselves. I hope Eric's photos bring you a little closer to all of these destinations, even if you can't visit them all yourself.

We visited almost all of the spots listed in this book, which gave me a firsthand look and allowed me to write confidently about the people, breweries, and beers herein. Occasionally I had to look back at some other works to confirm small details, and I owe a debt of gratitude to my fellow beer writers: Anne-Fitten Glenn, author of *Asheville Beer: An Intoxicating History of Mountain Brewing*; Timmons Pettigrew, author of *Charleston Beer: A High-Gravity History of Lowcountry Brewing*; Erik Lars Myers, author of *North Carolina Craft Beer and Breweries*; and Dave Tollefsen and

Glenn Cutler, whom most know as the NC Beer Guys and founders of the very popular NCBeerGuys.com. I am proud to call all of them my colleagues, and encourage you to check out their work as well.

Of course, I have to thank the Globe Pequot Press for asking me to write the book. As this and their other Beer Lover's volumes show, this is a publisher that really values its readers and takes great pains to ensure they put out the best product possible. A special thanks goes to my editor, Tracee Williams, for her knowledge and patience during the entire process.

And lastly, I have to thank *you* for reading this book. Just as our thirst for local craft beer has led to scores of breweries springing up in both Carolinas, so too does it inspire a project like this one. Whether you're a brewer, distributor, bartender, retailer, representative, drinker, or reader, you have played a part in bringing this book to life. The craft beer industry is nothing without its people, and I thank you.

Introduction

As a lifelong North Carolinian, I've spent my entire life visiting spots across my home state as well as South Carolina. My beer experience, however, had been fairly myopic before writing this book. I've lived in Charlotte for most of my life, and know its beer scene very well. I went to school in Asheville, and I owe a special debt of gratitude to that city for turning me on to craft beer in the first place. But aside from these two cities and a handful of other individual breweries, I had yet to really explore all that the Carolinas had to offer.

Don't make that same mistake.

North Carolina boasts more breweries than any other Southern state. The state has developed a reputation as a serious beer state thanks in part to the many breweries that call Asheville home, and to the masses that successfully voted Asheville as "Beer City USA" for three years running in an online poll. That city's beer scene is just the tip of the iceberg, though, as you can find breweries large and small across the Old North State, in small towns and bustling metropolises alike.

And North Carolina's neighbor to the South is no slouch, either. More and more breweries are popping up in South Carolina, and the passing of the "pint bill" has made the breweries themselves greater destinations by allowing visitors to enjoy full pints at the breweries, rather than just small samples with tours. Like North Carolina, the state boasts a mix of new and old breweries. Some are in small towns, and others in larger cities like Greenville, Columbia, and Charleston.

There has long been a playful contention between the two Carolinas, as if merely crossing the border signified some polar shift of values or culture. We're not so different, though. North and South Carolina are states united by mountains and beaches, with rolling foothills in between. We both love our 'cue, even if we have different ideas about how to prepare it. And greater than all these is our love for good beer made locally.

While touring all over both states, it became clear to me that I was no longer drinking Charlotte beer, Asheville beer, or whatever label we apply to these smaller beer scenes. No, I was drinking beer brewed in the Carolinas, a beautiful pair of states home not just to hundreds of destinations for beer but also the wonderful people that produce it, serve it, sell it, distribute it, and drink it. A trip like the one I took makes you rethink community, and I can say with no hesitation that the Carolina beer community is one of the finest in the nation.

In my first book, I noted that chronicling Charlotte's beer scene was a bit like trying to hit a moving target. Imagine how I felt when tasked with writing about breweries and beer bars across two states instead of just one city. Suddenly, I needed to hit lots of little targets, with new ones springing up every month or so.

You will find most of the new breweries in this book, though there's a chance one or two may have opened up by the time this book is published. And that's a great thing. The beer scene in the Carolinas is ever changing, and we the beer drinkers are fortunate for that. Please use this guide in your travels, but know that new breweries, brewpubs, and beer bars are always on the horizon. An appendix in the back of this book lists many of the breweries that have, at the time of this writing, not yet opened. Keep an eye out for them and make it a point to see what they are bringing to the Carolinas.

I know I will.

How to Use This Guide

This book was written to serve as a comprehensive guide to the beer scene in North and South Carolina. Both states lay claim to a wealth of excellent beer destinations, and in writing this book I quickly learned that visiting all of them is quite the challenge. That being said, it is a challenge very much worth pursuing, and this book is organized in a way that should make the journey a little easier.

The breweries, brewpubs, and beer bars featured in *Beer Lover's the Carolinas* are organized alphabetically according to their city or region. In North Carolina, this means a look at establishments in Asheville, Western North Carolina, the Foothills, the Triad, Charlotte, Raleigh, the Triangle, Eastern North Carolina, and Coastal North Carolina. South Carolina is broken down into four sections: Upstate South Carolina, the Midlands, Charleston, and the Lowcountry. Not all places fit neatly into any one geographical scene, but the book is structured in a way that makes the most sense for anyone visiting these areas.

The book distinguishes between breweries and brewpubs. Breweries usually brew and package their beer for distribution to off-premise accounts, though most do have taprooms where you can sample their beers. Brewpubs, on the other hand, typically sell their beer only at that location and often have a kitchen or a restaurant component. That is painting with a broad brush, though, as there are breweries that only sell their beer at the taproom and brewpubs that distribute theirs to other accounts as well.

Brewery sections offer a brief account of that brewery's history and philosophy, as well as a description of the atmosphere of the location and the beers offered there. Tasting notes are provided for a handful of beers at each brewery, but do not feel confined to trying just those recommended. Everyone has different tastes, so order up a flight and explore all these breweries have to offer!

For each brewery, a Beer Lover's Pick is also listed. Sometimes such beers are flagships or year-round beers that are easy to find on tap or in bottles, while other times they are seasonals or special releases that are a bit tougher to track down. It may be that the beer is a perfect, dead-on example of its respective style, or it could be something so creative and innovative that you would be remiss not to try it. Whatever the beer, though, the Beer Lover's Pick represents a shining achievement that you must try if you come across it.

The brewpub sections are laid out in much the same way as the breweries, though they do include food recommendations when applicable. Some of the best beer bars in the state are profiled as well, though with as many as we have in North and South Carolina, some inevitably were left out.

The breweries and bars listed in this book span many miles across two states, and I probably spent more time on the road between them than I did at the establishments themselves. If you are looking to keep it simple and hit a select few destinations all within walking distance of one another, you will enjoy the pub crawl features. You will find a crawl listed for the beautiful South Carolina city of Charleston, and in North Carolina there are crawl routes for Asheville, Charlotte, and Raleigh.

In addition to providing short guides for all of breweries, brewpubs and beer bars, you will also find chapters on:

Beer Festivals: Some of the finest beer festivals in the nation take place in North and South Carolina. The festivals listed herein are ones that take place every year, almost always during the months they are listed under. This section should help in planning your beer events for the year. Keep your ears open for others, too, as new beer festivals are being planned all the time.

BYOB: Brew Your Own Beer: Almost all professional brewers got their start homebrewing on a much smaller scale. In this book's "Brew Your Own Beer" section, you will find a comprehensive listing of homebrew shops in the area. In most cases, these shops have everything you need to brew as well as friendly staff that can help you along, whether you are a beginner looking to start with extract or a seasoned all-grain homebrewer. Following the listing of shops, you will find a selection of clone beer recipes that will give you the opportunity to clone some of the best beers in the Carolinas.

In the Kitchen: Beer pairs well with a number of foods, and it can also be used to enhance dishes. The "In the Kitchen" section features recipes from breweries and brewpubs that incorporate their beer. You might be surprised at how versatile a cooking ingredient it is when used in everything from appetizers to entrees, dressings to desserts. Use the beer that is recommended when you can, but feel free to substitute a beer in the same style if the beer that is listed is not available to you.

Glossary of Terms

ABV: Alcohol by volume—the percentage of alcohol in a beer. A typical mass-market domestic beer is a little less than 5 percent ABV.

Ale: Beer brewed with top fermenting yeast. Ales are quicker to brew than lagers, which can require weeks of aging at cold temperatures. Popular styles of ales include pale ales, amber ales, stouts, and porters.

Altbier: A German style of ale, typically brown in color, smooth, and malty.

Barleywine: Not a wine at all but a high-ABV ale that originated in England. English versions are usually sweeter than American versions, which are often brewed with more hops.

Barrel of beer: Production of beer is measured in barrels. A barrel equals 31 gallons.

Beer: An alcoholic beverage brewed with malt, water, hops, and yeast.

Beer bar: A bar that focuses on carrying craft or fine imported beers.

Bitter: An English bitter is an English-style ale, more hoppy than an English mild, but less hoppy than an IPA.

Bock: A German-style lager, typically stronger than the typical lager.

Bomber: Most beers are packaged in 12-ounce bottles. Bombers are 22-ounce bottles.

Brewpub: Typically a restaurant, but sometimes a bar, that brews its own beers on premises.

Cask: Also known as real ales, cask ales are naturally carbonated and are usually served with a hand pump rather than forced out with carbon dioxide or nitrogen.

Clone beer: A homebrew recipe based on a commercial beer.

Contract brewery: A company that does not have its own brewery and pays someone else to brew and bottle its beer.

Craft beer: High-quality, flavorful beer made by small breweries.

Double: The word double most often refers to a higher-alcohol version of a beer, most typically used in reference to a double, or imperial, IPA. It can also be used as an American translation of a Belgian dubbel, a style of Belgian ale.

ESB: Extra special bitter. A traditional malt-heavy English pub ale with low bitterness, usually served on cask.

Gastropub: A beer-centric bar or pub that exhibits the same amount of care selecting its foods as it does its beers.

Growler: A half-gallon jug of beer. Many brewpubs sell growlers of their beers to go.

Gypsy brewer: A company that does not own its own brewery, but rents space at an existing brewery to brew it themselves.

Hops: Hops are flowers used in beers to produce aroma, bitterness, and flavor. Nearly every beer in the world has hops.

IBU: International bittering units, which are used to measure how bitter a beer is.

Imperial: A higher-alcohol version of a regular-strength beer.

IPA: India pale ale. A popular style of ale created in England that has taken a decidedly American twist over the years. Often bitter, thanks to more hops used than in other styles of beer.

Kölsch: A light, refreshing German-style ale.

Lager: Beer brewed with bottom-fermenting yeast. Lagers take longer to produce than ales. Popular styles of lagers include black lagers, doppelbocks, pilsners, and Vienna lagers.

Malt: Typically barley malt, but sometimes wheat malt. Malt provides the fermentable sugar in beers. The more fermentable sugar, the higher the ABV in a beer. Without malt, a beer would be too bitter from the hops.

Microbrewery: A brewery that brews fewer than 15,000 barrels of beer a year.

Nanobrewery: A brewery that brews four barrels of beer per batch or less.

Nitro draft: Most beers that are served on draft use kegs pressurized with carbon dioxide. Occasionally, particularly with stouts, nitrogen is used, which helps create a creamier body.

Pilsner: A style of German or Czech lager, usually light in color. Many mass-produced beers are based on this style.

Porter: A dark ale, similar to the stout but with less roasted characters.

Pounders: 16-ounce cans.

Quad: A strong Belgian-style ale, typically sweet and high in alcohol.

Regional brewery: A brewery that brews up to 6 million barrels of beer a year.

Russian imperial stout: A stout is a dark, heavy beer. A Russian imperial stout is a higher-alcohol, thicker-bodied version of regular stouts.

Saison: Also known as a Belgian or French farmhouse ale. It can be fruity, and it can also be peppery. Usually refreshing.

Seasonal: A beer that is brewed only at a certain time of year to coincide with the seasons.

Session beer: A low-alcohol beer, one you can have several of in one long drinking "session."

Stout: A dark beer brewed with roasted malts.

Strong ale: A style of ale that is typically both hoppy and malty and can be aged for years.

Tap takeover: An event where a bar or pub hosts a brewery and has several of its beers on tap.

Triple (Tripel): A Belgian-style ale, typically lighter in color than a dubbel but higher in alcohol.

Wheat beer: Beers, such as hefeweizens and witbiers, that are brewed using wheat malt along with barley malt.

Yeast: The living organism in beer that causes the sugars to ferment and become alcohol.

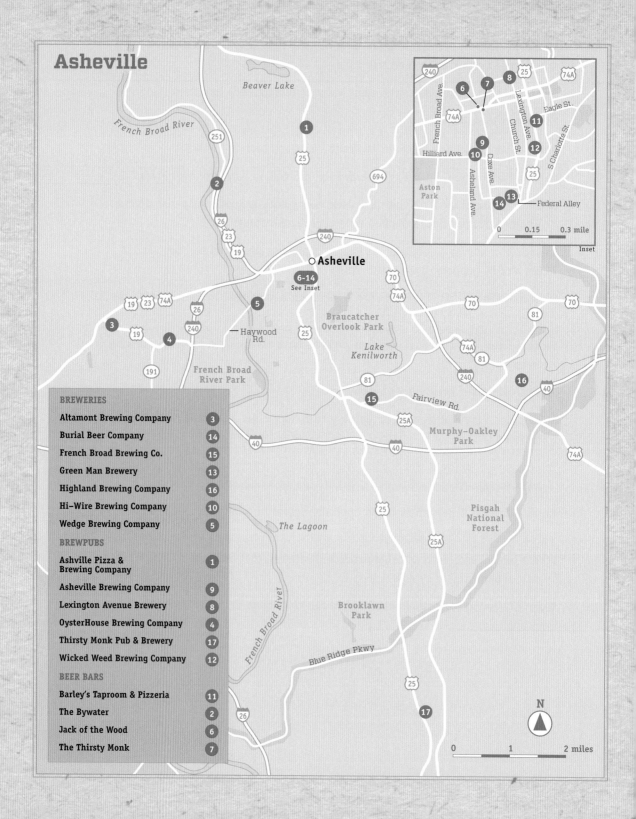

Asheville

Beaver Lake

French Broad River

Asheville

6-14
See Inset

Braucatcher Overlook Park

Lake Kenilworth

Haywood Rd.

French Broad River Park

Fairview Rd.

Murphy-Oakley Park

The Lagoon

Pisgah National Forest

French Broad River

Brooklawn Park

Blue Ridge Pkwy

Inset

French Broad Ave.

Hilliard Ave.

Asheland Ave.

Doxe Ave.

Lexington Ave.

Church St.

Eagle St.

S Charlotte St.

Federal Alley

Aston Park

0   0.15   0.3 mile

Inset

BREWERIES

Altamont Brewing Company	3
Burial Beer Company	14
French Broad Brewing Co.	15
Green Man Brewery	13
Highland Brewing Company	16
Hi-Wire Brewing Company	10
Wedge Brewing Company	5

BREWPUBS

Ashville Pizza & Brewing Company	1
Asheville Brewing Company	9
Lexington Avenue Brewery	8
OysterHouse Brewing Company	4
Thirsty Monk Pub & Brewery	17
Wicked Weed Brewing Company	12

BEER BARS

Barley's Taproom & Pizzeria	11
The Bywater	2
Jack of the Wood	6
The Thirsty Monk	7

N

0   1   2 miles

Asheville

The mountain city of Asheville is a haven for anyone who appreciates true beauty, whether that beauty comes in the form of the arts, Mother Nature's breathtaking views, or a pint of beer. While Asheville receives a variety of accolades every year from many sources, it has for years enjoyed a serious reputation as one of the nation's best beer cities. Asheville is frequently mentioned in the same breath as established beer destinations like Portland and San Diego, and for good reason. Asheville boasts a similar beer culture, but with far fewer residents. It has one of the highest numbers of breweries per capita in the nation, and that ratio only stands to grow as more breweries open their doors.

Breweries

ALTAMONT BREWING COMPANY

1042 Haywood Rd., Asheville, NC 28806; (828) 575-2400; AltamontBrewingCompany.com
Founded: 2011 **Founders:** Gordon Kear, Ben Wiggins **Brewer:** Gordon Kear **Flagship Beer:** India Pale Ale **Year-Round Beers:** India Pale Ale, Pale Ale **Seasonals/Special Releases:** Hefeweizen, Porter, Pale Ale, ESB, Golden Ale **Tours:** No **Taproom:** Mon through Sun, 2 p.m. to 2 a.m.

Though Thomas Wolfe's *Look Homeward, Angel* was set in the fictionalized town of Altamont, that town and its people were based on his hometown of Asheville. Some friends and family felt they were painted in an unfair light in the novel, a situation he also deals with in a later novel appropriately titled, *You Can't Go Home Again*.

Gordon Kear went to school at Warren Wilson College in Swannanoa, a neighboring town to Asheville. A few years after college he moved to Arizona to become a brewer for Flagstaff Brewing Company, where he worked for around six years before he, too, began to look homeward. With Ben Wiggins, whom he had first met at Warren Wilson, he founded the Altamont Brewing Company in West Asheville. When

they opened in January of 2011, Altamont was simply a neighborhood bar filled with a table-tennis table and, quite often, live bands. From day one, though, the plan was to eventually brew beer in the building that dated back to 1937. They poured their first Altamont beer in December of 2012. The brewery's seven-barrel brewhouse and fermenting tanks now sit just past the table-tennis table.

Of the brewery's 16 taps, four are usually pouring the brewery's beers, with the other 12 taps devoted to more craft options (with lots of local love). The **Pale Ale** is a milder take on the West Coast style, with lots of citrus and grapefruit but little bitterness. The **Porter,** on the other hand, actually seems to have more bitterness than most examples of the style, but it works very well with the chocolate and roasted coffee flavors. A good warm weather option is the brewery's **Hefeweizen,** which has the bubblegum and clove notes you expect of the German style, but a cleaner finish more reminiscent of an American wheat beer. Altamont frequently will have "charity beers" on, with a portion of that beer's sales benefitting a nonprofit. They also host monthly events benefiting area schools. The way Gordon and his brewery have embraced their local community just goes to show Thomas Wolfe wasn't always right—sometimes you *can* go home again.

Beer Lover's Pick

India Pale Ale

Style: India pale ale
ABV: 6 percent
Availability: On tap year-round
If you enjoy Altamont Brewing Company's Pale Ale but long for a little more hop flavor and bitterness, reach for their IPA. Like the pale, the IPA is in the West Coast camp, with notes of tangerine, grapefruit, and pine. It has a lighter body and is quite refreshing, an ideal beer to have while sitting back and enjoying a live band at the brewery.

BURIAL BEER COMPANY

40 Collier Ave., Asheville, NC 28801; (828) 475-2739; BurialBeer.com; @BurialBeer
Founded: 2013 **Founders:** Tim Gormley, Doug Reiser, Jess Reiser **Brewers:** Tim Gormley, Doug Reiser **Flagship Beer:** Scythe Rye Pale Ale **Year-Round Beers:** Scythe Rye Pale Ale, Hatchet NC Lager, Hacksaw Dark Lager, Billhook Farmhouse Ale, Pitchfork Saison, Reaper Tripel, Voorhamer Imperial Stout **Seasonals/Special Releases:** Bucksaw Belgian IIPA, Drawknife Dubbel, Tomahawk Mountain Ale, Skillet Donut Stout, Millstone White IPA, Cultivator Fresh Hop Black IPA, Spade IPA, Matchstick Petite Abbey, Twine Fresh Hop Saison **Tours:** No **Taproom:** Thurs and Fri, 4 to 10 p.m.; Sat, 2 to 8 p.m.

Burial Beer Company is yet another brewery in Asheville's beer-rich South Slope neighborhood, an area they share with Green Man Brewing, Hi-Wire Brewing and Asheville Brewing Company. The three founders—Tim Gormley and Doug and Jess Reiser—are no strangers to areas with a high concentration of breweries. They all met in Seattle and, after taking a trip to Belgium together in 2010, knew they wanted to open a brewery together. They all relocated to Asheville, a city they thought could support even more good beer.

Through their beers and the brewery itself, the three have done much to distinguish Burial Beer from its compatriots. They set up shop in a tiny brick warehouse and constructed their brewery using what they call a "new farmhouse" aesthetic. They used tin from an old barn to mimic a barn's ceiling inside the taproom, and then used that same tin to wrap the bottom of the bar. On white brick walls hang rusted, antique farm tools, which are also used as tap handles (most of the beers are named after farm tools as well). The brewery's small one-barrel system sits in the room next to the taproom, which also holds a couple of barrels. Out back, there is a small outdoor section with a few tables and chairs. There is a vending machine, too, but don't expect to grab a bag of chips. The machine is filled with much miscellany: action figures, toothpaste, empty whiskey bottles, a

Billhook Farmhouse Ale
Style: Saison
ABV: 7 percent
Availability: On tap year-round
The brewers at Burial Beer consider themselves ambassadors of a "new farmhouse" style, so you know they take a lot of inspiration from Belgium's farmhouse ales and saisons. The Billhook Farmhouse Ale departs from tradition a bit in that is brewed with Nelson Sauvin, Pacific Jade, and Motueka hops from New Zealand. These hops combine to create notes of citrus fruit, melon rind, and white grape, and all of these flavors work well with the dry saison base. Kiwis are added as well to add tartness, resulting in a beer that is as complex as it is refreshing.

Asheville

discarded pizza crust and more. And yes, the machine works, but you'd do better to spend your money on the beers inside.

Most of the beers brewed at Burial fall under three categories: German lagers, Belgian ales, and American styles. The brewery's flagship, the **Scythe Rye Pale Ale,** is as good a choice as any. Notes of pine and grapefruit pair well with rye malt, which contributes a nice spiciness, and the beer has a crisp, fresh quality to it. The **Hacksaw Dark Lager** is a far smoother beer than its name implies, with just a bit of roast and dark bread. One of the brewery's most sought after beers is the **Skillet Donut Stout,** which is brewed with the brewery's own exclusive coffee blend from Biltmore Coffee Traders.

The small space on Collier Avenue is just the beginning for Burial Beer Company, as the three hope to open a larger farmhouse-style taproom and production brewery in the coming years.

FRENCH BROAD BREWING CO.

101-D Fairview Rd., Asheville, NC 28803; (828) 277-0222; FrenchBroadBrewery.com; @FrenchBroadBrew

Founded: 2001 **Founder:** Andrew Dahm **Brewer:** Aaron Wilson **Flagship Beer:** Wee-Heavy-Er Scotch Ale **Year-Round Beers:** 13 Rebels ESB, Gateway Kölsch, IPA, Rye Hopper, Anvil Porter, Wee-Heavy-Er Scotch Ale **Seasonals/Special Releases:** Zepptemberfest **Tours:** By appointment **Taproom:** Mon through Sun, 1 to 8 p.m.

Just outside Biltmore Village is the French Broad Brewing Co., one of Asheville's oldest breweries. Established in 2001, the brewery is perhaps best known for its **Wee-Heavy-Er Scotch Ale.** The taproom is small, and it becomes even smaller on the nights live bands take to the tasting room stage. That usually happens from Thursday through Saturday, as the 25-seat taproom—or "listening room," as they call it—is a great place to sit back and enjoy live music with a beer brewed just feet away. Color-changing lights reflect a variety of colors off of the fishscale fermenting tanks as well as the shiny disco ball above them.

13 Rebels ESB
Style: Extra special bitter
ABV: 5.2 percent
Availability: Year-round on tap and in bottles and cans

13 Rebels ESB is named for those 13 rebellious colonies that broke away from England, where the Extra Special Bitter style originated. French Broad's take on the style isn't so rebellious, thanks to the use of Goldings hops from across the pond. The malt steals the show in this beer, though, contributing notes of toast, biscuit, and caramel. With beers like these in England, why did our original colonists leave in the first place?

Andrew Dahm opened Asheville Brewing Supply, a local homebrew store, in 1994. When 2001 rolled around many years later and his friend Jonas Rembert from Jack of the Wood was looking to start his own brewery, Andrew joined him. They opened with the intention of producing European styles and have, for the most part, stayed true to that vision. Their **Gateway Kölsch** is a perfect beer for novices and longtime craft beer drinkers alike, with notes of bread, honey, and freshly cut grass. At French Broad, they have been brewing **Rye Hopper** long before it became trendy to brew with this spicy grain. The beer's slightly peppery quality works well with its sweet malt base. The previously mentioned **Wee-Heavy-Er Scotch Ale** pours dark brown, with notes of caramel, toffee, brown sugar, and just the tiniest bit of smoke.

French Broad Brewing recently started canning several of their beers and getting their 22-ounce bottles out into new markets. You can find French Broad's beers across North Carolina and into Tennessee, as well as Georgia, Alabama, Louisiana, and Missouri.

GREEN MAN BREWERY

23 Buxton Ave., Asheville, NC 28801; (828) 252-5502; GreenManBrewery.com; @Green
ManBrewing

Founded: 1997 **Founders:** Joe Eckert, Joan Cliney-Eckert **Brewers:** John Stuart, Mike
Karnowski, Tyler Downey **Flagship Beer:** Green Man IPA **Year-Round Beers:** Green Man
IPA, ESB, Pale Ale, Porter **Seasonals/Special Releases:** The Dweller, Rainmaker Double
IPA, Harvester, Wheat, Stout, Wayfarer White IPA **Tours:** No **Taproom:** Mon through
Thurs, 3 to 9 p.m.; Fri through Sat, 2 to 10 p.m.; Sun, 3 to 9 p.m.

"The Green Man" is not just a name given to English pubs, but also a common
motif seen throughout many of the world's cultures. It is most often seen
as a symbol of rebirth, which is fitting since Green Man Brewery helped to kick off
Asheville's own brewing renaissance. Green Man Brewery is Asheville's second oldest

Beer Lover's Pick

The Dweller
Style: Imperial stout
ABV: 7.5 percent
Availability: Seasonal
The Dweller is so named because
this imperial stout lurked in
the brewery's cellar for so long
that the brewers felt it a fitting
moniker. They brought it out
for the first time in 2012 and
made it the first Green Man beer
to be bottled. That first batch
was 9.5 percent and subsequent
batches have been 7.5 percent,
but no matter the vintage you
can expect notes of roasted coffee, dark chocolate, raisins, and
tobacco. Drink it fresh, or let
it dwell in your own cellar for a
special occasion.

brewery, opening just a few years after Highland. And, like Highland, they have their origins in a local bar. Whereas Highland got its start in the basement of Barley's Taproom, the Green Man Brewery first brewed in the Jack of the Wood pub for many years before moving out in 2005 and finding its own space just down the road on Buxton Avenue.

The tasting room portion of the brewery is now referred to as Dirty Jack's, and if you visit today you're likely to see a lot of lighthearted nods to the Green Man motif. Look closely enough and you will find legendary green men like Shrek, Hulk, Robin Hood, and Green Lantern. Plenty of green paint and other verdant decor help bring the theme home in a fun and comfortable space. On one side of the tasting room is a nice covered patio with lights strung overhead; on the other is a warehouse space that holds Green Man's 30-barrel brewhouse. This system is much larger than the seven-barrel one Green Man started with at Jack of the Wood, but it is needed to get Green Man's beers to market. They now distribute their IPA, ESB, and Porter in six-packs, as well as the occasional seasonal in 750-ml bottles.

The **ESB** is one of the original beers that Green Man has brewed since 1997, and it's one of the most authentic extra special bitters this side of the pond. It is immensely drinkable, with notes of almond and toffee derived from British-grown malts. Green Man's **Porter** is another spot-on attempt at a British style. This English porter is smooth and refined, with notes of bittersweet chocolate and an earthiness that makes this one an easy drinker.

HIGHLAND BREWING COMPANY

12 Old Charlotte Hwy., Ste. H, Asheville, NC 28803; (828) 299-3370; HighlandBrewing
.com; @HighlandBrews
Founded: 1994 **Founder:** Oscar Wong **Brewers:** John Lyda, Joey Justice **Flagship
Beer:** Gaelic Ale **Year-Round Beers:** Gaelic Ale, St. Terese's Pale Ale, Kashmir
IPA, Oatmeal Porter, Black Mocha Stout **Seasonals/Special Releases:** Razor Wit,
Clawhammer Oktoberfest, Cold Mountain Winter Ale, Thunderstruck Coffee Porter, Little
Hump Spring Ale, Devil's Britches IPA **Tours:** Mon through Fri, 4 and 4:45 p.m.; Sat, 2:45,
3:30, 4, and 4:45 p.m. **Taproom:** Mon through Fri, 4 to 8 p.m.; Sat, 2 to 8 p.m.

Now one of North Carolina's largest production breweries, Highland Brewing Company began life as a motley assemblage of pieced-together dairy equipment in the basement of Barley's Taproom in Asheville. When founder Oscar Wong opened the brewery in 1994, Highland became the city's first brewery since Prohibition.

They have grown tremendously since that time. One of the largest shifts came when they left their small, dank space beneath Barley's and moved into a 35,000-square-foot building that previously housed Blue Ridge Motion Pictures.

They continued to focus on production for many years, installing a 50-barrel brew-house and enough fermenting tanks to produce up to 50,000 barrels annually. In 2010, they dressed the front of the building up with landscaping and a beautiful patio, and they left no stone unturned when it came time to build out a tasting room inside as well. From the bar, you can see the brewery's three-barrel pilot system, on which are crafted small batch "Brewer's Stache" beers that are usually only served in the tasting room. Here they also frequently have barrel-aged beers or cask beers on tap.

As big as they have grown, however, Highland has still stayed true to its roots. They continue to brew favorites like their iconic **Gaelic Ale** as well as four additional year-round beers. The **Oatmeal Porter** is incredibly smooth, with notes of chocolate, coffee, and a creaminess from the oats. They brew old favorites from the past while adding new ones nearly every year, such as the **Thunderstruck Coffee Porter,** a beer brewed with coffee from Dynamite Roasting Company in nearby Black Mountain.

Highland has always been committed to Asheville, and they have created a beautiful space for people to enjoy their beers. In a meadow beside the brewery, they added a large outdoor stage as well as an outdoor bar fashioned out of an old shipping container. The brewery hosts a variety of events and concerts here throughout the year. Tours are free, but the brewery appreciates donations (cash or canned food) to Manna Food Bank. Highland continues to grow as a regional brewery, with distribution across North and South Carolina as well as Georgia, Tennessee, Florida, Alabama, Virginia, Kentucky, Ohio, and Washington, DC.

Beer Lover's Pick

Cold Mountain
Style: Winter warmer
ABV: 5.2 percent
Availability: On tap and in bottles (12-ounce, 22-ounce, and liter swingtops) during winter

Because the recipe changes subtly each time it is brewed, Highland Brewing's Cold Mountain can be tough to pin down into a description that is relevant from year to year. No matter what secret ingredients they use, though, this highly coveted beer is always one that embodies the holiday season in which it is released. Expect a blend of holiday spices and other ingredients like vanilla and hazelnut, all set against a malty base and plenty of cheer.

HI-WIRE BREWING COMPANY

197 Hilliard Ave., Asheville, NC 28801; (828) 575-9675; HiWireBrewing.com; @hiwire brewing

Founded: 2013 **Founders:** Adam Charnack, Chris Frosaker, Matt Kiger **Brewer:** Luke Holgate **Flagship Beer:** Hi-Wire Lager **Year-Round Beers:** Hi-Wire Lager, Bed of Nails Brown Ale, Prime Time Pale Ale, Hi-Pitch IPA **Seasonals/Special Releases:** Ringmaster Red Rye, The Strongman Coffee Milk Stout, S'mores Stout, The Firebreather **Tours:** No **Taproom:** Mon through Thurs, 4 p.m. to 12 a.m.; Fri, 2 p.m. to 2 a.m.; Sat, 10 a.m. to 2 a.m.; Sun, 11 a.m. to 11 p.m.

One of Asheville's newest breweries, Hi-Wire Brewing Company sits in the Hilliard Avenue building that was home to Craggie Brewing before they closed in late 2012. The old Craggie equipment is still there, but the guys at Hi-Wire have redone the taproom in a very tasteful circus theme, with wood painted in muted colors that mirror those found on the brewery's labels. Rough brick in alternating patterns

makes up one wall, and much of the taproom's space is also covered with tin from a reclaimed barn.

The brewery distinguished itself right off the bat by packaging its four "Main Attraction" beers in six-packs before they were even open. Asheville has no shortage of breweries, yet only a handful of them package their beer, and fewer still do so on a consistent basis. Hi-Wire's four core beers are of different styles, and yet all are well balanced, drinkable, and relatively low in alcohol. They continued to stray from the conventional route by brewing a lager in an industry dominated by ales. Their **Hi-Wire Lager** is crisp and clean, with a bready malt base and just a hint of the German noble hops. The **Bed of Nails Brown** is the darkest of the brewery's core four, offering a smooth taste of caramel, toffee, and earthy flavors.

Hi-Wire also brews a selection of "Side Show Seasonals" that can only be found on tap at the brewery. If that's not enough reason to visit, the brewery has a large projector screen upon which they show soccer games, and they also host Nintendo nights where those old eight-bit classics are displayed on the big screen for all to see. Speaking of classics, old VW bugs and buses can often be found outside the brewery during their Volkswagen cruise-ins. These are just a few of the ways that Hi-Wire Brewing has established itself as a favorite local hangout in its short history.

Beer Lover's Pick

Ringmaster Red Rye
Style: Rye beer
ABV: 7 percent
Availability: Seasonal
One of their original Side Show Seasonals, Hi-Wire's Ringmaster Red Rye has a strong backbone of caramel malt and spicy rye that supports a trio of Amarillo, Centennial, and Columbus hops. The latter contribute juicy notes of grapefruit, orange peel, and pine. This one comes in at 90 IBUs (international bitterness units), but it does not drink like an exceptionally bitter beer.

WEDGE BREWING COMPANY

125B Roberts St., Asheville, NC 28801; (828) 505-2792; WedgeBrewing.com; @wedge
brewingco

Founded: 2008 **Founder:** Tim Schaller **Brewer:** Carl Melissas **Flagship Beer:** Iron Rail
IPA **Year-Round Beers:** Iron Rail IPA, Payne's Pale Ale, Julian Price Pilsner, Witbier,
Derailed Hemp Ale, Dark Imperial Pilsner **Seasonals/Special Releases:** Golem, The Third
Rail, Super Saison, Vadim Bora Russian Imperial Stout **Tours:** No **Taproom:** Mon through
Thurs, 4 to 10 p.m.; Fri, 3 to 10 p.m.; Sat and Sun, 2 to 10 p.m.

Located in Asheville's River Arts district, Wedge Brewing Company offers one of
Asheville's finest outdoor spots in which to grab a beer. The brewery sits in the
bottom floor of a three-story, wedge-shaped building (hence the name) that is also
home to Wedge Studios. The artistic sensibility from the studios above has trickled
down to the brewery, where the expansive outdoor patio is separated by welded walls
of recycled chains, gears, crankshafts, and other pieces of scrap metal turned into
art. Some of this is the work of the late John Payne, a sculptor and metal artist who
passed away shortly after the brewery opened in 2008. John's vision for the brewery
and the River Arts District lives on through the metal as well as through Wedge
Brewing's **Payne's Pale Ale.**

The taproom inside is small, but when the weather's nice most opt to sit outside
and take in all of the metal work or watch a train pass by. Food trucks are usually

parked outside, and the brewery often hosts outdoor cinema nights once the sun goes down. Carl Melissas, formerly of Green Man Brewing, has been Wedge's head brewer since the day they opened. He brews a variety of beers, most of them the sort of balanced and lower-alcohol styles that are well suited to outdoor drinking. The **Derailed Hemp Ale** is brewed with 150 pounds of toasted hemp seeds as well as rye malt and just enough black malt to render it dark, and then it is pushed through a nitro tap. The **Julian Price Pilsner** is a flavorful example of a style rarely brewed by craft brewers, and at 5 percent ABV it's the sort you can enjoy a few of. The same is true of Wedge's **Witbier,** which comes in at 4.6 percent.

Not all of Wedge's offerings are so sessionable, mind you. **The Third Rail** is brewed with twice the hops used in the **Iron Rail IPA,** and it's a big 11.6-percent monster. Almost as monstrous is the **Golem,** a popular Belgian golden brewed with a bevy of fermentables, including Pilsen malt, oats, wheat, corn, and Belgian candi syrup. **Vadim Bora Russian Imperial Stout,** named after late Asheville artist Vadim Bora, is brewed with 168 pounds of raspberries and is one of the brewery's most popular limited-release beers.

Beer Lover's Pick

Iron Rail IPA
Style: English India pale ale
ABV: 7 percent
Availability: On tap year-round
Wedge Brewing Company's Iron Rail IPA is so popular, the brewery has an express window devoted exclusively to that beer. It has aspects of both English and American IPAs, and is brewed with Centennial, Cascade, and Kent Golding hops as well as Maris Otter, Canadian Honey, and Belgian Crystal malts. The beer is exceptionally well balanced, with notes of oranges, mangoes, and bread.

Brewpubs

ASHEVILLE PIZZA & BREWING CO.

675 Merrimon Ave., Asheville, NC 28804; (828) 254-5339; AshevilleBrewing.com; @AshevilleBrewin

Founded: 1998 **Founders:** Mike Rangel, Leigh Lewis, Doug Riley **Brewers:** Doug Riley, Pete Langheinrich **Flagship Beer:** Shiva IPA **Year-Round Beers:** Shiva IPA, Red Light IPA, Roland's ESB, Escape Artist, Fire Escape, Stuntman Brown, Rocket Girl Lager, Ninja Porter, Scout Stout **Seasonals/Special Releases:** Christmas Jam White Ale, Moog Filtered Ale, Ashe Villain Black IPA

In 1998, Doug Riley moved from an established beer city in Portland to one that was just putting down roots in Asheville. He did so for the chance to help start up Two Moons Brew and View on Merrimon Avenue, but he ended up doing far more than that. A year after opening, the original owners sold Two Moons Brew and View to Doug Riley and his partners, Leigh Lewis and Mike Rangel.

Of course, you don't just abandon a concept as cool as a movie theater and brewpub. Instead, the trio rebranded the building as Asheville Pizza & Brewing Company, though to this day many still call it the "brew and view." The kitchen turns out great pizzas and other dishes, the seven-barrel brewery produces excellent beer, and the large movie screen displays films not long gone from other theaters, for just $3 a ticket. Oh, and there's also a game room. What's not to love?

Asheville Pizza brews a diverse selection of beers, offering something not just for every taste but to pair with seemingly every pie. The most popular offering is the **Shiva IPA,** a clean and citrus-filled beer that they started canning in 2011. The **Escape Artist Extra Special Pale Ale** is another popular option, and if you like a little spiciness in your beer you can opt for the **Fire Escape,** which is Escape Artist infused with freshly roasted jalapeños. You get the wonderful flavor of the pepper, along with a bit of heat on the finish. It's a very food-friendly beer. The **Ninja Porter** is a mild, English-style porter with notes of coffee and chocolate. That's just the beginning of the brewery's portfolio. The demand for these beers led Asheville Pizza to open their production brewery on Coxe Avenue in 2006.

ASHEVILLE BREWING CO.

77 Coxe Ave., Asheville, NC 28801; (828) 255-4077; AshevilleBrewing.com;
@AshevilleBrewin

Founded: 2006 **Founders:** Mike Rangel, Leigh Lewis, Doug Riley **Brewers:** Doug Riley,
Pete Langheinrich **Flagship Beer:** Shiva IPA **Year-Round Beers:** Shiva IPA, Red Light
IPA, Roland's ESB, Escape Artist, Fire Escape, Stuntman Brown, Rocket Girl, Ninja Porter,
Scout Stout **Seasonals/Special Releases:** Christmas Jam White Ale, Moog Filtered Ale,
Ashe Villain Black IPA

In 2006, the folks behind Asheville Pizza and Brewing Company opened their production brewery on Coxe Avenue. This brewery shares a food and beer menu with the original location, but it lacks the Brew and View's movie theater. It makes up for its absence, though, with a larger brewery capable of producing much more beer. In 2011, the brewery also added a canning line that packages **Ninja Porter, Rocket Girl Lager,** and the much-loved **Shiva IPA.**

The brewpub has a massive covered patio where games of cornhole or giant Jenga are wont to break out. Inside, the beers are often infused with additional ingredients, creating exclusive concoctions that can only be found at the brewpub. The Coxe Avenue location is close to downtown and a host of other breweries, and like the original Asheville Pizza it is a great spot to grab a beer and pizza.

LEXINGTON AVENUE BREWERY

39 N. Lexington Ave., Asheville, NC 28801; (828)252-0212; LexAveBrew.com; @LAB_Asheville

Founded: 2010 **Founders:** Mike Healy, Steve Wilmans **Brewers:** Jonathon Chassner, Bruce Cottingham **Flagship Beer:** India Pale Ale **Year-Round Beers:** India Pale Ale, Cream Ale, Brown Porter, Amber Ale **Seasonals/Special Releases:** White Ale, Pale Ale, Hefeweizen, Roggenbier, Rye Pale Ale, Imperial Rye, Marzen, Pumpkin Porter, Raspberry Porter, Nitro Porter, Chocolate Stout, Black Lab IPA, Out of Bounds Double IPA

Lexington Avenue Brewery has a great location in downtown Asheville, making it a popular spot not just for the dedicated beer geeks and locals who seek it out but also for visitors who might happen to be passing by and in need of good food and beer. The patio outside provides a prime venue for people-watching, or stay inside to get a glimpse of the copper brewhouse behind a wall of curved glass. A beautiful bar built of glossy wood twists about nearby, and just above this bar is a circular shelf displaying growlers and some of the medals the brewpub has garnered at various competitions.

At the 2011 Great American Beer Festival, one of the largest festivals and beer competitions in the world, the brewpub received a bronze medal for its **Brown Porter.** That beer is usually one of the eight you can find on tap at the brewpub,

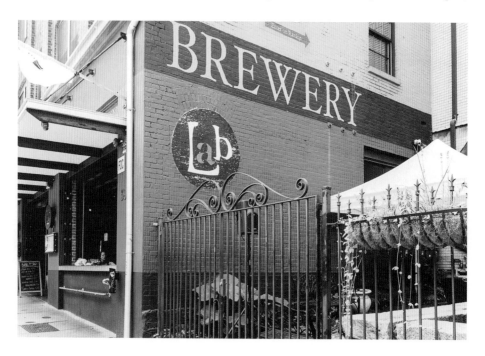

where they cycle through a few core beers with an interesting mix of seasonals. One of their most popular beers is the **Roggenbier,** a German rye beer fermented with a weizen yeast that results in a wonderful blend of spice and malty sweetness. A lighter option than the two previously mentioned beers would be the **Cream Ale.** It's brewed with two-row and pilsner malts as well as corn, as is typical of the style. The corn adds a subtle sweetness that balances out the German hops.

Most of the beers LAB brews are classic styles that pair well with the brewpub's extensive menu. Whether you are ordering an appetizer, soup or salad, a full entree or a dessert, it is likely that the dish incorporates local ingredients. LAB actually owns a nearby cattle farm, where cows consume the brewpub's spent grain before finding their way onto the menu in the form of steaks, burgers, and sandwiches. There is also a late-night menu for those wandering downtown well into the night. Founders Mike Healy and Steve Wilmans also opened the Sweet Peas hostel on the building's second floor, just above LAB. It serves as a no-frills place to stay if you're visiting their brewpub or the many others that call Asheville home.

OYSTERHOUSE BREWING COMPANY

625 Haywood Rd., Asheville, NC 28806; (828) 575-9370; OysterHouseBeers.com; @oyster housebrew
Founded: 2009 **Founder:** Billy Klingel **Brewer:** Billy Klingel **Flagship Beer:** Moonstone Oyster Stout **Year-Round Beers:** Moonstone Oyster Stout, OysterHouse Vegan Stout, IPA, Patton Ave. Pale Ale, Upside Down Brown, Ole Dirty Blonde **Seasonals/ Special Releases:** Majestic IPA, Oyster Stout with Celtic Sea Salt, Bourbon Barrel-Aged Moonstone Oyster Stout

Despite working at Asheville's The Lobster Trap and seeing oysters almost every day, Billy Klingel had never heard of an oyster stout until a coworker told him about them. Billy was immediately fascinated by the briny style, brewing countless version of an oyster stout until he felt he had one that would convince his manager to serve it at The Lobster Trap. Convince her he did, and soon Billy was brewing it half a barrel at a time for the restaurant on a SABCO BrewMagic system that he could wheel around behind the bar. He threw 5 pounds of unshucked oysters into each batch.

Turns out most of the patrons enjoyed the beer as much as Billy, and so he set his sights on expanding outside of The Lobster Trap and its small space. He found a location within walking distance from his home in West Asheville and opened his own establishment in 2013. The brewpub's dark blue walls contrast with the tin ceiling above. He now brews his stout and other beers on a larger five-barrel system.

Oysters find their way not just into the beer, but into the bar itself. OysterHouse Brewing Company has a dozen taps plus a cask, and of course a handful of taps are usually devoted to OysterHouse beers. The **Moonstone Oyster Stout** remains the brewery's most well known beer, but Billy also brews a **Patton Avenue Pale Ale** and an **Ole Dirty Blonde** that are popular. For vegans or those allergic to oysters, Billy brews the **OysterHouse Vegan Stout.** OysterHouse offers a menu of small bites, which includes a selection of oysters from around the country as well as appetizers, salads, sandwiches, and a handful of entrees.

THIRSTY MONK PUB & BREWERY

20 Gala Dr., Asheville, NC 28803; (828) 505-4564; MonkPub.com; @monkpub
Founded: 2011 **Founder:** Barry Bialik **Brewer:** Norm Penn **Flagship Beer:** Coco-Norm Coconut Porter **Year-Round Beers:** Coco-Norm Coconut Porter, India Pale Ale, American Pale Ale **Seasonals/Special Releases:** Imperial Red, Maple Pecan Belgian Brown, Winter Warmer, Chocolate Stout, Thirsty Goat Weizenbock

Of the four Thirsty Monk locations, Thirsty Monk South in Gerber Village is the only one at which beer is brewed. Founder Barry Bialik and brewer Norm Penn started brewing at this location in 2011. Norm was a homebrewer who spent a lot of time at the Thirsty Monk's popular downtown location. With space in the new location at a premium, they initially brewed on a small one-barrel system in the brewpub's kitchen. They expanded in 2013, adding on a four-barrel brewhouse that greatly increased the amount of beer they could produce at one time.

Even with the expansion, the system is small enough that the brewpub can afford to experiment a little from week to week by brewing new beers. They continue to brew house favorites like the **Coco-Norm Coconut Porter,** a smooth and quaffable porter with a blend of chocolate and toasted coconut that calls to mind a Mounds candy bar. Norm rotates through a variety of other favorites that he brewed prior to expanding, as well as completely new recipes.

The atmosphere of the South location is beer bar meets coffee shop, with plenty of bar space, a sofa, and tap handles hanging from the ceiling. Like all of the Thirsty Monk locations, the brewpub also features an excellent selection of additional craft beer, whether on draft or in bottles. They continue to hold pint nights and a variety of other craft beer events. This brewpub does not actually have a kitchen; their menu was created in partnership with nearby Frankie Bones, which delivers food to Thirsty Monk from just around the corner. It includes appetizers, salads, sandwiches, burgers, and a few other entrees. When the weather is nice, patrons can enjoy beer and food on the patio outside.

WICKED WEED BREWING COMPANY

91 Biltmore Ave., Asheville, NC 28801; (828) 575-9599; WickedWeedBrewing.com; @wickedweedbeer

Founded: 2012 **Founders:** Luke Dickinson, Walt Dickinson, Rick Guthy, Denise Guthy, Ryan Guthy **Brewers:** Luke Dickinson, Walt Dickinson **Flagship Beer:** Freak Double IPA **Year-Round Beers:** Freak of Nature Double IPA, Zealot IPA People's Choice Pale, Sir Ryan the Pounder, Infidel Porter, Tyrant Double Red, Black Angel Cherry Sour, Udderly Milk Stout **Seasonals/Special Releases:** Serentiy, Napolean Complex IPA, Transcendence, Pu-er Saison, XIV Rooted Saison, XIX Tamarind Saison, Coolcumber Saison, Pumpkanne Wicked Fest Beer, Dark Age Rum Stout

One of the first things you'll see upon entering Wicked Weed Brewing is a mural of King Henry VIII, who is rumored to have called hops "a wicked and pernicious weed." This quote inspired the name for the brewery, which opened beside Asheville's Orange Peel music venue in late December of 2012. It is hard to imagine the building as anything other than the beautiful brewpub it is, but it once held a hardware store and, before that, an auto repair shop. The interior has a modern feel yet uses lots of reclaimed materials, including a bar made from centuries-old black gum with two musket balls buried in it. The upstairs is considered the restaurant portion, while the downstairs is where you will find the brewery and tasting room.

The tasting room is as impressive visually as the upstairs, with stone-covered walls and a giant chalkboard. Coming out of the chalkboard are five wooden barrel ends turned on their sides, and from them are five taps per barrel pouring beers that fall into different series: Hops are Heresy, Beautiful and Belgian, Wicked Wood Aged Beers, and Small Batch. The beers are crafted by brothers Luke and Walt Dickinson,

who founded the brewery with Rick, Denise, and Ryan Guthy. Luke worked as a tour guide at Dogfish Head, and before opening Wicked Weed he and his brother toured the country visiting breweries for inspiration.

The 15-barrel brewery sits behind a small stack of barrels beside the tasting room. An open fermenter that is used for some saisons is sealed off behind glass, but you might be able to glimpse the fermentation through a mirror above it. Anything sour, funky, or brewed with wild yeast is pumped directly from the brewhouse to a separate building out back called the funkatorium. This keeps those wild yeasts from contaminating other styles. This building also includes a collection of barrel-aged beers. The **Black Angel Cherry Sour** is brewed with an abundance of Italian plums and a mix of sweet and tart cherries before spending time in bourbon barrels. The result is a dark, sour ale with notes of vanilla and an assertive tartness. If you're more interested in the brewery's West Coast styles (and there are plenty of them), try the **Freak of Nature Double IPA**, which is brewed with 48 pounds of hops per batch. It is one of the dankest IPAs you will find.

And that's all just the half of it. The brewpub's kitchen turns out lots of interesting twists on standard pub fare and Southern cuisine, such as its fried chicken sandwich with kimchee and miso mayonnaise. And Belgian inspiration isn't reserved only for the beers, as Wicked Weed's brussels sprouts are absolutely delicious.

Beer Bars

BARLEY'S TAPROOM & PIZZERIA

42 Biltmore Ave., Asheville, NC 28801; (828) 255-0504; BarleysTaproom.com;
@BarleysTapPizza
Draft Beers: 43 **Bottled/Canned Beers:** 50

Barley's Taproom & Pizzeria was the first bar to sell Highland Brewing's Gaelic Ale (then called Celtic Ale), which should come as no surprise since it was brewed in the building's basement. So it was that Barley's has been committed to local beer long before Asheville would come to be known nationally as "Beer City USA."

To this day you will find Highland's beers and plenty of other local options in Barley's Taproom, which occupies two stories in a building that was constructed in the 1920s. Asheville was dry at that time, but the building has served up plenty of beer since Barley's Taproom came in 1994. Downstairs, there is the restaurant portion of the taproom, with 24 taps and a stage for live music. Upstairs, you will find the billiard room with four beautiful regulation pool tables, five dart boards and, most importantly, 19 taps. At both the upstairs and downstairs bars, you will find an excellent selection of North Carolina beers.

Of course, the beer is just one half of Barley's. The taproom offers a menu of sandwiches, salads, wraps, and New York–style pizzas, which is what they are best known for (outside of the beer, of course).

THE BYWATER

796 Riverside Dr., Asheville, NC 28801;
(828) 232-6967; BywaterBar.com
Draft Beers: 18 **Bottled/Canned Beers:**
20+

The Bywater, located right on the banks of the French Broad River, is one of Asheville's most scenic and relaxing spots at which to have a beer. It is essentially a small park-like area that just so happens to have 18 well-chosen taps of craft beer inside. You can enjoy said beer in the small bar area, but if the weather's nice you would be silly not to take it out by the river's edge or on the bar's acre of green grass. Many outdoor games are played here, including horseshoes and cornhole. There are hammocks for those more content to bask in the Asheville sun. You can tube or kayak to and from the bar's location on the French Broad, and many people do just that by starting at Carrier Park a few miles downstream and then stopping to have beers at The Bywater.

The Bywater frequently has live music and open mic nights, and often there are food trucks out in the parking lot. There is no kitchen here, but there are outdoor grills for use by anyone who wishes to bring charcoal and something to cook. Because they serve liquor and no food, The Bywater has to operate as a private club. This means new visitors will have to pay $5 to become members unless they are the guest of another member.

JACK OF THE WOOD

95 Patton Ave., Asheville, NC 28801; (828) 252-5445; JackoftheWood.com; @JackoftheWood
Draft Beers: 16 **Bottled/Canned Beers:** 20+

Jack of the Wood is a Celtic-style pub that boasts the distinction of also being the birthplace of Green Man Brewing, before they expanded just a few blocks south. You can still find Green Man's beers among the bar's 16 taps, as well as several other NC locals. Lots of wood lends the pub a truly warm atmosphere, made warmer when visitors are dancing around to live bluegrass or Irish music.

It almost goes without saying that an establishment like Jack of the Wood should serve fish-and-chips and shepherd's pie, and you will indeed find those Irish favorites here. The menu also features a variety of other options ranging from small to large, all prepared with fresh and local ingredients.

THE THIRSTY MONK
92 Patton Ave., Asheville, NC 28801; (828) 254-5470; MonkPub.com; @MonkPub
Draft Beers: 36 **Bottled/Canned Beers:** 100

Shortly after he moved to Asheville in 2007, Barry Bialik decided to open a bar that reflected his own passion for Belgian beer. He found an ideal location in the bottom of a downtown Patton Avenue building, and in 2008 he purchased the building and opened the Thirsty Monk in its basement. The dimly lit, stone-walled space has a cellar-like quality to it, and it is a great place to enjoy any number of Belgian beers, from the more routine to the rare.

Not long after opening, the space above the basement became available. Since he already owned the building, Barry added a bar above that carries a good selection of American craft beers. He also opened a cocktail bar on the roof of the building called Top of the Monk. In addition to the downtown location, the Thirsty Monk empire also includes beer bars in Biltmore Park, Reynolds Village, and Gerber Village (they have their own brewery at this last location, which is often called Thirsty Monk South).

Whether upstairs or downstairs, Thirsty Monk prides itself on a tap lineup that is ever changing. The downtown location's menu features a large selection of appetizers, small plates, salads, sandwiches, and pizzas. Almost every single one of these items is made with beer, with the particular beer used listed right alongside. Green Man's Porter, brewed just a few blocks away, is used in the porter-chipotle brisket tacos. Highland Brewing's Black Mocha Stout, a classic of the Asheville beer scene, is used in the stout beef sliders. Even the pizza dough uses Fat Tire from New Belgium Brewing, which hopes to open its Asheville facility in 2015.

Pub Crawl

Asheville

The first half of this four-stop pub crawl hits two popular beer bars, the last half two breweries. It takes you out of the heart of downtown and into the city's South Slope neighborhood, which is fast becoming a brewing mecca.

Jack of the Wood, 95 Patton Ave., Asheville, NC 28801; (828) 252-5445; JackoftheWood.com. Jack of the Wood is a Celtic-style pub and also the original home of Green Man Brewing, before they opened their own brewery a few blocks south. Belly up to the beautiful black walnut bar and order a pint of Green Man for old time's sake, or choose another beer from Jack's 16 taps. Jack features lots of live bands, including traditional Irish music and bluegrass. If you're hungry, the menu features sandwiches, burgers, and entrees, the latter broken down into small, medium, and large. Of course, you will find Irish favorites like shepherd's pie and fish-and-chips.

Walk out of Jack of the Wood and look across Patton Avenue and to the left. A purple building with a mural and monk on the side signify your next destination.

Thirsty Monk, 92 Patton Ave., Asheville, NC 28801; (828) 254-5470; MonkPub.com. If you didn't eat at Jack of the Wood, Thirsty Monk has a tasty menu filled with appetizers, small plates, salads, sandwiches, and pizzas, almost all of which are prepared to some degree using beer.

Leave Thirsty Monk and head south down Coxe Avenue. Asheville Brewing Company will be on the right, about a five-minute walk away.

Asheville Brewing Company, 77 Coxe Ave., Asheville, NC 28801; (828) 255-4077; AshevilleBrewing.com. The first thing you'll see when approaching Asheville Brewing Company's Coxe location is the huge covered patio. When the weather's nice, this is the place to be. This building houses Asheville Brewing Company's production brewery, so rest assured all of the beers are fresh. Most are fairly sessionable, which is always a good thing toward the end of a pub crawl. If you still haven't eaten, Asheville Brewing Company serves up a variety of delicious pizzas.

Leave Asheville Brewing and continue heading south down Coxe Avenue until it intersects with Hilliard Avenue. Turn right and you will find Hi-Wire Brewing before the next intersection. It is only a two-minute walk from Asheville Brewing Company to Hi-Wire Brewing.

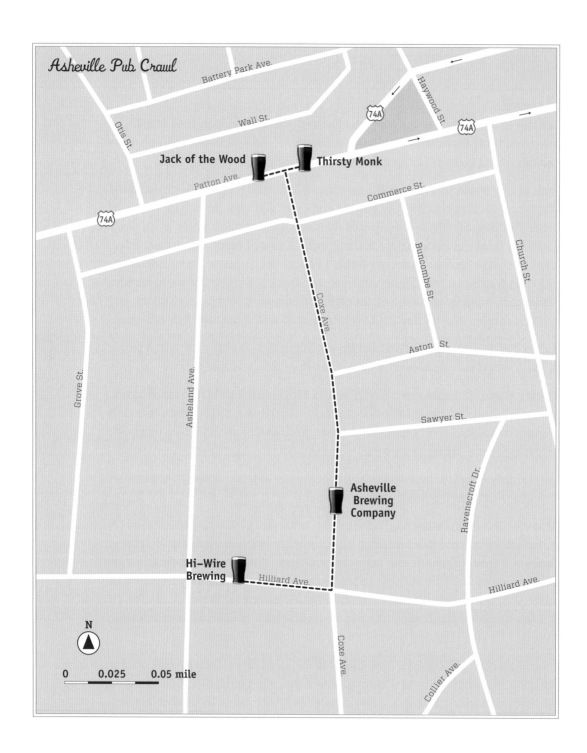

Asheville Pub Crawl

Battery Park Ave.

Wall St.

Jack of the Wood

Thirsty Monk

Patton Ave.

Commerce St.

Haywood St.

74A

74A

74A

Otis St.

Grove St.

Asheland Ave.

Coxe Ave.

Buncombe St.

Church St.

Aston St.

Sawyer St.

Ravenscroft Dr.

Asheville
Brewing
Company

Hi-Wire
Brewing

Hilliard Ave.

Hilliard Ave.

Coxe Ave.

Collier Ave.

N

0   0.025   0.05 mile

Hi-Wire Brewing, 197 Hilliard Ave., Asheville, NC 28801; (828) 575-9675; HiWire Brewing.com. One of Asheville's newest breweries, Hi-Wire Brewing took over the spot left vacant when Craggie Brewing closed its doors. The building has a really fun feel to it, thanks to muted colors reminiscent of the brand's six-pack packaging. Close the night with one of their four main attraction beers or whatever side show seasonal happens to be on. If you can, get in a game of shuffleboard or Super Nintendo, or just check out what's on the big screen. With the night coming to a close, make sure to grab a six-pack while you're there to enjoy later.

Asheville

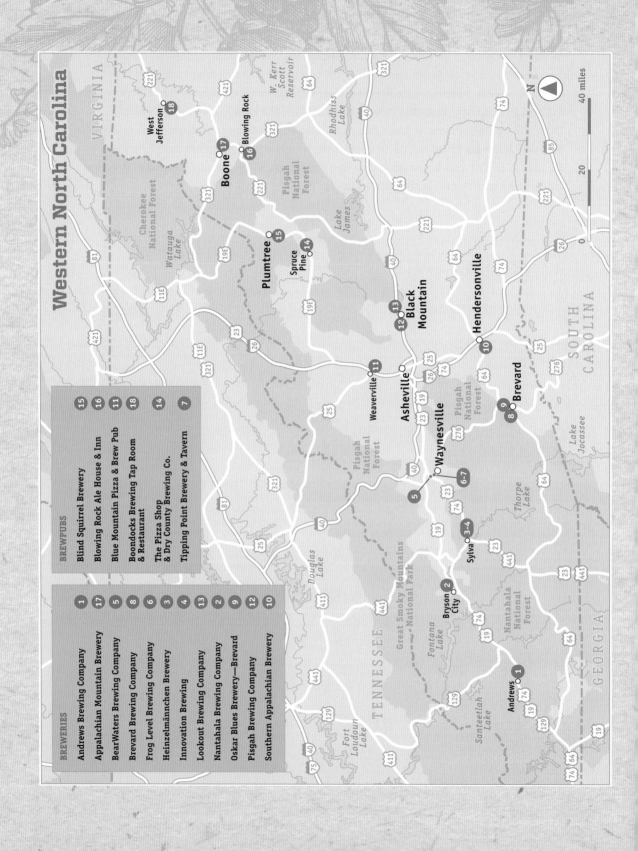

Western North Carolina

VIRGINIA

TENNESSEE

SOUTH CAROLINA

GEORGIA

Cherokee National Forest

Pisgah National Forest

Great Smoky Mountains National Park

Nantahala National Forest

Pisgah National Forest

West Jefferson ⓲

Blowing Rock

⓱ Boone ⓰

⓯ Plumtree
⑮

Spruce Pine ⓮

⑬ Black
⑫ Mountain

Weaverville ⑪

Asheville

Hendersonville ⑩

⑨ Brevard
⑧

Waynesville
⑥-⑦

⑤

Sylva ③-④

② Bryson City

① Andrews

W. Kerr Scott Reservoir

Rhodhiss Lake

Lake James

Watauga Lake

Douglas Lake

Fort Loudoun Lake

Fontana Lake

Santeetlah Lake

Thorpe Lake

Lake Jocassee

N

40 miles
0   20

BREWERIES

Andrews Brewing Company	①
Appalachian Mountain Brewery	⑰
BearWaters Brewing Company	⑤
Brevard Brewing Company	⑧
Frog Level Brewing Company	⑥
Heinzelmännchen Brewery	③
Innovation Brewing	④
Lookout Brewing Company	⑬
Nantahala Brewing Company	②
Oskar Blues Brewery—Brevard	⑨
Pisgah Brewing Company	⑫
Southern Appalachian Brewery	⑩

BREWPUBS

Blind Squirrel Brewery	⑮
Blowing Rock Ale House & Inn	⑯
Blue Mountain Pizza & Brew Pub	⑪
Boondocks Brewing Tap Room & Restaurant	⑱
The Pizza Shop & Dry County Brewing Co.	⑭
Tipping Point Brewery & Tavern	⑦

Western North Carolina

Asheville might have won "Beer City USA" a few times, but don't devote all of your attention to just one city in the beer-filled landscape of Western North Carolina. Whether you are up north in the High Country, to the east in Black Mountain, down south in Hendersonville or Brevard, or out west in Waynesville or the Nantahala National Forest, Western North Carolina is sure to have a brewery for you just over that next mountain.

Breweries

ANDREWS BREWING COMPANY

565 Aquone Rd., Andrews, NC 28901; (828) 321-2006; AndrewsBrewing.com
Founded: 2013 **Founders:** Eric and Judy Carlson **Brewer:** Eric Carlson **Flagship Beer:** American Red **Year-Round Beers:** American Cream Ale, American Red, Irish Red **Seasonals/Special Releases:** Pumpkin Amber, Double American IPA, Blueberry Wheat, FBI Rye, American Red, ESB, Arrowhead Red IPA **Tours:** During open hours **Taproom:** Thurs, 12 to 5 p.m.; Fri and Sat, 12 to 5 p.m. (or later, weather permitting)

Andrews is a small town, and its brewery is even smaller. In a 300-square-foot stone building that once served as the town's jailhouse, Eric and Judy Carlson built Calaboose Cellars, one of the nation's smallest wineries, in 2007. You would think that tiny space would be cramped with winemaking equipment, but in 2013 they found enough room to bring in what is essentially an advanced homebrewing setup capable of brewing 20 gallons at a time.

The building has only about 50 square feet devoted to a tasting room, as the rest of it is filled with fermenting tanks of various sizes, a sink, lab, bathroom, and storage room. Above all of this is a loft filled with even more brewing and winemaking equipment. Needless to say, when crowded this small space can indeed begin to feel like the prison it once was. Break out of that tiny room's rusty iron bars, however, and you will find a wraparound deck that adds plenty of space for those looking to enjoy a beer. There are a few barrels that serve as decor and a spot on which to set a glass, as well a tables and chairs. In front of the deck is a stone patio and a fireplace, and all of this is just feet away from rows and rows of grapes.

Arrowhead Red IPA
Style: Red IPA
ABV: 7.2 percent
Ever the innovative bunch, breweries continue to put new spins on the India pale ale. New colorful approaches include white IPAs, black IPAs, and red IPAs, and it's the latter that Andrews Brewing Company's Arrowhead Red IPA falls under. At 73 IBUs, it has an assertive punch of citrus and pine, balanced with a sturdy backbone of caramel malt.

The winery plays up the old jailhouse theme quite a bit: Eric is known as the warden, others are inmates, and their wines have names like Revinoor's Red and Wardin's White. Andrews Brewing Company's offerings, however, are for the most part listed by their style (aside from a few beers, like **FBI Rye**). They try to keep six beers on at any given time, which they rotate through quite often. Like other nano-brewers across the Carolinas, their small size allows them the flexibility and creative freedom to constantly try new things. At the 2013 NC Brewers' Cup, a competition held at the NC State Fair, their **Irish Red** took second place and their **ESB** third in their respective categories.

APPALACHIAN MOUNTAIN BREWERY

163 Boone Creek Dr., Boone, NC 28607; (828) 263-1111; AppalachianMountainBrewery .com; @AMBrewery

Founded: 2013 **Founders:** Sean and Stephanie Spiegelman **Brewers:** Nathan Kelischeck, Chris Zeiber **Flagship Beer:** Long Leaf IPA **Year-Round Beers:** Honey Badger Blonde Ale, Long Leaf IPA, The 71 IPA, Switchback Amber, Black Gold Porter, Kilt Lifter, **Seasonals/Special Releases:** King's Kölsch, Crooked Common, Good Deal Pale Ale, Session IPA, Skipping Stone ESB, Rye'd That, Golden Nugget, Belay On Saison, Daniel's Double IPA, Nut Brown Ale, Autumn Brown, Brown Vanilla Porter, Von Watzdorf, Corruption Imperial Stout **Tours:** Times vary, check website **Taproom:** Mon, 4 to 10 p.m.; Tues through Fri, 4 to 11 p.m.; Sat, 3 to 11 p.m.; Sun, 3 to 9 p.m.

Boone attracts its fair share of tourists, but one look at Appalachian Mountain Brewery assures you this is a spot for leaf-watchers and locals alike. The brewery's motto of "Act Local, Drink Local" can be found throughout the building, which maintains a comfortable and unpretentious aesthetic. A massive garage door on the back of the building hints at the building's industrial past as a welding shop, and concrete blocks and pallet wood cover most of the wall space inside. On the side of the building, a covered patio offers the perfect spot for outdoor imbibing all year, as it is kept enclosed and heated during the winter. An outdoor bar spans a length of 120 feet.

Appalachian Mountain Brewery has brewed many different styles since opening in early 2013, and they keep a diverse lineup of beers on tap. The **Honey Badger,** a blonde brewed with orange zest and local wildflower honey, won a gold medal at the 2013 US Open Beer Championship. On the darker end of the spectrum is **Black Gold,** a porter that gives just a hint of roast and has a dry finish that leaves you wanting more, not unlike an Irish stout. And if you want a **Good Deal,** just ask for it—the pale ale of that name boasts lots of grapefruit and citrus flavors with a prickly finish.

No matter how good the deal, there are few deals better than ordering a good beer for a good cause. You can do just that through the brewery's Pints for Non-Profits

PHOTO BY AUTHOR

Long Leaf IPA
Style: India pale ale
ABV: 6.8 percent
Availability: On tap year-round
At its foundation, Long Leaf IPA has a solid caramel malt presence upon which Appalachian Mountain Brewery has thrown plenty of hops, resulting in a 75 IBU beer with notes of grapefruit, pine, and orange. Behind that are smooth notes of honeysuckle, making this an incredibly refreshing and drinkable IPA.

program, which delivers a portion of a pint's proceeds to nonprofits (most of them in the High Country). Wood plaques bearing the names of these nonprofits hang beneath the plaques of the beers they are associated with. The brewery has been dedicated to their local community since the day they opened. While they do not have a kitchen, it is not uncommon to find a food truck or barbecue smoker just behind the brewery, their wonderful smells wafting in through that big garage door.

BEARWATERS BREWING COMPANY

130 Frazier St., Ste. 7, Waynesville, NC 28786; (828) 246-0602; bwbrewing.com
Founded: 2012 **Founders:** Kevin Sandefur, Heidi Dunkelberg **Brewers:** Kevin Sandefur, Jim Sandefur **Flagship Beer:** Heady Eddy Pale Ale **Year-Round Beers:** Heady Eddy Pale Ale, White Water Hefeweizen, Stiff Paddle IPA, Upper Falls IPA, Angler's Amber Ale **Seasonals/Special Releases:** Sliding Rock Ale, Delta Blonde Ale, Big Sky Rye, Rip Current Red, River Dog ESB, Skipping Stone Stout, Barrel Roll Bourbon Porter, Paint Rock Porter, Brown Mountain Dark Ale, Snownado Chocolate Peppermint Stout, Mud Bug Chocolate Barrel-Aged Stout **Tours:** No **Taproom:** Mon through Fri, 2 to 9 p.m.; Sat, 1 to 10 p.m.

BearWaters Brewing Company is headquartered in a Waynesville warehouse, yet you can't help but feel you're in the great outdoors upon entering the taproom.

Kayaks hang from the ceiling and picnic tables line one of the walls, the entire length of which is covered in a mural of a lakeside scene. It's as close to outdoor drinking as you can get without actually being outdoors.

Kevin Sandefur, the brewery's owner and brewer, won $8,000 from the Haywood County Chamber of Commerce Business Startup Competition. He used this money to purchase much of his equipment, and soon he was operating Waynesville's second brewery (with Frog Level being the first). The brewery opened in May 2012 under the name "Headwaters Brewing Co.," but was soon asked to stop using the name by Pennsylvania's Victory Brewing Company, maker of Headwaters Pale Ale. Not even a year after opening, Headwaters underwent a rebranding and emerged as BearWaters Brewing Co.

The brewery's new name was close enough to the old that it still worked well with all of their water-related beer names. Their flagship, **Heady Eddy Pale Ale,** is a very drinkable, English-style pale with notes of citrus and a slight malty sweetness. If you want something a little hoppier, opt for their popular **Stiff Paddle IPA.** Kevin

Upper Falls Double IPA

Style: Double IPA

ABV: 11 percent

Availability: On tap year-round

When almost all of your beers take their names from waterways, it makes sense that one of your biggest offerings is named after the Upper Falls, those higher, faster, more dangerous rapids than can be daunting to the uninitiated. BearWaters Brewing's Upper Falls Double IPA is 11 percent ABV, and certainly could prove punishing if you had more than one. That being said, one by itself is not a rough ride, as the beer has a sweet malt backbone to balance out the massive hop presence.

brews on a small system and as such rotates his beers out very frequently, so be sure to try some of his other styles when visiting the taproom. The **Skipping Stone Stout** is an easy-drinking attempt at the style that calls to mind Guinness, but with a kiss of smoke. The **River Dog ESB**, with its notes of caramel and toffee, is a spot-on attempt at an English style that is sometimes overlooked by American drinkers.

BREVARD BREWING COMPANY

63 E. Main St., Brevard, NC 28712; (828) 885-2101; Brevard-Brewing.com

Founded: 2012 **Founder:** Kyle Williams **Brewer:** Kyle Williams **Flagship Beer:** Bohemian Pilsner **Year-Round Beers:** Bohemian Pilsner, American Premium Lager, Munich Dunkel, American IPA **Seasonals/Special Releases:** American Red Ale, German Hefeweizen, Coriander Ale, Octoberfest Lager, Smoked Porter, Oatmeal Stout, ESB, Bock, American Wheat **Tours:** No **Taproom:** Mon through Thurs, 3 to 10 p.m.; Fri and Sat, 12 p.m. to 12 a.m.; Sun, 2 to 10 p.m.

After homebrewing for years and also working in Black Mountain's Pisgah Brewing Company, Kyle Williams decided to see his dream of opening his own

brewery into fruition in April of 2012. At Pisgah, Kyle was tasked with brewing a wide variety of styles, mostly big and bold American ales. When it came time to start his own brewery, though, he chose to pursue his own passion for drinkable, European-inspired lagers.

It was a bold move in today's craft beer climate, where bigger is often better and brewing seems more and more like an arms race to see who can out hop whom. This is not so with most lagers—subtlety and nuance are the name of the game. Lagers are stored at colder temperatures than ales and often for at least twice as long, meaning they take up fermentation space that Kyle can do nothing with except wait. Give lagers time, though, and you will be rewarded with a crispness that ales just can't match. The perfect example of this is Brevard Brewing's **Bohemian Pilsner,** a 4.9 percent lager with subtle floral and spicy notes derived from noble hops. A lighter alternative would be the **American Premium Lager;** it's flavorful enough for most craft beer geeks, but not so bold that it will scare away the uninitiated. While Brevard Brewing specializes in lagers, that's not all they brew. The **American IPA** is a subdued take on the style with a pronounced hoppiness and clean finish.

Brevard Brewing Company sits right on the town's Main Street, and the rustic stonework that adorns the building's façade continues into the taproom as well. The small, three-sided bar is conducive to good conversation, and on weekends the taproom is filled with live music. It is a warm, inviting space full of stone, wood and, more often than not, lovers of lagers and ales alike.

Munich Dunkel
Style: Dunkel
ABV: 5 percent
Availability: On tap year-round
Years of big beer commercials have beat the word "light lager" into our heads, and it's not surprising that many would think "dark lager" a contradiction in terms. Not so. Brevard Brewing Company's Dunkel offers flavors of caramel, dark bread, chocolate, and just the slightest hint of coffee, but in a well-carbonated and crisp beer that is just as drinkable as its lighter brethren.

FROG LEVEL BREWING COMPANY

56 Commerce St., Waynesville, NC 28786; (828) 454-5664; FrogLevelBrewing.com; @FrogLevelBrew

Founded: 2011 **Founders:** Clark and Jenny Williams **Brewer:** Clark Williams **Flagship Beer:** Lily's Cream Boy Ale **Year-Round Beers:** Lily's Cream Boy Ale, Catcher in the Rye, Nutty Brew-Nette, Salamander Slam IPA, Hop-Scotch Ale, Tadpole Porter **Seasonals/ Special Releases:** Cinco Ranas Picante, Bug Eyed Stout, Bufo Brown, Special Hoperations, Hoppy Thyme IPA, Hop Along Imperial IPA **Tours:** No **Taproom:** Tues and Wed, 2 to 6:30 p.m.; Thurs through Sat, 2 to 9 p.m.

Frog Level Brewing Company's taproom in downtown Waynesville is a long, straight space filled with sofas, artwork, cornhole boards, a foosball table and, of course, a bar. The taproom doesn't end there, however, but just outside it. There, Richland Creek babbles just feet away from the brewery's outdoor deck.

The creek, which frequently flooded, was said to turn the low-lying area into a "Frog Level." Since his building butts right up to that very creek, founder Clark

Williams felt it was only appropriate to name his brewery after this historic part of town. Don't worry: the creek doesn't flood as often as the legend suggests, and it provides a scenic backdrop upon which to enjoy any number of Frog Level Brewing's beers.

Many craft breweries avoid brewing with corn, which "the big guys" use as a cheaper, more neutral-tasting fermentable than malt. Clark puts it to good use, however, in his **Lily's Cream Boy Ale,** a slightly sweet and refreshing take on the cream ale style. That one's named after his sphynx cat, but the **Nutty Brew-Nette**—a brown ale brewed with roasted hazelnut—is named after his wife, Jenny. The brewery's **Salamander Slam IPA** pairs citrus and floral hop notes with a prominent breadiness from the malt. If you enjoy rye, give **Catcher in the Rye Ale** a try: The peppery spice of the rye works well with juicy grapefruit flavors derived from the Amarillo hops.

Whether you're relaxing in the taproom on a comfortable sofa or getting some sun out on the deck, Frog Level Brewing Company offers an idyllic setting in which to enjoy a beer. While food is not available, you can bring in food from nearby restaurants. Better yet, why not pack a picnic to enjoy out by the creek?

Tadpole Porter
Style: English porter
ABV: 5.8 percent
Availability: On tap year-round
Tadpole Porter is an English-style porter brewed with oatmeal that displays less roasted malt character than most others in this style. Instead, you can expect the usual hints of chocolate and coffee with a bit of licorice on the finish. Enjoy it by the creek outside the brewery or grab a growler to go.

HEINZELMÄNNCHEN BREWERY

545 Mill St., Sylva, NC 28779; (828) 632-4466; YourGnometownBrewery.com; @Heinzelmannchen
Founded: 2004 **Founders:** Dieter Kuhn, Sheryl Rudd **Brewer:** Dieter Kuhn **Flagship Beer:** Ancient Days Honey Blonde Ale **Year-Round Beers:** Ancient Days Honey Blonde Ale, Gopher Ale, Hoppy Gnome, Weise Gnome Hefeweizen, Middleworld Brown, Black Forest Stout **Seasonals/Special Releases:** Gnutty Gnome, Maibock Not Yours, Roktoberfest, Chocolate Covered Gnome, Gnarly Gnome, Big Amber Gnome, Merry Gnome, Kilted Gnome Scottish Ale **Tours:** No **Taproom:** Mon through Sat, 10 a.m. to 6:30 p.m. (Tues open until 9 p.m. for trivia)

In the middle of the night, gnomes creep into Dieter Kuhn's brewery in downtown Sylva. They mill the grain, heat the water, clean kegs, and fill growlers. They prepare everything so that when Dieter walks into Heinzelmännchen Brewery every morning, most of the work is already done.

Okay, so maybe not. Growing up in Germany, Dieter always heard the fairy tales of the Heinzelmännchen, good and honest gnomes that would complete most of a person's work for them while they were sleeping. While the gnomes aren't real, Dieter liked what they represented enough to make them the namesake for his brewery, which he and his wife Sheryl Rudd opened in 2004. He has modeled

Heinzelmännchen after the neighborhood breweries found in big cities and small towns across Germany. Like the Heinzelmännchen, he wants to do good things for his community.

The small storefront contains the brewery on one side and a few tables at which to drink on the other. There is no window or wall separating the brewery and modest taproom, but that adds to its charm. The **Hoppy Gnome** is a hoppier version of the **Gopher Ale;** both beers have a distinct crispness, with the former being just a bit more floral and bitter than the latter. The **Black Forest Stout,** which Dieter likens to a non-lagered German schwarzbier, is as dark and decadent as a cake from the Black Forest region itself. The two might make for a natural pairing, as Dieter and Sheryl put together an entire cookbook filled with recipes that use beers from the brewery, whose slogan is "The Beer Brewed for Food." Check the "In the Kitchen" section for their **Heinzelmännchen Brewery German Potato Salad** recipe, p. 308. It and others can also be found in "Your Gnometown Cookbook."

Ancient Days Honey Blonde
Style: Blonde ale
ABV: 5 percent
Availability: On tap year-round
A smooth and sweet blonde ale brewed with local Catamount honey, Ancient Days Honey Blonde is one of Heinzelmännchen Brewery's most popular beers. Besides the obvious sweetness from the honey, it also has a floral character and a cracker-like quality from the pilsner malt. It finishes crisp and clean, with a fleeting maltiness on the finish.

INNOVATION BREWING

414 W. Main St., Sylva, NC 28779; (828) 586-9678; Innovation-Brewing.com; @InnovationBrew

Founded: 2013 **Founders:** Chip Owen and Nicole Dexter **Brewers:** Chip Owen and Nicole Dexter **Flagship Beer:** Hop Bomb IPA **Year-Round Beers:** Hop Bomb IPA, Spare Parts Pale, Afternoon Delight Blonde Ale, Nut Brown **Seasonals/Special Releases:** Black IPA, Bourbon Barrel Imperial Stout, Apple Butter Brown, Vegan Smoked Maple Bacon Porter, Belgian Tripel **Tours:** No **Taproom:** Tues through Thurs, 4 to 11 p.m.; Fri, 2 p.m. to 12 a.m.; Sat, 12 p.m. to 12 a.m.; Sun, 2 to 10 p.m.

Innovation Brewing is appropriately named, given everything Chip Owen and Nicole Dexter took on themselves prior to opening their brewery in October of 2013. Across one wall they slathered green paint, and to cover their cold room they put up tall planks of dark wood, giving the small taproom a rustic feel that jives well with the beautiful mountain town of Sylva. They framed the bar themselves, and then on top of it they formed designs from grains that they had toasted to a variety of colors. Above that, they hung a few Edison lights. And finally, they constructed 50 barstools themselves before welcoming the community to come try their beers.

Much of this came naturally for Chip, who was a mechanical engineer before he and Nicole decided to open their own brewery. Brewing, too, is something he's quite comfortable with. He started homebrewing almost a decade before opening Innovation Brewing's doors in Sylva, which is also home to Heinzelmännchen Brewery. The beers, of course, are the most innovative part of the operation. Chip and Nicole brew several traditional styles, but also want to change the way people think about beer by experimenting with different techniques and ingredients. Their more traditional offerings include their **Hop Bomb IPA** and **Nut Brown Ale.** Less conventional beers include the **Apple Butter Brown** and **Vegan Smoked Maple Bacon Porter.**

Traditional or innovative, all of the beers are crafted on a small, 1.5-barrel system. As a result, Chip and Nicole have to brew frequently to fill their 12 taps, however it does allow them to keep a wide variety of styles on at any given time. They do not serve food, however food trucks can frequently be found parked outside.

LOOKOUT BREWING COMPANY

103 S. Ridgeway Ave., Black Mountain, NC 28711; (828) 357-5169; LookoutBrewing.com; @LookoutBrewing
Founded: 2013 **Founder:** John Garcia **Brewers:** John Garcia, Rich Jones, Chris Terwilliger **Flagship Beer:** Black Mountain IPA **Year-Round Beers:** Black Mountain IPA, Alison's Front Porch Pale Ale, Dark Town Brown, Dungadoon Blonde, Lookout Stout **Seasonals/Special Releases:** Whatever Wheat Pale, Spyglass Pilsner, Smokin' Scotty, Beer-B-Q Smoked Ale, Hoptometrist Double IPA, Jive Turkey **Tours:** No **Taproom:** Mon through Sat, 10 a.m. to 8 p.m.

As a homebrewer, John Garcia so enjoyed Pisgah Brewing's pale ale that he committed himself to cloning it. He hoped his homebrewed version would come close to Pisgah's, but he never expected to one day own a brewery just down the street from them. In a small warehouse in downtown Black Mountain, John built his taproom and brewery. It is a small but very comfortable space, with a beautiful copper bar and a patio outside by the treeline. True to his homebrewing roots, John also sells a variety of homebrewing ingredients and equipment.

The system on which John brews is closer to an advanced homebrew setup than most commercial examples. He brews on the same half-barrel SABCO BrewMagic system that Dogfish Head founder Sam Calagione and so many other brewers started on. By starting small, John was able to avoid loans and investors so that he could stay

true to his vision. He gets by with help from his family, too. His stepfather helps brew, his mother runs the books, and his wife, Allison, watches the kids so that John can do what he loves.

By brewing on a smaller level, John can also afford to use local malt and hops, something he is very committed to. Many of his beers feature grain from Asheville's Riverbend Malt House or local hop farms, like Hop 'n Blueberry Farm. To see what specific flavors different hops can impart, John keeps jars of whole-leaf hops on the copper bar. You can infuse your beer with them for a dollar.

One of the brewery's hoppiest and most popular beers is the **Hoptometrist Double IPA,** which reaches 80 IBUs (international bitterness units) through its use of Willamette, Warrior, Simcoe, Cascade, and Perle hops. While this and all of John's IPAs are excellent, he brews a variety of styles. His **Beer-B-Q** is described as a smoked ESB, or what John calls "an extra smoky bitter." It balances the smoke with a caramel-like sweetness. The **Lookout Stout** is medium-bodied and sessionable, with a dry finish and notes of roasted coffee and bitter dark chocolate.

Black Mountain IPA

Style: India pale ale

ABV: 5.5 percent

Availability: On tap year-round

Black Mountain IPA is brewed with rye, which provides a little bit of spice and earthiness. It is exceptionally well balanced, with a sturdy caramel backbone supporting the Cascade and Fuggle hops. This beer is one of Lookout's most popular offerings, and it is easy to see why.

NANTAHALA BREWING COMPANY

61 Depot St., Bryson City, NC 28713; (828) 488-2337; NantahalaBrewing.com; @NantahalaBrew

Founded: 2010 **Founders:** Joe Rowland, Ken Smith, Mike Marsden, Chris and Christina Collier **Brewer:** Greg Geiger **Flagship Beer:** Noon Day IPA **Year-Round Beers:** Noon Day IPA, Appalachian Trail Extra Pale Ale, Bryson City Brown, Dirty Girl Blonde, Up River Amber **Seasonals/Special Releases:** Little Tennessee Logger, 4 Foot Drop Pale Ale, Hellbender Hefeweizen, Rivers End Oktoberfest, Pattons Run Porter, Chocolate Covered Cherry Stout, Devil's Courthouse Belgian Golden Strong, 8 Foot Drop Double IPA, Trail Magic Series **Tours:** Mar through Oct, Fri at 1 and 2:30 p.m.; Sat, 1 and 2:30 p.m.; Nov through Feb, Sat at 1 p.m. and 2:30 p.m. **Taproom:** Mon through Fri, varies by season; Sat, 12 to 11 p.m.; Sun, 12 to 8 p.m.

Every year, thousands visit the Great Smoky Mountains to float down the Nantahala River, whether by raft or tube, kayak or canoe. Many of them, after a long but satisfying day on the water, inevitably make their way to nearby Nantahala Brewing Company in Bryson City.

The brewery sits just off the railroad tracks that shuttle open-air cars through the scenic mountains. The Quonset hut warehouse it is housed in dates back to 1945, when it was used to store lumber and other material. In a fortuitous meeting, Mike Marsden—who owned the tavern next door to the brewery—met Chris and Christina

Collier as they were riding their Harley through Bryson City. He had always thought the old warehouse would make a great space for a brewery, and eagerly showed it to the couple. Chris was a homebrewer, and he and his wife had long entertained the idea of opening a brewery. With fellow co-owners Joe Rowland and Ken Smith, they did just that in 2010. The taproom opened the next year.

The decor inside the taproom follows the theme of the great outdoors, with lots of wood and kayaks in abundance. Dartboards hang on one wall, and on the other side of the taproom is a stage used to host musicians. There is a large projection screen, which a lot of people park themselves in front of come college football season. The bar boasts more than 30 taps that are filled not just with the brewery's core offerings, but also with seasonals and more limited beers, like the brewery's Trail Magic Ales, which are released in March, June, and October of each year. These are always popular, as are year-round beers like the **Appalachian Trail Extra Pale Ale,** with citrus flavors and lighter body that lies somewhere between a pale ale and an IPA.

The open-air scenic train tours stop right in front of the brewery, dropping off folks for a quick visit to Bryson City. With any luck, they'll step into Nantahala for a beer before resuming their tour of the Great Smokey Mountains.

Noon Day IPA
Style: India pale ale
ABV: 6 percent
Availability: On tap year-round
The word "Nantahala" comes from the Cherokee language and means "Land of the Noon Day Sun." This IPA—the brewery's flagship—shines about as brightly as its namesake. While it was born and brewed in the mountains of North Carolina, it is firmly rooted in the West Coast style. Notes of pine, grapefruit, and orange peel are at the forefront, with caramel malt only peeking through occasionally. It is sometimes served on nitrogen, which mutes some of the hoppiness in favor of a creamier mouthfeel.

OSKAR BLUES BREWERY–BREVARD

342 Mountain Industrial Dr., Brevard, NC 28712; (828) 883-2337; OskarBlues.com; @OskarBluesWNC
Founded: 2012 **Founder:** Dale Katechis **Brewer:** Noah Tuttle **Flagship Beer:** Dale's Pale Ale **Year-Round Beers:** Dale's Pale Ale, Mama's Little Yella Pils, Old Chub, Deviant Dale's, G'Knight **Seasonals/Special Releases:** Gubna, Ten-FIDY **Tours:** Mon through Thurs, 4 p.m.; Fri through Sun, 2, 3, 4, and 5 p.m. **Taproom:** Sun through Thurs, 12 to 8 p.m.; Fri through Sat, 12 to 10 p.m.

The Oskar Blues Brewery in Brevard sits on "Mountain Industrial Drive," which is appropriate for the Colorado-based brewery's new space. The setting *is* industrial—the brewery dwarfs most any other in North Carolina. Don't think for a second,

though, that this is simply a manufacturing plant, devoid of soul. The brand has grown exponentially over the years, but never abandoned the humility and humor that got them there in the first place.

There is a closeness to the beer here, a proximity to the process. The outside patio sits in the shade of hundreds of kegs. Upon walking in, cans of beer tower to your right, while an archway made of discarded cans serves as the portal for all heading to the Tasty Weasel tasting room upstairs. Up there, you are drinking right beside the 200-barrel fermenters that stretch to the ceiling, and you can see the roller coaster of a canning line snaking its way through the brewery. Chances are you'll spy a few bicycles, too, as many of the employees are avid mountain bikers. They share this passion with Oskar Blues founder Dale Katechis, the man whose name graces every can of **Dale's Pale Ale.**

The Brevard brewery brews Dale's and the rest of the brewery's core year-round and seasonal beers. Their **Old Chub** is a Scottish ale with smooth, sweet notes of figs, raisins, chocolate, and a little smoke. The seasonal **Ten-FIDY** is one of the thickest imperial stouts out there. In that viscous, syrupy body, you will find notes

Deviant Dale's

Style: American IPA

ABV: 8 percent

Availability: Year-round on tap and in
16-ounce cans

Deviant Dale's, as the name implies, is a
darker, danker, and decidedly more bitter
version of Dale's Pale Ale. Pine, grapefruit,
and juicy orange dominate this beer, which
has a lip-smackingly sticky character to it.
The caramel malt prevents the hops from
being too deviant, and even though it is
more bitter and boozy than "regular" Dale's,
it is still a balanced-yet-big beer.

of sweet fudge and dark-roasted coffee. All of the regular offerings are available in
cans, save for any small batch beers served only at the Tasty Weasel during Tasty
Tuesdays and Firkin Fridays. The brewery offers free trolley rides back and forth from
Asheville (check their website for pickup locations).

PISGAH BREWING COMPANY

150 Eastside Dr., Black Mountain, NC 28711; (828) 669-0190; PisgahBrewing.com;
@PisgahBrewing

Founded: 2005 **Founders:** David Quinn, Jason Caughman **Brewers:** David Quinn, Ryan
Frank **Flagship Beer:** Pisgah Pale Ale **Year-Round Beers:** Pisgah Pale Ale, India Pale Ale,
Tripel, Nitro Stout **Seasonals/Special Releases:** ESB, Porter, Belgian Witbier, Mexican
Lager, Red Devil, Cosmos, Valdez, Vortex I, Vortex II, Hellbender Barleywine, Baptista,
Benton's Bacon Snout **Tours:** Sat at 2 and 3 p.m. **Taproom:** Mon, Tues, and Weds, 4 to 9
p.m.; Thurs and Fri, 2 p.m. to 12 a.m.; Sat, 12 p.m. to 12 a.m.; Sun, 2 to 9 p.m.

The mural painted across a concrete wall with the Pisgah Brewing logo is the only
indication that a brewery lurks behind the doors of this industrial warehouse.
Once you make your way down the dimly lit hall, though, the space opens up to
reveal a long bar with many taps, and as many medals hanging above them.

There are a couple of couches lining the back wall, but most of the floor is left open for people during the many concerts. Music is a heavy focus here, as Pisgah Brewing has an inside stage and a large outside stage in the pasture behind the warehouse. There is also a small patio outback with a few picnic tables.

From the day they opened in 2005, Pisgah Brewing took pride in brewing certified-organic beers. They lost their certification from the USDA in 2013 due to not being able to find sufficient quantities of organic hops. Rather than change their recipes, they decided to continue brewing as they always have. They still use organic grain and whole-leaf hops exclusively. The only thing that has changed is the way the USDA goes about its certifications.

The brewery was founded by David Quinn and Jason Caughman in 2005. David left to head out west for a few years, but returned when Jason left the company in 2013. The brewery brews a variety of styles, with many year-rounds and season-als. The **Pisgah Pale Ale** is one of the area's finest in that style, and it accounts for a huge volume of the brewery's sales. They brew a host of much-loved seasonal and limited beers, including **Valdez,** an imperial stout brewed with coffee beans from Black Mountain's Dynamite Coffee Roasters. It might make a good breakfast when paired with **Benton's Bacon Snout,** a stout brewed with molasses from Coates Family Farms and bacon from Benton's Smokehouse Farms.

Vortex I
Style: Double India pale ale
ABV: 9.2 percent
Availability: Seasonal
As a brewer that uses only whole-leaf hops, Pisgah lets you know it takes its hoppy offerings seriously. They say Vortex I is the hoppiest beer in Buncombe County, which is a bold claim given that county's many brewers. Lots of Chinook and Nugget hops are used, resulting in a wealth of mango, grapefruit, and pine in a beer that belies its 9.2 percent ABV.

SOUTHERN APPALACHIAN BREWERY

822 Locust St., Ste. 100, Hendersonville, NC 28792; (828) 684-1235; SABrewery.com;
Founded: 2011 **Founders:** Andy and Kelly Cubbin **Brewer:** Andy Cubbin **Flagship Beer:** Copperhead Amber Ale **Year-Round Beers:** Copperhead Amber Ale, Pilsner, Belgian Blonde Ale, India Pale Ale, Black Bear Stout **Seasonals/Special Releases:** Raspberry Wheat, Peach Wheat **Tours:** No **Taproom:** Weds through Fri, 4 to close; Sat and Sun, 2 to close

The Southern Appalachian Brewery dates back to 2003, when two gentlemen started a small brewery called Appalachian Brewery in Rosmon, North Carolina. Years later, they put their brewery and brand up for sale. Andy and Kelly Cubbin—two photographers from Chicago—bought the brand in 2006 and started brewing in Fletcher, just south of Asheville. Andy had been homebrewing prior to this, and the five-barrel system was a good way for him to adjust to commercial brewing before moving up to something larger, which he and Kelly knew they would have to do eventually.

Western North Carolina

They looked at space in Asheville, but after seeing brewery after brewery open up in that city they set their sights a little farther south. They changed the brewery's name to Southern Appalachian Brewery and opened in Hendersonville, about a block away from that city's historic district.

A food truck is likely to be the only car you'll find in the large parking lot directly beside the brewery, as the regular parking lot is across the street. You will find people of all ages hanging in this lot beside the brewery, which is about as family-friendly as it gets. Kids ride around on bikes and trikes or play games, while adults grab plastic chairs and tables from big stacks and find themselves a seat. Chalk covers the asphalt as well as the concrete walls that cut the lot off from the rising road beside it.

Underneath that road is a tunnel behind a locked wooden door. The building the brewery sits in used to be a Coca-Cola bottling plant, and the plant's employees would drive their forklifts through the tunnel to the other side. Andy hopes to use this as a cellar space for his sour program and barrel-aged beers. The 15-barrel brewhouse that Andy brews on, as well as rows of fermenting tanks, are within full view of the taproom. The taproom usually has at least six beers on tap, including the flagship **Copperhead Amber Ale.** It is a smooth, well-balanced amber with notes of caramel and just a kiss of citrus. At 6 percent ABV, Southern Appalachian's **Pilsner** is a bit more potent than most, but it rings true to style with a light cracker quality and a bit of spiciness from the Saaz hops. In addition to what is offered by the food trucks, soft pretzels from nearby Underground Baking Company are often available. The brewery also invites visitors to bring in food or have it delivered.

Beer Lover's Pick

Black Bear Stout
Style: American stout
ABV: 5.5 percent
Availability: On tap year-round
Southern Appalachian Brewery's Black Bear Stout is a smooth, lower-alcohol stout that offers up notes of coffee and milk chocolate on the front of the palate before transitioning to a dry finish. This finish helps the stout remain quaffable despite its full body.

Brewpubs

BLIND SQUIRREL BREWERY

4716 S. US Hwy. 19E, Plumtree, NC 28664; (828) 765-9696; BlindSquirrelBrewery.com
Founded: 2012 **Founders:** Cleve and Robin Young **Brewer:** Will Young **Flagship Beer:**
Nut Brown Ale **Year-Round Beers:** Pale Ale, IPA, Amber Ale, Tripel, Stout and Nut Brown
Ale **Seasonals/Special Releases:** Cream Ale, Hefeweizen, Belgian IPA, and Wee Heavy

The building that now houses the Vance Toe River Lodge was built in 1919 as the T. B. Vance General Store. It changed hands over the years, becoming a "tack and critter" store and even once providing housing for workers in the rural Appalachia area. The building had a rich history, yet it had been abandoned when Cleve and Robin Young stopped to explore the site during a family trip. They were enamored with the building and the picturesque location—so much so that, in 1992, they bought the building and began a three-year renovation process before moving to Plumtree and opening what is now the Vance Toe River Lodge.

PHOTO BY AUTHOR

In the years since, the Young family has grown the lodge from a remote mountain outpost to a destination offering visitors a wide array of activities—a bed and breakfast, a restaurant, a campground, various cabins, fishing, rafting, disc golf, canopy tours, and the Plumtree Valley Vineyards. In 2012 the Youngs decided to add a brewery to their long list of attractions, and so far it has brought many a visitor to the lodge. Cleve and Robin's son, Will Young, brews all of Blind Squirrel Brewery's beers on a mobile three-barrel system in front of the small taproom. Therein you can find eight taps, all of them brewed true to style and immensely drinkable. Hungry? Try the beer-battered fried trout po'boy if you enjoy seafood, as the trout is harvested, cleaned, and cooked on the property. The clean and crisp **Cream Ale** would help to cut through that batter and remoulade, making for a nice pairing.

BLOWING ROCK ALE HOUSE & INN

152 Sunset Dr., Blowing Rock, NC 28607; (828) 414-9600; BlowingRockBrewingCo.com; @BRBrewingCo
Founded: 2013 **Founders:** Jeff Walker, Todd Rice, Rob Dyer, Lisa Stripling **Brewer:** Ray Hodge **Flagship Beer:** Pilsner **Year-Round Beers:** Double IPA, Extra Special Bitter, Wheat **Seasonals/Special Releases:** Chocolate Porter, Cherry Chocolate Porter, Stout, Russian Imperial Stout, Scottish Ale, Wee Heavy

A block away from Blowing Rock's bustling Main Street sits the Blowing Rock Ale House & Inn. Having opened in 2013, the brewery itself is new even if the building it occupies is not. What was formerly the Maple Lodge bed and breakfast now houses the restaurant and inn, while the former carriage building around back houses the brewery itself, a five-barrel system manned by industry veteran Ray Hodge.

PHOTO BY AUTHOR

The brewery's brand has been around since 2005, when Jeff Walker and Todd Rice created the Blowing Rock name and had their beers contract brewed in Pennsylvania while they built a brand and sought a home of their own. You will find two of those beers listed under the Legacy Brand section of the menu, though those are brewed at another much larger production brewery.

When visiting the Blowing Rock brewpub, opt instead for the Ale House Series that Ray creates in the brewery behind the restaurant. Some base styles will remain on tap throughout the year, but go through "seasonal expressions." You might not think a **Chocolate Porter** is an ideal summer beer, but Blowing Rock's is light in both body and alcohol (it's only 4.2 percent ABV). In the winter, this beer becomes a **Cherry Chocolate Porter.** The **Scottish Ale,** which is brewed with just a touch of peat-smoked malt, becomes a **Wee Heavy** when the weather turns cold. And the **Stout,** of the dry and drinkable Foreign Export style, gives way to an imperial iteration when winter descends upon the mountains.

The menu at the Blowing Rock Ale House & Inn is small, but satisfying. If you simply need something to curb your hunger before getting back to your excursion, opt for the pair of pretzels. Both the mustard and cheese that accompany these perfectly baked knots are made with the brewery's beer. Want something more substantial? The bison burger with smoked mozzarella is a fine choice.

BLUE MOUNTAIN PIZZA & BREW PUB
55 N. Main St., Weaverville, NC 28787; (828) 658-8777; BlueMountainPizza.com
Founded: 2012 **Founder:** Matt Danford **Brewers:** Mike Vanhoose, Joey Cagle **Flagship Beer:** North Main Pale Ale **Year-Round Beers:** North Main Pale Ale **Seasonals/Special Releases:** The Creep, Lil' Creep, Daydream Belgian Blonde, Fire Wheel Red IPA, Cesspool Saison, Summit Saison, Belgian Tripel, Zwart Belgian Black IPA

Blue Mountain Pizza has long been a favorite among Weaverville locals, who often pack into this neighborhood spot to eat pizza and enjoy live music. In December of 2012, founder Matt Danford gave residents yet another reason to come in: beer.

He and brewers Mike Vanhoose and Joey Cagle installed a two-barrel system in the basement on the backside of the building. Because it is a smaller setup, Mike and Joey rotate through a lot of different recipes to keep things fresh and interesting. The brewpub's flagship is the easy drinking **North Main Pale Ale,** and that one's on fairly regularly. While Blue Mountain brews a variety of styles, their IPAs are among the most popular. Notables include **The Creep** double IPA and **Lil' Creep,** a slightly less hoppy version of the former. Belgian styles are on tap often, too, including the **Summit Saison** and **Belgian Tripel.**

You can create your own pizza or choose from several delicious pies, such as the Banks Classic (pepperoni, ham, red onion, portobello mushrooms, feta, Gorgonzola, and pesto) or the Islander (barbecue sauce, pork, red onion, pineapple, jalapeños, and smoked Gouda, encircled by a Parmesan and black-pepper crust). The brewpub also offers 14-inch Chicago-style pizzas and a selection of salads, pastas, and appetizers.

While pizza is quite obviously Blue Mountain's specialty, Mike—who in addition to brewing beers and managing the restaurant has a degree in culinary arts—hosts special dinners called "The Other Side of the Mountain" on the third Monday of every month. The tables are draped in white linen, and upon them Mike serves a four-course meal to an intimate group of only 20 people.

BOONDOCKS BREWING TAP ROOM & RESTAURANT

108 S. Jefferson Ave., West Jefferson, NC 28694; (336) 246-5222; Boondocks-Brewing.com
Founded: 2012 **Founder:** Gary Brown **Brewer:** Gary Brown **Flagship Beer:** Kölsch
Year-Round Beers: N/A **Seasonals/Special Releases:** Kölsch, Belgian Tripel,
Cinnamon Basil Blonde Ale

Venture northeast past Blowing Rock and Boone and you will find West Jefferson, a small mountain town surrounded in every direction, it sometimes seems, by Christmas tree farms. While West Jefferson doesn't draw the amount of tourists those two cities do, its downtown is full of coffeehouses, art galleries, gift shops, a cheese factory, and several restaurants.

One of those restaurants was Frasers, a place Gary Brown and his wife frequented whenever they left their home in Rocky Mount for West Jefferson, where they have had a vacation home since the early '90s. On one trip, the Browns learned that the owners of Frasers were going to let the lease run out in December. They couldn't let that happen.

Frasers closed on July 31, 2012, and the very next day Gary Brown introduced himself to the staff as the new owner. Most already knew him and his wife from

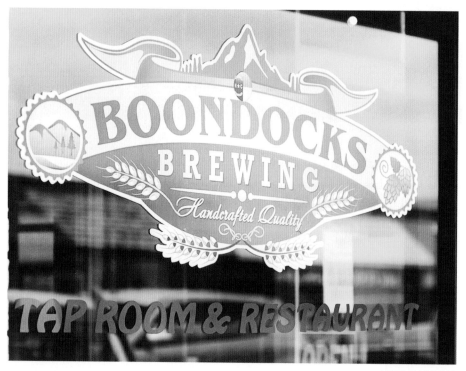

PHOTO BY AUTHOR

their years of coming to Frasers. One of the biggest things to change after Gary opened up was the beer. Gary had homebrewed for decades prior, and installed a 15-gallon SABCO Brewmagic system to handle brewing for the restaurant. So far, he hasn't worked through enough recipes to say what might be a flagship or even a year-round beer. His **Kölsch** has been very well received, as was a **Cinnamon Basil Blonde Ale.** His **Belgian Tripel,** with its light body and notes of bubble gum and malt sweetness, is sneakily drinkable for such a high-ABV style.

The Boondocks' beers go quickly, but patrons can rest easy knowing Gary has 34 taps to choose from, many of them devoted to local or limited release beers. Flights are available for all, making it easy to try several great beers in a single sitting. The brewpub has an extensive menu as well, and they pride themselves on steaks that are cut in-house from locally raised beef. The Ultimate BLT lives up to its name with avocado, pesto mayonnaise, cheese, and a fried egg joining the standard bacon, lettuce, and tomato.

THE PIZZA SHOP & DRY COUNTY BREWING CO.
585 Oak Ave., Spruce Pine, NC 28777; (828) 765-4583; DryCountyBrewing.com
Founded: 2010 **Founders:** Chad Mohr and Jennifer Rambo **Brewer:** Chad Mohr
Flagship Beer: N/A **Year-Round Beers:** N/A **Seasonals/Special Releases:** Sorachi Ace IPA, Scotch Ale, Extra Special Bitter, Farmhouse Ale, Nugget IPA, Belgian Dubbel, Rye Pale Ale, Black Lager, Rye Bock

The mountains of Spruce Pine are known for their gemstone mines, but head into the small downtown nestled between those big mountains and you'll find a gem of a different sort. In an unassuming and nondescript building sits The Pizza Shop & Dry County Brewing Co. The Pizza Shop itself was founded in 2009, the same year Spruce Pine voted to allow the sale of alcohol in an otherwise dry county. The next year, Chad Mohr assembled a small 10-gallon brew system in one of the restaurant's rooms just off the kitchen, and it is there that he brews The Pizza Shop's beers.

From the road, you would never think that beer is brewed inside the nondescript, ranch-style building. Even when you get inside, you won't find a window overlooking a stainless steel brewhouse, as is often the case. What you will find is a chalkboard detailing the six beers that are currently on tap. Of those six taps, Chad usually has a lager, IPA, farmhouse, and Belgian beer on at all times. Because he cycles through 45 different recipes, it is not often that you'll come across the same beer twice.

Chad does have a penchant for using rye in his beers, and his **Rye Pale Ale** pairs well with a mozzarella and bacon-laden pizza, pesto as its base. Rather than listing

specific pizzas, Dry County allows you to select a base sauce (pesto, white, or traditional) and then select the toppings of your choice. All of the food served at The Pizza Shop is made from scratch, and quite often locally grown or sourced from the farmer's market that sets up in the brewpub's parking lot during warmer months. On the third Thursday of each month, Dry County hosts a popular team trivia event that they call Quizzo. They also host live music and open mic nights.

TIPPING POINT BREWERY & TAVERN

190 N. Main St., Waynesville, NC 28786; (828) 246-9230; TippingPointTavern.com
Founded: 2010 **Founders:** Doug Weaver, Jenny Weaver, Dan Elliot, Jon Bowman
Brewer: Scott Peterson **Flagship Beer:** Chunky Gal Amber **Year-Round Beers:** Chunky Gal Amber, Punch in the Face IPA, Hiking Viking Blonde **Seasonals/Special Releases:** Edelweiss Wheat, Mayor Brown, 1736 Porter

Tipping Point Tavern was founded in 2010, and then added the brewery in 2012. The downtown Waynesville tavern seems much older than it is, thanks in part to old beer signs, movie posters, and lots of dark wood and exposed ductwork spanning the length of the building.

On a small three-barrel system in the brick-lined basement, Scott Peterson brews the tavern's three staples: **Chunky Gal Amber, Punch in the Face IPA,** and **Hiking Viking Blonde.** The Chunky Gal is nowhere near as heavy as it sounds, with a malt sweetness that makes it a smooth and easy-drinking choice that would work well with much of the tavern's food. Likewise, the Punch in the Face IPA isn't a bruiser of a beer by any stretch, though it displays nice citrus notes alongside the bitterness that is typical of the style. The Hiking Viking Blonde is the lightest beer they brew, and it would surely be a good thirst-quencher if you had spent all day hiking nearby trails. In addition to those three, Scott—who previously worked for Ska Brewing and Wynkoop Brewing in Colorado—also brews several seasonals throughout the year.

The tavern also has a good bottle selection and keeps many other NC beers on tap. And if you're touring Waynesville's other breweries, make a point to stop by Tipping Point Tavern to grab some lunch or dinner first. There's nothing fun about drinking on an empty stomach, and it's virtually impossible to leave Tipping Point with one. The massive pulled pork burrito is stuffed with pork, peppers, and onions before being drowned in the tavern's spicy ranchero sauce. The Mexican pulled pork sandwich is popular, too, as are the fish tacos.

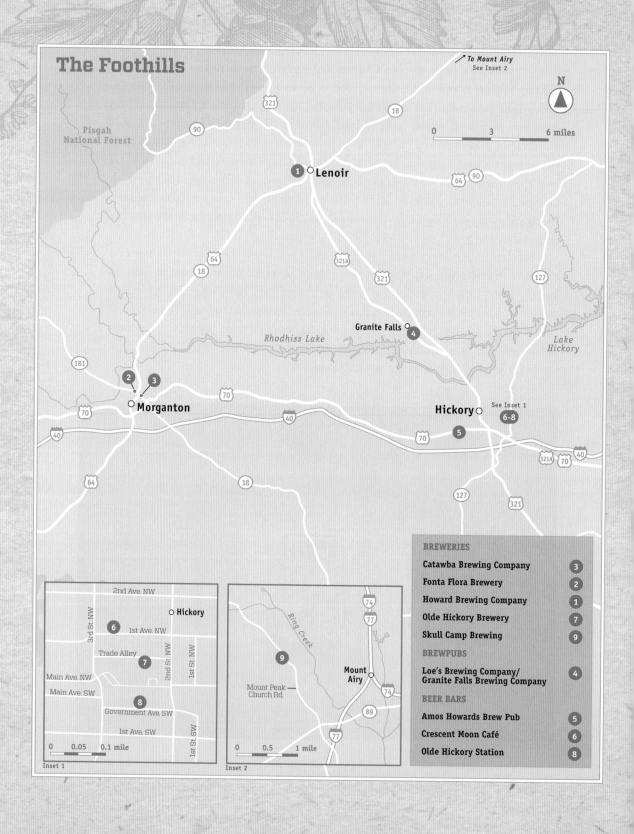

The Foothills

To Mount Airy
See Inset 2

N

Pisgah
National Forest

321

90

18

321

64 90

○ Lenoir 1

64

18

321A

321

Granite Falls 4

Rhodhiss Lake

Lake
Hickory

127

181

2 3

○ Morganton

70

70

40

Hickory ○

See Inset 1

6-8

40

64

18

70

5

321A 70 40

127

321

Inset 1

2nd Ave. NW

○ Hickory

3rd St. NW

6

1st Ave. NW

2nd St. NW

1st St. NW

Trade Alley

7

Main Ave. NW

Main Ave. SW

8

Government Ave. SW

1st Ave. SW

1st St. SW

0   0.05   0.1 mile

Inset 1

Inset 2

Ring Creek

74

77

9

Mount
Airy

Mount Peak
Church Rd.

74

89

77

0   0.5   1 mile

Inset 2

BREWERIES	
Catawba Brewing Company	3
Fonta Flora Brewery	2
Howard Brewing Company	1
Olde Hickory Brewery	7
Skull Camp Brewing	9
BREWPUBS	
Loe's Brewing Company/ Granite Falls Brewing Company	4
BEER BARS	
Amos Howards Brew Pub	5
Crescent Moon Café	6
Olde Hickory Station	8

0   3   6 miles

The Foothills

As the mountains of North Carolina give way to the foothills, fewer breweries dot the scenic landscape. As these breweries show, though, it's not just about the number of breweries but the quality of beer they are producing. From the Hickory area all the way up to Mt. Airy near the state's northern border, the foothills are filled with breweries brewing great beer.

Breweries

CATAWBA BREWING COMPANY

212 S. Green St., Morganton, NC 28655; (828) 430-6883; CatawbaBrewingCompany.com; @CatawbaBeer

Founded: 1999 **Founders:** Scott Pyatt, Billy Pyatt, Jetta Pyatt **Brewer:** Kevin B. Sondey **Flagship Beer:** Firewater IPA **Year-Round Beers:** Firewater IPA, Brown Bear Ale, Farmer Ted's Farmhouse Cream Ale, Mother Trucker Pale Ale, Revenuer's Red Ale, White Zombie Ale, Black Dome Stout **Seasonals/Special Releases:** King Don's Pumpkin Ale, King Coconut Porter, Le Sexxxy Saison, Chocolate Saison, Arlo's PB&J, Brewberry Stout, Hooligan Scotch Ale, King Winterbolt Winter Ale **Tours:** During tasting room hours **Taproom:** Wed through Fri, 5 to 11 p.m.; Sat, 1 to 6 p.m.

Catawba Brewing Company has its roots in the basement of an antiques mall in Glen Alpine, where Scott Pyatt first started his brewery in 1999. The brewery has grown quite a bit since then, and in 2007 Scott left the basement for a large warehouse space in nearby Morganton.

Two large garage doors off the loading dock serve as the entryway, not just for guests but also grain, hops, and anything else that needs to be unloaded when the tasting room is not open. The taproom is large, with plenty of seating at the bar and tables throughout the building. Scott is a graduate of Appalachian State University, and his pride in his alma mater can be seen in the bright yellow ASU Mountaineer booths bolted to the floor. Those with a real interest in college football, however, would do better to sit on the other side of the taproom, where a massive screen lights up with games every Saturday. The brewery also hosts a huge potluck-style party for the Super Bowl. The stage in front of the screen is quite often filled with bands, and the brewery's open mic nights are popular.

Catawba offers three of its beers in cans—Firewater IPA, White Zombie, and Farmer Ted's Farmhouse Cream Ale—which you can find at bottle shops around NC. The IPA is something of a cross between the English and American IPA, with a biscuity malt backbone and hops from both countries. Those English hops also find their way into the brewery's **White Zombie Ale,** a Belgian witbier that is also brewed with orange peel and coriander. Completing the trio of cans is **Farmer Ted's Farmhouse Cream Ale,** a light and crisp beer brewed with wheat, corn, and American-grown hops—ingredients all available to Appalachia's early settlers.

At the taproom you will find a lot of other year-round and seasonal offerings that don't often appear outside of Morganton. If the concept of a peanut butter and jelly sandwich in liquid form appeals to you (and why wouldn't it?), you owe it to

PHOTO BY AUTHOR

King Don's Pumpkin Ale
Style: Pumpkin ale
ABV: 5.7 percent
Availability: On tap during the
fall

Catawba's King Don's Pumpkin Ale is the brewery's fall seasonal, but the first pours actually occur during their big Halloween in July celebration. It doesn't matter if it's summer or fall, fans swarm the taproom for a taste of this beloved autumn treat. King Don's is a heavily spiced pumpkin ale, with notes of cinnamon, brown sugar, and a bit of nutmeg. A sturdy caramel malt base rounds the beer out and renders those spices smooth and drinkable. The beer lingers on the palate, leaving the

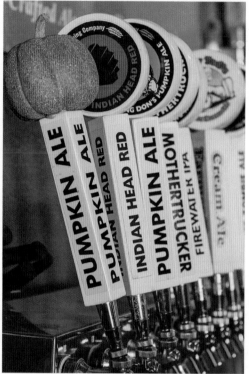

PHOTO BY AUTHOR

sensation that you just chewed a stick of Big Red gum. If you prefer to enjoy your pumpkin beers in the fall instead of July, the brewery has a very popular Halloween party in October as well.

yourself to try **Arlo's PB&J,** a beer that really is a peanut butter and jelly sandwich in a glass.

Catawba Brewing Company has seen a lot of growth since its days in the basement, and it continues to expand. They started life as Catawba Valley Brewing company, but dropped the "valley" when they rebranded in 2013. In 2014, they will open an Asheville location just across from Biltmore Village that will feature a brewery, tasting room, and distribution center.

FONTA FLORA BREWERY

317 N. Green St., Morganton, NC 28655; (828) 413-1183; FontaFlora.com; @FontaFloraBrew
Founded: 2013 **Founders:** Mark Bennett, David Bennett, Todd Boera **Brewer:** Todd Boera **Flagship Beer:** N/A **Year-Round Beers:** N/A **Seasonals/Special Releases:** English Table Beer, Belgian Table Beer, American Table Beer, Scottish Table Beer, Hop Beard Series, Foraged Fig Saison, Black Apple Saison, Scuppernong Saison, Appalachian Grisette **Tours:** No **Taproom:** Thurs and Fri, 5 to 10 p.m.; Sat, 12 to 10 p.m.; Sun, 12 to 7 p.m.; Mon, 5 to 10 p.m.

Todd Boera spent four years at Morganton's Catawba Brewing Company, and when he wanted to do his own thing he didn't have to look far. In 2013, he and founders Mark and David Bennett opened Fonta Flora Brewery in a small building just about a mile down the road from Catawba.

In that building, they installed light-blue wainscoting beneath the brick walls. There is a bar, of course, and behind it a wood-covered wall with the available beers scrawled across two chalkboard sections. The heart of Fonta Flora, the brewery itself, sits a few feet away, no railings or glass walls separating it from the rest of

PHOTO BY AUTHOR

English Table Beer

Style: English mild

ABV: 3.8 percent

Availability: Rotating

Fonta Flora's English table beer shatters the myth that dark beers must be thick, heavy, and full of alcohol. This true-to-style English mild features subtle notes of chocolate and coffee, along with biscuity malt and the faintest wisp of smoke. The mouthfeel is thin, the finish dry. This beer is a perfect example of a style you don't often see brewed on this side of the pond. It is sessionable and exceptionally food-friendly, making this an ideal choice for watching the game or having dinner with family and friends.

PHOTO BY AUTHOR

the establishment. It includes a 3.5-barrel system and four 7-barrel fermenters, all manufactured in America by Portland Kettle Works. The system is much smaller than the one on which he brewed at Catawba, but it enables Todd to craft a larger variety of styles. Like Erik Lars Myers of Mystery Brewing, Todd is reticent to name any one beer as a flagship or year-round offering. He may not always have a specific beer on tap, but visitors should still be able to find certain styles on tap, such as a dark beer, an IPA, or a saison.

The saisons are all openly fermented, as they used to be when brewed so long ago by farmers in Belgium and France. Doing so takes some of the control away from Todd, but it can lead to more interesting flavors. His **Black Apple Saison** is brewed with 70 pounds of heirloom apples, and his **Foraged Fig Saison** features local figs. Since Todd is as well known for his beard as he is his beers, it's only fitting that the brewery's IPAs will often fall under the **Hop Beard IPA** series.

Another type of beer you might regularly find at Fonta Flora is table beer, which is really less of a particular style and more a name given to a low-alcohol beer that you could have a few of at lunch or dinner, family gathered 'round. Table beers are popular in Europe, and Todd would like to see these sessionable beers catch on state-side. Todd also infuses water with hops and grapefruit zest, making for a refreshing, nonalcoholic option.

HOWARD BREWING COMPANY

1001 West Ave. NW, Lenoir, NC 28645; (828) 572-4449; HowardBrewing.com; @HowardBrewing
Founded: 2012 **Founder:** Jason Howard **Brewer:** Jason Howard **Flagship Beer:** Action Man Lager **Year-Round Beers:** Action Man Lager, Lake Fever Black IPA, Trail Maker Pale Ale, The Weekender Pilsner **Seasonals/Special Releases:** Mistletoe, General Lenoir's Old Ale, Jalapeño Action Man, Single Hop Session Wheat IPA, Twisted Trail IPA **Tours:** No **Taproom:** Thurs through Sat, 5 to 9 p.m.; Sun, 1 to 4 p.m.

Howard Brewing is located in historic downtown Lenoir, in a building they share with Carolina Distillery. Many oak barrels—a common bridge between the beer and spirits worlds these days—serve as tables, with small stools pulled up to them.

The brewery's namesake—founder Jason Howard—started homebrewing while working in the construction business in Michigan. When he moved to North Carolina, it didn't take him long before he became the president of a local homebrew club. When the homebuilding industry stalled, he saw an opportunity to turn his passion into a profession. In 2012, he built the brewery and small tasting room in downtown Lenoir.

The tasting room often features live music on Friday and Saturday nights. And, true to his homebrewing roots, he invites the local club to host meetings there. Through three windows in the taproom, visitors can look in on the 15-barrel brewery and stacks of aluminum cans. The brewery cans both its **Action Man Lager** and **Trail Maker Pale Ale,** and both are exactly the sort of low-alcohol and easy-drinking beers you would want in such a package.

Of course, the brewery has some hoppier options as well. The **Lake Fever Black IPA** is a well-executed example of a style that is becoming more and more popular. Howard's iteration tastes of medium-roast coffee, just a hint of chocolate, and piney hops. One of the brewery's most sought-after beers is **Mistletoe,** a porter brewed

Action Man Lager

Style: Vienna lager

ABV: 5.5 percent

Availability: On tap and in cans year-round

True to its name, Howard Brewing's Action Man Lager is well suited to a life spent in action, thanks to its aluminum can and relatively low ABV. Action Man pours a rich amber color, and one whiff lets you know this is a beer that focuses on the malt. The beer has notes of toasted bread and sweet honey, and it is a crisp, easy drinker. German hops keep all that malt from becoming too sweet, making this well-balanced beer one just about anyone could appreciate.

PHOTO BY AUTHOR

with raspberries from North Carolina and aged in barrels that once held Carolina Distillery's apple brandy. This results in an interplay of chocolate, coffee, tart raspberries, and a caramel-like sweetness from the barrel. As the name suggests, this one is released around the holidays every year.

OLDE HICKORY BREWERY (OLDE HICKORY TAPROOM)

222 Union Sq., Hickory, NC 28601; (828) 322-1965; OldeHickoryBrewery.com; @OldeHickory

Founded: 1994 **Founder:** Steven Lyerly **Brewer:** Steven Lyerly **Flagship Beer:** Table Rock Pale Ale **Year-Round Beers:** Table Rock Pale Ale, Piedmont Pilsner, Hickory Stick Stout, Ruby Lager, Brown Mountain Light, Hefe-Weizen **Seasonals/Special Releases:** Wilson Creek ESB, Black Raven, Death by Hops, Redeemer, Southern Cross, Irish Walker, Imperial Stout, Event Horizon, Seven Devils, Lindley Park, Daniel Boone Brown Ale, Bestway IPA, Oktoberfest, Christmas Ale **Tours:** By appt. at the brewery **Taproom:** Mon through Sun, 11 a.m. to 2 a.m.

The Olde Hickory Brewery only offers tours by appointment, so your best bet to enjoy their beers is to visit the Olde Hickory Taproom just around the corner in downtown Hickory's Union Square (the address above is for the taproom, while the brewery is around the corner at 2 Third St.). The taproom has the feel of a cozy

English pub. Hundreds of pewter mugs hang above and beside the long bar, waiting patiently for any number of regulars to come in and have a pint. Above the tap-room's many comfortable booths are mirrors with Olde Hickory beer names or iconic Hickory places, and between these mirrors and the ceiling are staggered tap handles. The taproom offers an extensive menu, and features live music frequently.

No beer is brewed here, but being within walking distance from the production brewery ensures plenty of fresh Olde Hickory beer is on tap and in bottles. It is here that Olde Hickory brews one of the largest portfolios in the state, with an extensive selection of year-round and seasonal beers running the gamut of styles and flavors. The **Table Rock Pale Ale** is well balanced, with notes of bready and sweet malts as well as fruity and floral qualities from the hops. If you are craving more bitterness, opt for **Death by Hops.** It was based on Alex Buerckholtz's winning recipe from the first Olde Hickory Pro Am homebrew competition (Alex owns Hops and Vines in Asheville, and this isn't the first competition he's won!). This double IPA is awash with orange, grapefruit, and pine resin. Caramel malts battle for attention, but they are no match for the likes of Chinook, Columbus, Centennial, Cascade, Simcoe, Amarillo, Falconer's Flight, and Zythos hops. The malt here plays a supporting role, wisely choosing to relent to the hops and the 108 IBUs they provide.

The brewery produces many big beers, including their **Imperial Stout** and **Irish Walker** barleywine. They also boast one of the largest barrel-aging programs in the state, which turns out such limited and lovely beers as the **Seven Devils** Scottish Ale and **Lindley Park,** an imperial stout brewed with honey and raspberries.

Beer Lover's Pick

The Event Horizon
Style: Imperial stout
ABV: 8.5 percent
Availability: On tap and
    in 22-ounce bottles
    in the winter

An event horizon is a point in space where gravity renders escape impossible, otherwise known as a "point of no return." Fortunately this imperial stout is one Olde Hickory returns to year after year. It is brewed with 10 different types of malt as well as local honey, and then aged in oak barrels that once held bourbon. All of this combines to create an incredibly complex stout, filled with notes of molasses, tobacco, espresso, and fudge, with the oak barrel contributing

vanilla and coconut. It is a rich and rewarding beer, unfolding new flavors with each passing sip.

SKULL CAMP BREWING

765 Round Peak Church Rd., Mount Airy, NC 27030; (336) 352-5595; SkullCampBrewing
.com

Founded: 2012 **Founders:** Ken Gulaian, Kari Heerdt **Brewers:** Kent Yocco, Jeff Leftwich
Flagship Beer: 11th Hour Amber **Year-Round Beers:** Dusk 'til Dawn Black IPA, Cave
Dweller Porter, Spilled Milk Centennial IPA, Tongue-Tied Rye IPA **Seasonals/Special
Releases:** Black Jack Black Saison, Day Tripper Tripel, Knuckle Dragger DIPA, Easy RYEder
Session Rye, Black Belt Stout, Dr. Doctoberfest Oktoberfest **Tours:** No **Taproom:** Sun to
Thurs, 12 to 5 p.m.; Fri, 12 to 8 p.m.; Sat, 11 a.m. to 6 p.m. (or until sunset from June
to Aug)

North Carolina's Yadkin Valley may be wine country, but that didn't stop Mount Airy's Round Peak Vineyards from opening up a brewery in 2012. Skull Camp Brewing takes its name from Skull Camp Mountain, which looms large in the distance past Round Peak's 13 acres of vineyards. The view from the back patio is spectacular, whether you have a glass of wine or beer in your hand.

The beers are brewed on a 10-gallon system by Kent Yocco and Jeff Leftwich. While Kent favors Belgian styles, Jeff is all about IPAs. Couple this with the fact they have to brew frequently due to their small brew system, and chances are you're likely to find something new on at Skull Camp Brewing each time you visit. In the taproom the brewery shares with the winery, you can usually find four taps on at a time. The **Black Jack Black Saison** also offers a unique twist on a traditional style, somehow melding what some may say are disparate flavors—tartness, roast, and pepper spice—into a complex and refreshing beer. Citra hops were used heavily in the brewery's **Knuckle Dragger DIPA** until hop shortages necessitated the use of Falconer's Flight, a newer hop blend that imparts notes of lemon, grapefruit, and spice.

Skull Camp Brewing has purchased a building in Elkin, NC, where they are in the process of installing a 10-barrel system. This much larger brewery will also feature a taproom and beer garden, but if you are fond of the view at Round Peak Vineyards—and you will be—you will still be able to have a pint of Skull Camp beer there.

11th Hour Amber
Style: Amber ale
ABV: 6.9 percent
Availability: Year-
round on tap

Skull Camp Brewing's 11th Hour Amber is an imperial amber, which in this case means it is hoppier and has a higher ABV than most amber ales. Due to generous hop additions, this one has lots of the citrus character usually reserved for a West Coast IPA. It finishes dry and should appeal to amber and IPA drinkers alike.

The Foothills

Brewpub

LOE'S BREWING COMPANY / GRANITE FALLS BREWING COMPANY

47 Duke St., Granite Falls, NC 28630; (828) 781-5761; LoesBrewing.com; @LoesBrewing
Founded: 2010 **Founders:** Stephen Loe, Robert Loe **Brewer:** Stephen Loe **Flagship Beer:** Punch Clock Pale Ale **Year-Round Beers:** Punch Clock Pale Ale, Southern Divinity Red IPA, Carolina Bootleg Kölsch **Seasonals/Special Releases:** Punch Clock Chocolate Orange Ale, Chocolate Moose Imperial Stout, Born 2 Poor Cherry Porter, Electric Octopus Purple Thai IPA

In 2010, the father and son pair of Robert and Stephen Loe first opened Loe's Brewing Company's doors in Hickory. They soon outgrew that space, and found themselves with a unique opportunity to go home to Granite Falls, where they had both lived in a small brick building behind a building that once housed the Granite

Bottling Works plant that was built in 1903. Around 110 years later, the Loes jumped at the chance to brew and bottle in a space that had significance not just as a former bottling plant, but as a part of their family history.

The 32,000-square-foot space is vast, and most of it is devoted to the brewery and warehouse space that will accommodate future expansion. Upon walking in, signed celebrity photos hang in a lobby area, and a stack of self-guided tour instructions invite patrons to walk throughout the large space and identify a number of interesting pieces. The restaurant portion, located in the front of the building, is done in a 1940s–60s theme. One mural shows Granite Falls as it looked in the '40s, and another shows the founders of the original Granite Bottling Works. In one corner of the restaurant is a 1948–49 booth that once sat patrons in an old Alabama soda shop. In addition to a number of booths, there is a three-sided bar built from copper pennies, wine corks, and the Charleston chestnut bar that was in place at Loe's Brewing's original location.

Another long stretch of bar continues into the tasting room, done in a 1970s–80s theme. When it's all added up, the brewery has an impressive 103 feet of bar space. A collection of 1,102 beer cans is displayed behind glass, and you could spend quite a bit of time marveling at the old labels. A large baseball glove chair sits beside an old jukebox, and above them both hangs a 1976 disco ball sourced from NBC studios that glimmered high over such shows as *American Bandstand* and *Soul Train*.

With more than 150 recipes, the brewpub almost always has something different and unique on. The **Chocolate Moose Imperial Stout,** aged in Jack Daniel's barrels, is one of the brewery's most praised beers. Those looking for something lighter will find it in the **Carolina Bootleg Kölsch,** which has floral notes and just a touch of sweetness. Stephen is a graduate of the Culinary Institute of America and has worked in many Carolina kitchens, so it should come as no surprise that the restaurant turns out some great pizzas, sandwiches, and burgers.

Beer Bars

AMOS HOWARDS BREW PUB
2828 US Hwy. 70 SW, Hickory, NC 28602; (828) 323-8753; AmosHowards.com
Draft Beers: 19 **Bottled/Canned Beers:** 200+

It's not uncommon to walk by a brewery and see shiny, silver tanks gleaming behind glass. As you approach Amos Howards Brew Pub, you will see the big, wooden barrels—and you'll likely see people sitting in them. These barrel booths are spread throughout the brewpub, and they are the most distinctive feature of this very charming establishment. The entryway into the restaurant is a barrel turned

PHOTO BY AUTHOR

on its side, and the green-and-white checkered floor contributes to the English pub feel.

Amos Howards is best known as the birthplace of Olde Hickory Brewing. Steve Lyerly was the brewer at Amos Howards, and ended up purchasing it from the original investors before he built Olde Hickory's taproom and brewery in downtown Hickory. Their brewery on Third Street is a production brewery capable of supplying all of their accounts, so they no longer brew any beer at Amos Howards. Their beers still make up almost all of the restaurant's 19 taps, though, and they boast a bottle selection of more than 200 additional beers. Of course, you can purchase Olde Hickory bottles here as well.

The food menu contains some of the pub-standard appetizers, as well as a variety of wings, sandwiches, and burgers. One of the more interesting burgers is the Aviemore, which is named after a town in Scotland and topped with a fried egg and pickled beets. The restaurant also smokes its own ribs and pulled pork.

CRESCENT MOON CAFÉ
256 1st Ave. NW, Hickory, NC 28601; (828) 322-1456; CrescentMoonCafeHKY.com; @CrescentMoonHKY
Draft Beers: 28 **Bottled/Canned Beers:** 20+

Walking by Crescent Moon Café's storefront, you would never know the restaurant boasts one of the best beer selections in Hickory; the outside does not do the inside of the building justice. The atmosphere is modern, with dark blue walls over gray wainscoting. Behind a concrete, crescent-shaped bar are 28 taps, with which the restaurant rotates through an ever-changing selection of craft beers. In keeping with the theme, a small decorative moon hangs above the bar, and moons are painted all over the wall behind it.

Crescent Moon Café holds weekly pint nights that feature one brewery and occasionally some of that brewery's more limited selections. Because they are open until 2 a.m. Monday through Saturday, Crescent Moon Café is as good a late night spot as it is a lunch destination. The menu consists of several appetizers, salads, flatbreads, and sandwiches. Options like the soft pretzel and meat and cheese plates are especially beer-friendly. The cafe has several vegan options and usually keeps a handful of gluten-free beers on tap. There is a smaller late-night menu available from 10 p.m. to close.

OLDE HICKORY STATION

232 Government Ave. SW, Hickory, NC 28602; (828) 322-2356;
OldeHickoryStation.com
Draft Beers: 49 **Bottled/Canned Beers:** 200+

Set in an old train station just across the tracks from the Olde Hickory Taproom and right around the corner from Olde Hickory Brewing is the Olde Hickory Station, the brewery's newest venture. The station features 49 taps of well-selected craft beers, including offerings from Olde Hickory Brewing. There is an extensive food menu that utilizes local produce and meats throughout, which can be enjoyed in the station, out on the covered deck, or on the patio overlooking the train tracks and Union Square, the heart of Hickory. Candied bacon is just one appetizer that would be great with beer, especially porters and stouts.

The station's staff handles a number of tasks, including curing many of the meats and baking bread and pastries. You can purchase the meats, breads, desserts, and cheeses in the station's retail market, which also includes a decent selection of craft beer to take home.

The Triad

BREWERIES

- ③ Hoots Roller Bar & Beer Co.
- ② New Sarum Brewing Company
- ⑫ Red Oak Brewery
- ⑥ Small Batch Beer Co.
- ① Westbend Brewhouse

BREWPUBS

- ④ Foothills Brewing
- ⑧ Liberty Steakhouse & Brewery
- ⑪ Natty Greene's Pub & Brewing Co.

BEER BARS AND BOTTLE SHOPS

- ⑦ The Brewer's Kettle
- ⑤ Hops Burger Bar
- ⑨ Mellow Mushroom
- ⑩ Potent Potables

The Triad

Smack dab in the middle of North Carolina is the Triad region, which encompasses the three cities of Greensboro, Winston-Salem, and High Point as well as many other surrounding towns. The region is home to three of the state's largest-production breweries in Foothills Brewing, Natty Greene's Brewing, and Red Oak Brewery, with Foothills and Natty Greene's also operating brewpubs in Winston-Salem and Greensboro respectively.

These longtime veterans of the Triad beer scene have been joined in recent years by a host of additional breweries and brewpubs, and the area has no shortage of great beer bars to support them all. Once it was that the Triad was known for its furniture industry, but today's band of brewers have given the region another craft to call its own.

Breweries

Hoots Roller Bar & Beer Co.
840 Manly St., Winston-Salem, NC 27101; (336) 608-6026; Hootspublic.com;
@HootsBeerCo
Founded: 2013 **Founders:** Eric Weyer, Eric Swaim, Ralph Pritts **Brewer:** Chad Leiser
Flagship Beer: GasHopper IPA **Year-Round Beers:** GasHopper IPA, Lionheart ESB,
Das Hoots Pilsner, Leiser's Evening Stout **Seasonals/Special Releases:** N/A **Tours:** No
Taproom: Tues through Sat, 2 p.m. to 2 a.m.; Sun, 12 p.m. to 12 a.m.

The Hoots Roller Bar & Beer Co. opened in 2013 as one of the first tenants of the West End Mill Works, a collection of artists and businesses operating out of a historic mill in Winston-Salem's West End neighborhood. The Hoots family built the Hoots Roller Mill in 1935, with the surrounding buildings being erected all the way

into the '50s. Since a roller bar is used to make flour, the founders of Hoots Roller Bar and Beer Co. felt their name was a fitting homage to the mill and the family who ran it.

The brick building that houses Hoots Roller Bar & Beer Co. sits across from the old mill itself. This is where the mill stored its flour, which would be loaded onto trains that ran between the two buildings. No trains come through today, and the space between the buildings is now a nice grassy area with hanging lights stretching above. Peter's Creek babbles on quietly beside the mill.

The inside of Hoots Roller Bar & Beer Co. is even more scenic, thanks to some impressive woodwork and interesting items. It's a small but eclectic space, and the three founders—Eric Weyer, Eric Swaim, and Ralph Pritts—handled most of the construction and decor, including the sunburst-style wood wall behind the bar. On top of the bar itself sits an antique brass diving helmet that disguises four taps. Continuing the maritime theme are five portholes that look into the 10-barrel brewery. There's a thrift-store piano, a jukebox that plays 45s, and a Judge Dredd pinball machine.

The brewery's initial tasting events showcased beers like **GasHopper IPA, Lionheart ESB, Das Hoots Pilsner,** and **Leiser's Evening Stout,** brewed with coffee from Winston-Salem's Krankies Coffee. Hoots will continue to brew a mix of "blue collar classics" and "pioneering new American styles."

Leiser's Evening Stout
Style: American stout
ABV: 5 percent
Availability: On tap year-round
Stouts that feature coffee are often called breakfast stouts, but Hoots has gone in a different direction with theirs. At 5 percent ABV, Leiser's Evening Stout has plenty of roasty notes thanks to the addition of coffee from Winston-Salem's Krankies Coffee. The coffee is well integrated and the beer is a smooth drinker, whether for breakfast, lunch, or dinner.

NEW SARUM BREWING COMPANY

117 S. Lee St., Salisbury, NC 28144; (704) 633-1101
Founded: 2013 **Founders:** Gian Moscardini, Andy Maben **Brewer:** Andy Maben
Flagship Beer: 142 Blonde Ale **Year-Round Beers:** 142 Blonde Ale, Old Stone House
IPA, Roundhouse Robust Porter **Seasonals/Special Releases:** Honey Brown, Belgian
Tripel **Tours:** No **Taproom:** No

If asked to name a beverage made in Salisbury, most self-respecting Carolinians would probably say Cheerwine. Despite the name, this iconic cherry-flavored soda contains no alcohol, and it's popular not just in Salisbury but throughout the south.

Salisbury residents can now be just as proud of the beers made in their city, thanks to New Sarum Brewing Company.

The beers are brewed right next door to Salisbury's Salty Caper, a restaurant and bar specializing in gourmet pizzas. That restaurant has always been committed to serving craft beer, and in 2013 founder Gian Moscardini and manager Andy Maben started New Sarum Brewing Company. For now, you can only find New Sarum's beers at the Salisbury and Mooresville Salty Capers, as well as at La Cava, which the Moscardini family also owns.

The name New Sarum is a reference to the city of Salisbury in England, which was once known by that name. Some of New Sarum's beers refer to historical ties to the NC city. The **Old Stone House IPA,** for example, is named after the oldest structure in Rowan County. This IPA was one of the first beers that New Sarum put out, and it pairs well with any number of pizzas prepared next door at the Salty Caper. Other early offerings include the **Roundhouse Robust Porter,** a **Honey Brown** and **Belgian Tripel.**

142 Blonde Ale
Style: Blonde ale
ABV: 5.5 percent
Availability: On tap year-round
New Sarum's name may come from an English city, but its flagship beer is distinctly tied to the South. The 142 Blonde Ale is brewed with grits, which contribute a corn-like sweetness that works well with the light and refreshing blonde base. That sweetness lingers on longer than it does in most blonde or cream ales, making this one of the more interesting and flavorful in its style.

RED OAK BREWERY

6901 Konica Dr., Whitsett, NC 27377; (336) 447-2055; RedOakBrewery.com; @RedOakBrew
Founded: 1991 **Founder:** Bill Sherrill **Brewers:** Chris Buckley, Al Wolf, Jorge Naveiro **Flagship Beer:** Red Oak Amber Lager **Year-Round Beers:** Red Oak Amber Lager, Hummin' Bird Golden Lager, Battlefield Bock **Seasonals/Special Releases:** Big Oak, Black Oak, Old Oak **Tours:** Fri at 3 p.m. **Taproom:** Open for growler fills and 12-pack sales, Mon through Fri, 9 a.m. to 5 p.m.

Four words, bright red against a steel blue building: "Red Oak, The Freshest." They have flagged down many thirsty motorists who have noticed the large brewery right off the stretch of interstate where I-40 and I-85 run together near Greensboro. Those curious (and smart) enough to take Exit 138 are rewarded with a view that cannot be seen from the road. At the building's entrance is a well-manicured landscape surrounding the brewery, filled with a variety of plants, a small pond and waterfall, plenty of tables and chairs, and several hop bines, all of them climbing their way to the top of a towering post.

This is a popular area after the brewery's tours, which are only given at 3 p.m. each Friday. For just $10 (cash only), visitors receive a collectible glass and several samples, as well as an entertaining and educational tour of the brewery. It is an immaculately clean, almost fully automated brewery that Red Oak built in 2007. The entire brewery was custom-designed, and then the building itself was designed around it. Red piping runs along the walls, and in another room horizontal fermenting tanks are stacked from the floor to the warehouse-high ceilings.

It's all a far cry from the brewery's humble beginnings in 1991, when they opened the Red Oak Brew Pub in Greensboro. What hasn't changed over the years is Red Oak's adherence to the *Reinheitsgebot,* which says that beer must be brewed with only malted barley, hops, water, and yeast. Their beer is unfiltered, unpasteurized, and naturally carbonated. The flagship **Red Oak Amber Lager** is so popular it accounts for around 90 percent of the company's sales, but other options, including the **Hummin' Bird Golden Lager** and **Battlefield Bock,** have their fervent followers as well. In addition to those three year-round beers, Red Oak brews three seasonals. In the spring there's **Big Oak,** a strong Vienna lager; for the fall, there's **Old Oak,** an Oktoberfest-style lager; and in the winter there's **Black Oak,** a dark doppelbock. While the brewery doesn't have a taproom, you can visit from 9 a.m. to 5 p.m. Monday through Friday for growler fills or to grab 12-packs of Red Oak Amber Lager.

Red Oak Amber Lager

Style: Amber lager

ABV: 5 percent

Availability: On tap and in 12-packs year-round

It's easy to see why Red Oak Amber Lager is the brewery's flagship, outselling the other beers by so large a margin. It is an exceptionally smooth take on the Munich Urtyp (old-style) lager. With notes of caramel, toast, and a malty sweetness, this is one to buy by the 12-pack.

SMALL BATCH BEER CO.

241 W. 5th St., Winston-Salem, NC 27101; (845) 337-8444; SmallBatchWS.com; @SmallBatchWS

Founded: 2013 **Founders:** Ryan Blain, Tim Walker, Cliff Etchason **Brewers:** Tim Walker, Cliff Etchason **Flagship Beer:** Limónhead IPA **Year-Round Beers:** Limónhead IPA **Seasonals/Special Releases:** Mr. Mizzle's Magical Elixir, Pumpkin Porter, Sweet Potato Pie, Oktoberfest, Ginger Wheat, Kranked Mocha Cappuccino Stout, The Bennett Saison, Cucumbière Saison, Strawberry Fields Saison, Purple Drank, El Lobo, Match Day, Big Beautiful Amber **Tours:** No **Taproom:** Weds through Fri, 2 p.m. to 2 a.m.; Sat, 12 p.m. to 2 a.m.; Sun, 12 p.m. to 12 a.m.

For the many years until they closed in 2011, the Kopper Kitchen was a Winston-Salem institution, turning out Southern home cooking with a smile to all who entered. In light of what they meant to the city, the guys at Small Batch Beer Co. decided to leave the iconic Kopper Kitchen sign on top of the building's roof when they moved in.

Though they left the sign, the brewery's founders—Ryan Blain, Tim Walker, and Cliff Etchason—changed practically everything else. They pulled slats of wood

The Triad

from pallets and covered the walls with them. They hung vintage-style cage lights below the exposed ductwork, and installed a backsplash of clean white tile behind the bar, where they pour from eight taps. True to their name, they brew just one barrel at a time. The advantage to brewing small batches is that they can constantly experiment and try new things. They can also afford to use premium ingredients that might be cost-prohibitive if brewed on a larger scale.

Such is the case with the **Strawberry Fields Saison,** a beer that required 25 pounds of local strawberries to produce. Tim enjoys brewing (and drinking) saisons, so that is a style you will find pretty regularly at Small Batch. The **Purple Drank** saison is brewed with blackberries, and another saison is brewed with kiwi. These are all very refreshing, easy-drinking beers, and that's even true of the brewery's **Kranked Mocha Cappuccino Stout.** This 4.9 percent stout is brewed with lactose, cacao nibs, and coffee from Krankies Coffee.

Limónhead IPA
Style: India pale ale
ABV: 8 percent
Availability: On tap year-round
Small Batch calls its Limónhead IPA "an IPA for people who don't like IPAs." It is not an overly bitter beer, but still abounds with all of the grapefruit and citrus flavors you expect in an IPA, thanks to seven different types of hops and lots of lemon zest in the boil.

WESTBEND BREWHOUSE

5394 Williams Rd., Lewisville, NC 27023; (336) 945-5032; WestbendVineyards.com; @WestbendBrews

Founded: 2012 **Founder:** Lillian Kroustalis **Brewer:** Jamie Mingia **Flagship Beer:** Pale Ale **Year-Round Beers:** Pale Ale, Golden Ale, IPA, Stout **Seasonals/Special Releases:** English Ale, Summer Wheat, Cucumber Wheat, Pumpkin Ale, Winter Ale, Ghost Pepper Pale Ale, Chocolate Stout **Tours:** N/A **Taproom:** Tues through Thur, 11 a.m. to 5 p.m.; Fri and Sat, 11 a.m. to 8 p.m.; Sun, 12 to 5 p.m. Growlers are available to go.

Westbend Vineyards is only about 15 minutes west of Winston-Salem, and yet the 60 sprawling acres of vineyards in the Yadkin Valley seem far more remote. In 1972, Jack Kroustalis planted several varieties of *Vitis vinifera*, the grapes used to make European-style wines. It was a bold move, as winemakers in the state at that time almost exclusively made muscadine wines. It paid off for Jack, and in 1988 Westbend became a bonded winery.

In 2011, Jack's wife Lillian and general manager Mark Terry decided to add a brewery and taproom to the vineyards. The taproom is elegant, featuring tables made from wine barrels, lots of dark wood, a TV, and diamond-style wine racks that hold empty growlers instead of the expected wine bottles. Jamie Mingia joined as

head brewer, and in February of 2012 they were serving up pints of their **Chocolate Stout.** That was brewed for Valentine's Day, but soon the brewery was pouring four core beers and working in seasonals as well.

The **Golden Ale** is light in body and flavor, but a fine choice for anyone looking for a refreshing pint. Citrus notes and a pleasant grassiness are present in the brewery's **Pale Ale,** while the **IPA** showcases piney hops against a solid malt backbone.

Enjoy spicy beers? Do not pass up the **Ghost Pepper Pale Ale,** which is brewed with half a pound of ghost peppers per 75-gallon batch. It exhibits the characteristic back-of-the-throat burn that one might expect, but not so much as to render it undrinkable.

While Westbend Vineyards does not have a kitchen, you can find the Vineyards Mobile Grill parked outside from Tuesday through Sunday, offering up a menu featuring both "wine fare" and "beer fare." The latter includes such foods as jalapeño bottle caps, golden-fried onion rings, and mac and cheese bites.

Beer Lover's Pick

Westbend Stout
Style: Stout
ABV: 4.5 percent
Availability: On tap year-round
Westbend Brewhouse's Stout is 4.5 percent ABV, and only their Golden Ale has less alcohol by volume. It drinks like it's twice that, though, and not because it's overly boozy. On the contrary, this sessionable stout boasts a complexity usually reserved only for its imperial brethren: It contains notes of dark chocolate, espresso, molasses, and tobacco. It is easy to see why this beer took home a silver medal at the Carolinas Championship of Beers in 2013.

Brewpubs

FOOTHILLS BREWING
638 West 4th St., Winston-Salem, NC 27101; (336) 777-3348; FoothillsBrewing.com; @FoothillsBeer
Founded: 2004 **Founders:** Jamie Bartholomaus, Matthew Masten **Brewers:** Jamie Bartholomaus, T.L. Adkisson, Dave Gonzalez **Flagship Beer:** Hoppyum IPA **Year-Round Beers:** Pilot Mountain Pale Ale, Torch Pilsner, People's Porter, Hoppyum IPA, Seeing Double IPA, Jade IPA, Carolina Blonde, Carolina Strawberry, Cottonwood Endo **Seasonals/Special Releases:** Foothills Stout, Gruffmeister Maibock, Sexual Chocolate, Bourbon Barrel Aged Sexual Chocolate, Foothills Red, Foothills Hefeweizen, Hoppy Medium, Oktoberfest, Cottonwood Pumpkin Spiced Ale, Cottonwood Low Down Brown, Cottonwood Frostbite Black IPA, Barrel–Aged People's Porter

Foothills has come a long way since 2004, when they opened their brewpub in downtown Winston-Salem. Jamie Bartholomaus and Mattew Masten have seen the brand grow from one that only brewed beer for that brewpub, to one that brews and packages beer for a variety of markets around the Southeast.

Foothills had been brewing at capacity in the brewpub for quite some time. When Carolina Beer and Beverage wanted to get out of the beer business, Foothills reached out to see about purchasing their equipment. They ended up working out a package deal, and Foothills purchased not just the equipment but also the Carolina Beer brands, such as the popular Carolina Blonde and Cottonwood lines.

In December of 2011, they moved the new equipment into a sprawling 48,000-square-foot facility at 3800 Kimwell Drive in the Stratford Industrial Park. This serves as the production brewery, where Foothills brews and packages their beers for distribution. Foothills continues to expand here, bringing in more and more

Beer Lover's Pick

Bourbon Barrel Aged Sexual Chocolate
Style: Imperial stout
ABV: 9.75 percent
Availability: On tap year-round
Every year, a small portion of Foothills' highly sought after Sexual Chocolate spends four months in bourbon barrels. As is the case with the original Sexual Chocolate, people show up in the wee hours of the morning—often spilling out of the downtown brewpub just after it closes at 2 a.m.—in hopes they will be able to grab their allotment of this very limited beer, with its complex notes of cocoa, vanilla, raisins, molasses, and bourbon. This beer won a gold medal at the Great American Beer Festival in 2010 and a silver at the same festival in 2011.

fermenters and barrels to keep up with demand. They hope to open a taproom at the production brewery by the end of 2014.

Of course, they are still brewing at the brewpub as well. The brewery can be glimpsed in the back of the establishment, past the dining room and long bar where the brewery's many year-round and seasonal beers are poured. Their flagship is **Hoppyum IPA,** a balanced beer with lots of citrus and a malt backbone that features subtle notes of both biscuit and caramel. If it's more hops you want, look to **Jade IPA,** a big India pale ale that features the juicy and tropical Pacific Jade hops. **People's Porter** is one of the state's best English versions of the style, with notes of cola, sweet bread, dark chocolate, and espresso, and a medium body. If you enjoy bourbon, you would be remiss not to try the **Barrel-Aged People's Porter,** which makes a great beer even more complex with notes of vanilla and oak. Jamie made a few tweaks to some of the Carolina Beer brands, such as changing **Carolina Blonde** from a blonde ale to a cream ale. The **Cottonwood Pumpkin Spiced Ale** is an excellent fall seasonal, proving so popular that the brewery started packaging it in 12-packs.

The brewpub has many great food items as well, and executive chef Shane Moore is constantly changing things up and offering new weekly specials. In this book's "In the Kitchen" section, you will find his recipe for **Pear & Arugula Salad with Candied Pecans & Stout Cranberries** (p. 304).

LIBERTY STEAKHOUSE & BREWERY
914 Mall Loop Rd., High Point, NC 27262; (336) 882-4677; LibertySteakhouseandBrewery .com
Founded: 2000 **Founder:** Homegrown Hospitality Group **Brewer:** Todd Isbell **Flagship Beer:** Miss Liberty Lager **Year-Round Beers:** Deep River Wheat, Blackberry Wheat, American IPA, Rocket's Red Ale, Nut Brown Ale **Seasonals/Special Releases:** Patriot Porter, Oatmeal Stout, Dry-Hopped Kellerbier, DeBeen Espresso Porter, Oktoberfest, Winterfest, White IPA, Belgian White

Liberty Steakhouse and Brewery features all of the patriotic decor and references you would expect of a brewery with such a name. Through the glass walls encasing the brewhouse, you can see the US and NC flags stretching down from the ceiling to the floor. Once inside, you see it reflected in the names of the beers, such as the brewery's **Miss Liberty Lager** and **Patriot Porter.** And a look at the beer lists assures you that Liberty gives head brewer Todd Isbell all the freedom he would want.

It has paid off in spades. Since Isbell joined the brewery in 2007, Liberty has been one of the most prolific medal winners at Hickory Hops' Carolinas Championships of

Beers, where he has taken home too many medals to list here. One such medal winner is Todd's **Dry-Hopped Kellerbier,** an unfiltered and more citrusy version of the crisp and clean Miss Liberty Lager. The **Blackberry Wheat** is a standard American wheat ale made more tart by the addition of blackberries, and it is a favorite at the brewpub.

You can find some of the same staple beers on tap at Liberty's High Point and Myrtle Beach locations, but Isbell takes pride in brewing many different beers with names as unique as they are. His craft take on malt liquor was called The Mullet, and variations on that beer included names like Joe Dirt, Swayze, and Billy Ray Cyrus. Again, what could be more patriotic?

NATTY GREENE'S PUB & BREWING CO.

345 South Elm St., Greensboro, NC 27401; (336) 274-1373; NattyGreenes.com; @Natty_Greenes

Founded: 2004 **Founders:** Chris Lester, Kayne Fisher **Brewers:** Sebastian Wolfrum, Scott Christoffel, Mike Rollinson **Flagship Beer:** Buckshot Amber Ale **Year-Round Beers:** Buckshot Amber Ale, Southern Pale Ale, Wildflower Witbier, Guilford Golden Ale, General Stout **Seasonals/Special Releases:** Old Town Brown Ale, Swamp Fox Belgian Blonde, Elm Street English IPA, Freedom American IPA, Hessian Hefeweizen, Summerfest Dortmunder Lager, Red Nose Winter Ale, Cannonball Double IPA

Before the pub in Raleigh, before the large-production brewery, there was the Natty Greene's Pub & Brewing Co. in downtown Greensboro. It is here, in this building dating back to 1892, that the brewery has its origins. The building has undergone some changes since it was built in the 19th century, of course, but not so much as to take away from its historical charm. The first thing you notice upon

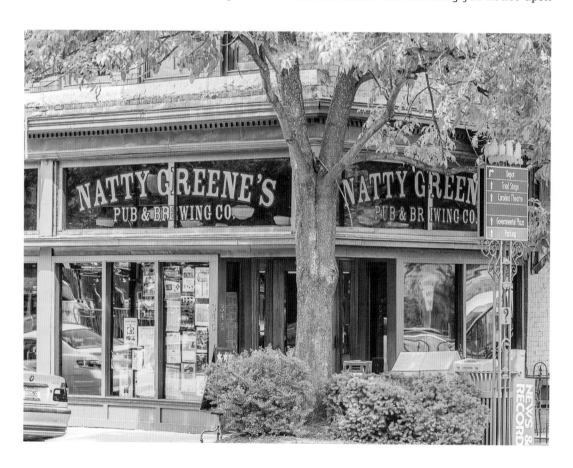

walking in is the mural, its scene of an "Old Greensborough" stretched in muted colors across the entirety of the lefthand wall. Time-worn bricks jut from the other walls, and exposed ductwork snakes across the ceiling.

The brewhouse itself is on the main floor, visible just past the bar and stairs leading to the upper level. Down in the basement, a dozen seven-barrel fermenters stretch all the way to the cramped basement's ceiling. While you can find many Natty Greene's in stores across the state, the brewpub provides drinkers with a chance to try a host of one-offs and seasonals. The **General Stout** is a perfect example of the dry Irish style, and at 4 percent ABV it's as sessionable as stouts come. The seasonal **Elm Street English IPA** and **Freedom American IPA** show two countries' approach to the same style, the former milder with a caramel sweetness, the latter with more of the typical American hops though still restrained. If you are fortunate enough to find the **American Sour,** be sure to try this limited edition beer from their Cellar Series. This oak-aged Flanders Red Ale ages for two years before being bottled in very limited numbers.

Before opening this brewpub, founders Chris Lester and Kayne Fisher had opened three area Triad bars, all of which focused heavily on good food and beer. It only made sense to offer a full kitchen at the new brewpub. As is often the case, some of the brewpub's best food is the messiest. The mesquite fries are topped with cheddar and Monterey jack cheese, scallions, and apple cider bacon (the latter pops up frequently throughout the menu). The Cohiba is essentially a Cuban sandwich slathered in barbecue sauce and then pressed, and you will need to make use of the large knife that accompanies it.

Every Friday from 5-9 p.m., Natty Greene's opens up their tasting room at their production brewery (1918 W. Lee St.). The "bunker," as it's called, features some of the brewery's more limited offerings.

The Triad

Beer Bars

THE BREWER'S KETTLE

2505 N. Main St., Ste. 101, High Point, NC 27262; (336) 885-0099; TheBrewersKettle
.com; @BrewersKettle
Draft Beers: 13 **Bottled/Canned Beers:** 400+

The Brewer's Kettle started life as a bottle shop, and has slowly developed into one of the Triad's better beer bars. The space is a small, cozy one, and it is filled with more than 400 beers. The bar seats about 10, while a leather couch and chair comfortably accommodate a few more. Behind the bar are 13 taps, usually consisting of a mix between NC beers and popular choices from around the nation. The Brewer's Kettle frequently hosts tastings and special beer events. They regularly tap special casks from Liberty Steakhouse and Brewery just down the road in High Point.

HOPS BURGER BAR

2419 Spring Garden St., Greensboro, NC 27403; (336) 235-2178; HopsBurgerBar.com
Draft Beers: 13 **Bottled/Canned Beers:** 25+

The name Hops Burger Bar alone is enough to suggest the restaurant is the perfect union of beers and burgers, ales and Angus. You will find a good selection of locals from breweries like Foothills, Red Oak, and Natty Greene's, as well as beers from other regional and national breweries. While there are only 13 taps, the restaurant carries a selection of bottles and cans as well.

Beer is just one part of the experience, of course, as the menu of burgers and fries is mouthwatering. The burgers are certified Angus, and can be ordered as 6-ounce or half-pound patties. While they routinely come up with daily or weekly specialty burgers, the menu includes favorites like The Hawaiian (sweet and spicy chile sauce, blue cheese, and grilled pineapple) and the Pickleback (fried onion, spicy barbecue, and bourbon-marinated pickles). The restaurant even offers several bun choices, including brioche, potato, pretzel, and gluten-free.

The Wall of Fries showcases the myriad ways you can have your *pommes frites* prepared, with options ranging from the standard and unadulterated sea-salt dusting to more creative approaches like Parmesan jalapeño, buffalo, or nacho.

MELLOW MUSHROOM

314 W. 4th St., Winston-Salem, NC 27101; (336) 245-2820; MellowMushroom.com;
@MellowWS
Draft Beers: 32 **Bottled/Canned Beers:** 50+

Mellow Mushroom is a chain of pizza restaurants known for its "Classic Southern Pizza" and an extensive selection of craft beers, both local and national. Winston-Salem's Mellow Mushroom is located just down the road from Foothills Brewing. You can almost always find a Foothills beer on the menu, and they occasionally tap that brewery's small-batch or more limited beers, like the highly sought after Sexual Chocolate imperial stout.

The restaurant's 32 taps also include a mix of popular national craft brands, and the Winston-Salem location frequently hosts special tappings, takeovers, and beer events. They will often use their Randall, a device first pioneered by Dogfish Head, to infuse beers with a variety of ingredients, including fruits, vegetables, herbs, and coffee.

Though the menu includes calzones and hoagies, salads and appetizers, pizza is naturally the most popular option here. Build your own, or choose from house constructions like Kosmic Karma, which features mozzarella, spinach, feta cheese, and both sun-dried and Roma tomatoes topped with a swirl of pesto.

POTENT POTABLES

115 E. Main St., Jamestown, NC 27282; (336) 882-9463; Facebook.com/PotentPotablesNC;
@PotentPotableNC
Draft Beers: 6 **Bottled/Canned Beers:** 500+

Like a few other establishments profiled in this book, Potent Potables is part bottle shop and part beer bar. The name is a reference to the popular *Jeopardy* category, and Potent Potables carries both beer and wine. It has been a popular hangout since opening, especially among Jamestown beer lovers who would have otherwise needed to drive to High Point or Greensboro to find a beer bar of this caliber.

While the draft selection is small, the shop's large retail selection ensures there are plenty of different beers to be enjoyed. The bar frequently has live music, and food trucks are often parked outside to ensure everyone has something to pair with their potables.

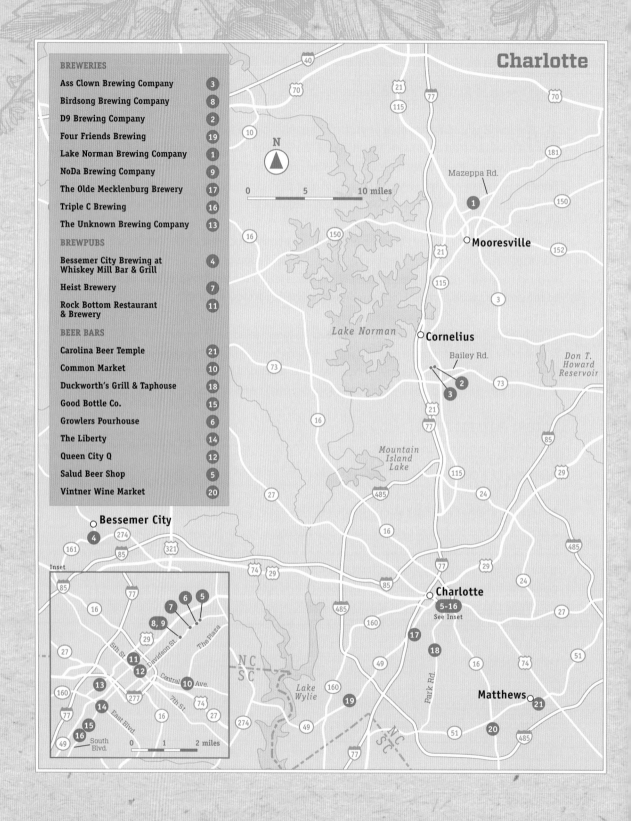

Charlotte

BREWERIES

Ass Clown Brewing Company	3
Birdsong Brewing Company	8
D9 Brewing Company	2
Four Friends Brewing	19
Lake Norman Brewing Company	1
NoDa Brewing Company	9
The Olde Mecklenburg Brewery	17
Triple C Brewing	16
The Unknown Brewing Company	13

BREWPUBS

Bessemer City Brewing at Whiskey Mill Bar & Grill	4
Heist Brewery	7
Rock Bottom Restaurant & Brewery	11

BEER BARS

Carolina Beer Temple	21
Common Market	10
Duckworth's Grill & Taphouse	18
Good Bottle Co.	15
Growlers Pourhouse	6
The Liberty	14
Queen City Q	12
Salud Beer Shop	5
Vintner Wine Market	20

Mazeppa Rd.

Mooresville

Cornelius

Bailey Rd.

Don T. Howard Reservoir

Lake Norman

Mountain Island Lake

Bessemer City

Inset

5th St

Davidson St.

The Plaza

Central Ave.

7th St

East Blvd

South Blvd.

NC
SC

Lake Wylie

Charlotte

5-16
See Inset

Matthews

NC
SC

Charlotte

A city once known for its banks has in recent years become revered for its beers, thanks to a host of new breweries as well as several bars and bottle shops dedicated to supporting the local craft beer movement. That movement transcends the Queen City's borders and has spread into other cities in the Charlotte metro area, such as Bessemer City, Cornelius, and Mooresville. The banking industry may have experienced a recession in recent years, but Charlotte's beer scene shows no signs of letting up.

Breweries

ASS CLOWN BREWING COMPANY

10620 Bailey Rd., Stes. E and F, Cornelius, NC 28031; AssClownBrewery.com;
@AssClownBrewing

Founded: 2011 **Founder:** Matt Glidden **Brewer:** Matt Glidden **Flagship Beer:** Orange Spiced IPA **Year-Round Beers:** Orange Spiced IPA, Vanilla Bean Chocolate Brown **Seasonals/Special Releases:** Buttered Apple Pie Amber, Lemon Spiced Wheat IPA, Dark Chocolate Blueberry Porter, Chipotle Pumpkin Stout, Coffee Tequila Oatmeal Stout, Bourbon Old Ale, Wet Hop Citra IPA, Wet Hop Simcoe IPA **Tours:** N/A **Taproom:** Tues through Thurs, 3 to 9 p.m.; Fri, 11 a.m. to 9 p.m.; Sat, 12 to 9 p.m.

Matt Glidden is a craft beer superhero. By day, he is the mild-mannered owner of Interesting Mortgages. By night, he is the founder and brewer at Ass Clown Brewing. These two businesses actually share the same office space in a nondescript business park in Cornelius. It might not look like much from the outside, but inside the taproom is a fun, eclectic, and comfortable space in which to enjoy Ass Clown's beers—and they are many.

Matt brews on a small system and cycles through over a hundred different recipes; the taproom boasts 32 taps to ensure a variety unmatched by most breweries. This is especially impressive considering the brewery's only two year-round beers are the **Orange Spiced IPA** and the **Vanilla Bean Chocolate Brown.** All of Ass Clown's beers are quite inventive and often prefaced by at least a couple of descriptors, as is the case with the **Oyster Wasabi Stout**, **Buttered Apple Pie Amber** or **Raspberry**

Cinnamon Sour Porter. As those names indicate, Matt takes much of his inspiration from food. The ingredients he brews with may be relatively unusual in the beer world, but they are often paired together flawlessly in food.

Fans of blueberry muffins, for example, would probably enjoy Ass Clown's sweet, tart, and roasty **Dark Chocolate Blueberry Porter.** If a breakfast of bacon and maple syrup–drenched pancakes sounds tasty, then you might try the brewery's **Smoked Bacon Maple Black Ale,** which is actually brewed with maple syrup and several pounds of bacon. Matt has even gotten into wines, and you know by the beers that he is not going to be bound by tradition. He ages styles like Pinot Noir and Cabernet on bourbon-soaked oak, resulting in an interesting interplay between whiskey and wine.

And the name? That's the question Matt gets most often. It's a term of endearment that Matt and his friend used to volley back and forth with one another. Never one to take himself too seriously, Matt assigned the name to his brewery. Whether you love or hate it, it is every bit as memorable as Ass Clown's beers.

Beer Lover's Pick

Raspberry Jalapeño Stout
Style: American stout
ABV: 7.1 percent
Availability: Rotating on-tap
Raspberries and jalapeños are used in several of Ass Clown's beers, but the perfect marriage of the two can be found in the Raspberry Jalapeño Stout. The tart raspberry works very well with notes of chocolate and jalapeño heat, which lingers on the finish.

BIRDSONG BREWING COMPANY

2315 N. Davidson St., Charlotte, NC 28205; (704) 332-1810; BirdsongBrewing.com; @BirdsongBrewing

Founded: 2011 **Founders:** Chris Goulet, Tara Goulet, Chandra Torrence, Jackie Mohrfeld, Tom Gillam, Michelle LeBeau, Ben Cauthen, Conor Robinson **Brewer:** Conor Robinson **Flagship Beer:** Higher Ground IPA **Year-Round Beers:** Higher Ground IPA, Jalapeño Pale Ale, Free Will Pale Ale, Lazy Bird Brown Ale **Seasonals/Special Releases:** Up on the Sun Saison, Doin' Thyme Witbier, Raise a Ruckus Dark Rye, The Pride Abbey Ale, MexiCali Stout, Honey Pie Double IPA, Red House Wheat, Carolina Common, Eat a Peach, St. Tuber Abbey Ale **Tours:** Weds at 6 p.m. **Taproom:** Wed through Fri, 5 to 10 p.m.; Sat, 2 to 10 p.m.; Sun, 2 to 7 p.m.

Less than two months after NoDa Brewing opened in 2011, Birdsong Brewing did the same just across the street. The two breweries are literally next-door neighbors, prompting many to refer to East 26th Street in Charlotte's funky and eclectic

NoDa neighborhood as "Brewers Alley." The brewer on Birdsong's side of the alley is Conor Robinson, a baker-turned-brewer who met Tara Goulet while working at Charlotte's Great Harvest Bread Company. Tara and her husband Chris were so impressed with Conor's homebrews, they offered him the head brewer position despite the fact he was 23 years old and lacking commercial brewing experience. He and the rest of the Birdsong crew have been creating lots of great beer ever since.

Most of these beers are lower in alcohol and are sessionable, so you could visit their side of Brewers Alley and have a few out on the patio or inside the laid-back vibe of the taproom. Grab some free peanuts while you're at it, or hit up a food truck if one's parked outside, as is often the case. **Higher Ground IPA** is billed as a West Coast example of the style, yet it is a well-balanced beer with a distinct

Jalapeño Pale Ale

Style: Chile beer

ABV: 5.5 percent

Availability: On tap year-round

What started as a quick experiment ended up becoming a cult favorite in the Charlotte area. When he didn't have a pilot batch to tap one Thursday, head brewer Conor Robinson used a Randall to infuse his Free Will Pale Ale with fresh jalapeños. It was so popular, fans of the beer demanded they brew it on the big system. Now, Conor throws eight pounds of peppers into every batch, taking care to remove most of the seeds to create a beer with lots of vegetal pepper flavor and practically no heat. Try it with nachos!

caramel malt backbone. Conor also has a deep appreciation for Belgian styles, which is reflected in **Up on the Sun Saison,** a farmhouse ale with notes of lemon and dill from the use of Sorachi Ace hops.

Birdsong brews a host of other much-loved seasonals. The **MexiCali Stout,** brewed with cinnamon and local coffee, provides plenty of warmth on those cold winter nights. In warmer weather, you might reach for **Red House Wheat.** American wheat beers are nothing unusual, but Birdsong uses red wheat malt and African rooibos tea to create a refreshing wheat beer with sweet and herbal characteristics.

D9 BREWING COMPANY

18627 Northline Dr., Unit E, Cornelius, NC 28031; D9Brewing.com; @D9Brewing
Founded: 2013 **Founders:** Andrew Durstewitz, John Ashcraft, Aaron Burton **Brewers:**
Andrew Durstewitz, John Ashcraft, Aaron Burton **Flagship Beer:** Battle Hymn Black IPA
Year-Round Beers: #12, Outpost Tea Ale, Peruvian Ale **Seasonals/Special Releases:**
Head of the Horseman Imperial Pumpkin, Singularity IPA, (Rye)it Ale, Barely Legal IPA
Tours: During open hours **Taproom:** Weds, 4:30 to 10:30 p.m.; Fri and Sat, 7 to 10:30 p.m.

Districts, by their very nature, are divisions. They are boundaries, borders, sections of land and labor meant to keep people in or out. The founders of D9 Brewing Company, though, think districts can be just the opposite: a way of uniting people of all types. Their very name calls to mind movies like *District 9* and *The Hunger Games* franchise, which focus on people that revolt against the powers that be.

It may seem a bit dramatic, but it is a fitting analogy for most craft brewers, and particularly one as small as D9 Brewing Company. In 2013, Andrew Durstewitz, John Ashcraft, and Aaron Burton opened up the nanobrewery in an office park just around the corner from Ass Clown Brewing, another small brewery in Cornelius. On warm nights, a raised garage door reveals the taproom portion of the building. The walls are painted in a seafoam green that gives the taproom a modern and homey feel. Strings of lights hang from one side of the taproom to another wall that sections off a small sitting area. Underneath them is bar and a handful of barstools.

Outpost Tea Ale
Style: Pale ale
ABV: 5.1 percent
Availability: On tap year-round

Tea is not commonly used in beer, but when it is many brewers add it to the boil with the hops. D9 Brewing Company takes a different route, choosing to steep black tea and hops in vodka for one week to extract their flavors

before adding them to a beer after fermentation. The flavors are more apparent this way, and the hops and tea stand out all the more against the light-bodied base.

The three brew in the back of the space on a one-barrel system not unlike some more advanced homebrewers use. The trio had been homebrewing for about six years each prior to going pro. The **Battle Hymn Black IPA,** the brewery's flagship, has notes of pine and black coffee. Like their neighbor in Ass Clown Brewing, the advantage of brewing on a small system is the creative freedom to experiment with different styles and ingredients. D9 Brewing Company plans to rotate through several seasonals and small batch beers, such as their **Head of the Horseman Imperial Pumpkin.**

FOUR FRIENDS BREWING

10913 C Office Park Dr., Charlotte, NC 28273; (704) 233-7071; FourFriendsBrewing.com; @4FriendsBrewing
Founded: 2010 **Founders:** Jon and Beth Fulcher, Mark and Allyson Kaminsky **Brewer:** Jon Fulcher **Flagship Beer:** i77 IPA **Year-Round Beers:** i77 IPA, Queen City Red, **Seasonals/Special Releases:** Race Day Pale Ale, Intimidator Imperial Red, Sunryez'd, Misty Mountain Hop IPA, Uptown Brown, 24kt Belgian Golden Ale, Dubbel D, Hot Damn, Afterglow, Punkin' Brewster **Tours:** N/A **Taproom:** Thu and Fri, 5 to 9 p.m.; Sat, 2 to 7 p.m.

Four Friends Brewing incorporated their business in 2007, but didn't open the doors to their brewery until 2010. The brewery was, as the name implies, the work of four friends and founders. One of those friends—Jon Fulcher—has served as the brewer and jack of all trades since opening. When the brewery was young, he would hand deliver kegs to local businesses around town. And that was the best way

to try Four Friends' beers for many years, as they only opened the brewery up for special events since they didn't have a true taproom.

When their neighbors next door left, the friends bought the space and built a proper taproom in 2013 where longtime fans could enjoy the beers and often talk with Jon or his wife Beth, another of the four friends. It is a comfortable taproom that sees its fair share of regulars, many of whom are part of the Fifth Friend membership club. The club is a way for fans to support the brewery while gaining access to exclusive benefits only available to Fifth Friends.

In their infancy, Jon had planned to brew predominantly British styles. They've changed their approach a bit over the years, now offering a mix of British, American, and Belgian styles. The **24kt Belgian Golden Ale** falls firmly in the latter camp, with the Belgian yeast adding bubble gum, pear, apple, and the tiniest bit of spice. The **Uptown Brown,** on the other hand, is distinctly British: Its notes of coffee,

---

Beer Lover's Pick

i77 IPA
Style: India pale ale
ABV: 7.7 percent
Availability: On tap year-round
Named for the interstate that runs through Charlotte, i77 IPA is one of Four Friends' hoppiest and most popular offerings. Several varieties of hops—Warrior, Willamette, Chinook, and Cascade—are used to call to mind flavors of grapefruit, orange zest, and pine. The hops and their accompanying bitterness are kept well in check by this well-balanced IPA's solid malt backbone. The ABV, appropriately, clocks in at 7.7 percent.

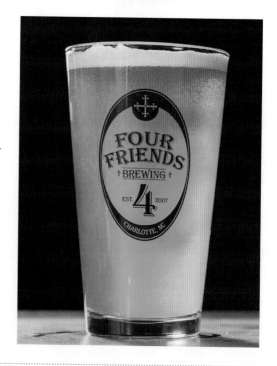

toast, and nuttiness make it an ideal fall seasonal. Another one to look for when the leaves begin to change is the **Punkin' Brewster,** a subtly spiced pumpkin beer fermented with an English ale yeast. Jon also brews a variety of small-batch, experimental beers, most of which are reserved for area festivals or the taproom.

LAKE NORMAN BREWING COMPANY

159 Barley Park Ln., Unit B, Mooresville, NC 28115; (704) 660-1182; LakeNormanBrewingCompany.com; @LKNBrewing
Founded: 2013 **Founders:** Mike Prascak, Andy Prascak **Brewer:** Andy Prascak **Flagship Beer:** Outboard Amber Ale **Year-Round Beers:** Outboard Amber Ale, Dockside Blonde Ale, Pontoon Pale Ale **Seasonals/Special Releases:** Wakeboard Wheat Ale **Tours:** No **Taproom:** Check website

When Carolina Beer and Beverage signed on to be the anchor tenant in a Mooresville business park, the road they were on was named Barley Park Lane. That company sold their popular Carolina Blonde and Cottonwood Brands to Foothills and is now known as Carolina Beverage Group, but thanks to the father-son team of Mike and Andy Prascak, a brewery is once again calling Barley Park Lane home.

Pontoon Pale Ale

Style: American pale ale

ABV: 5.5 percent

Availability: On tap year-round

Pontoon Pale Ale is the hoppiest of Lake Norman Brewing Company's three core beers, thanks to generous additions of three popular "C" hops: Chinook, Cascade, and Centennial. A sweet maltiness helps to balance the beer, and this one's about as true to style as they come. It has a very clean, semi-dry finish that leaves you wanting more.

Their name, too, calls to mind another brewery from Charlotte's past. A Lake Norman Brewing Company operated out of Cornelius from 1996 to 2000. The Prascaks have no relation to this brewery, but are committed to again establishing a brewery that locals around the Lake Norman area can call their own. The brewery is a fraction of the size that their neighbors used to brew on, but Lake Norman is brewing on a smaller scale and the 3,000-square-foot space will allow them to grow if and when they need to. A third of that space is devoted to the taproom.

Mike and Andy did almost all of the work in the brewery themselves. They tore down old walls and put up new ones. They fashioned their own boat-motor tap handles. They even built their own five-stage keg cleaner, and also managed to eliminate a lot of wasted water by recirculating the water they use to chill their wort back into the walk-in cooler.

The Prascaks opened up with three core beers: the **Outboard Amber Ale,** a toasty and smooth amber; the **Dockside Blonde Ale,** a refreshing, clean beer with a hint of sweet malt; and the **Pontoon Pale Ale,** a well-balanced and true-to-style American pale. Once they get their sea legs under them, expect to see a variety of seasonal and one-off beers in the taproom. They do not have any bottled offerings, but you can find them on draft in better beer bars around the Lake Norman area.

NODA BREWING COMPANY

2229 N. Davidson St., Charlotte, NC 28205; (704) 451-1394; NoDaBrewing.com; @NoDaBrewing

Founded: 2011 **Founders:** Todd and Suzie Ford **Brewer:** Chad Henderson **Flagship Beer:** Hop Drop 'n Roll **Year-Round Beers:** Hop Drop 'n Roll, Coco Loco Porter, Ramble on Red, Jam Session Pale Ale, Woody and Wilcox IPA **Seasonals/Special Releases:** Ghost Hop White IPA, Gordgeous Pumpkin Ale, Midnight Madness, NoDaRyeZ'd, Cold Crash, Monk's Trunks, NoDajito, Hope's Stout, TriUmphant Tripel, Imperial Coco Loco, Santa Baby **Tours:** Mon through Fri at 6 p.m.; Sat at 5 p.m. **Taproom:** Mon and Tues, 4 to 8:30 p.m.; Weds, 4 to 9 p.m.; Fri, 4 to 9:30 p.m.; Sat, 12 to 10 p.m.; Sun, 1 to 6 p.m.

When NoDa Brewing Company opened in Charlotte's NoDa neighborhood in 2011, they helped to fill a void in Charlotte's craft beer scene. The Olde Mecklenburg Brewery and Four Friends Brewing were producing great beers before this, but neither of those breweries specialized in the West Coast styles that so many craft beer drinkers crave.

Todd and Suzie Ford saw the need for such a brewery, and their philosophy on beer and brewing was much in line with Chad Henderson's, who Todd met through the Carolina BrewMasters homebrew club. Despite his lack of commercial brewing experience, Chad was hired as the head brewer, and no one who has ever tried his

Hop Drop 'n Roll
Style: American India pale ale
ABV: 7.2 percent
Availability: Year-round on tap
and in 16-ounce cans

NoDa Brewing's Hop Drop 'n Roll is an IPA brewed in the West Coast style and hopped before, during and after the boil. Citra and Amarillo hops contribute juicy flavors of tangerines, oranges, grapefruit, pungent pine, and just a little bit of mint. An assertive bitterness lingers on through the finish, yet it invites further sipping. Make sure to grab a growler or a four-pack of 16-ounce cans.

beers would question the Fords' decision to entrust him with such a role. After being open for only a year, the brewery's **Coco Loco Porter** won a silver medal in the robust porter category at the Great American Beer Festival in 2012.

That beer gets plenty of accolades back home in Charlotte, too, as do a host of other NoDa Brewing beers. The brewery is Charlotte's most prolific, brewing several year-round beers and recurring seasonals. **Jam Session** is a well-hopped pale ale with a cracker-like maltiness, and at 5.1 percent ABV it is one you can enjoy two or three of. One of the brewery's most raved about seasonals is the **NoDajito,** a witbier that is brewed with mint and lime zest to create the beer version of a mojito. That beer and a few others began life as NoDable Series beers, which are small-batch beers brewed on a pilot system that are tapped every Tuesday. Because these kegs usually only last through the night, Tuesdays are popular nights to visit the brewery.

Wednesday nights are, too, as that's when the brewery's run club hits the streets of NoDa. Spearheaded by Director of Community Optimism Brian Mister, this group of more than 200 runners shows that beer and a healthy lifestyle can easily coexist. The run club is just one example of the many ways the brewery has reached out to the community. There is no food in the NoDa taproom, but there are food trucks outside most nights.

THE OLDE MECKLENBURG BREWERY

4150 Yancey Rd., Charlotte, NC 28217; (704) 525-5644; OldeMeckBrew.com; @OldeMeckBrew

Founded: 2009 **Founder:** John Marrino **Brewer:** Carey Savoy **Flagship Beer:** Copper **Year-Round Beers:** Copper, Captain James Jack Pilsner **Seasonals/Special Releases:** Fat Boy Baltic Porter, Früh Bock, Rein Pale Ale, Hornet's Nest Hefeweizen, Mecktoberfest, Bauern Bock, Dunkel, Yule Bock **Tours:** Fri at 6 p.m.; Sat at 1, 2, 3, 4, and 5 p.m.; Sun at 2, 3, and 4 p.m. **Taproom:** Mon, 12 to 9 p.m.; Tues through Sat, 12 to 10 p.m.; Sun, 12 to 8 p.m.

Water, barley, hops, and yeast. Those are the four ingredients that the German beer purity law of 1516 dictates beer must be brewed with, and The Olde Mecklenburg Brewery follows it. That might seem limiting to brewers accustomed to using fruit, chocolate, coffee, or any number of other additives, but the folks at OMB (as the locals call it) have actually taken the untraditional route by brewing more traditional German styles.

Founder John Marrino came to love those styles while working in Germany. More specifically, he fell in love with Altbier, a malty, lagered ale that originated in the city of Düsseldorf. He grew accustomed to having fresh altbier right at the source, but when he returned to the states he found that almost all of the German beers on store shelves were old, shells of their former selves. Later, while on a cross-country RV trip with his family, he read about how someone was resurrecting the Narragansett brewery in Rhode Island. He wondered why a city of Charlotte's size didn't have its own local brewery, and then he realized that by building a brewery in Charlotte he could supply an entire city with the German-style beer he so loved. He opened The Olde Mecklenburg Brewery in 2009.

The brewery's flagship **Copper** is as true to the altbier style as you'll find in the states. It is an amber ale brimming with notes of dark bread, caramel, and just a touch of roast and noble hop bitterness. It is lagered to impart a clean and crisp character that has almost come to define everything The Olde Mecklenburg Brewery puts out. The brewery's other year-round offering is **Captain James Jack Pilsner,**

Mecktoberfest
Style: Märzen
ABV: 5.4 percent
Availability: On tap and in
bottles during the fall

The Olde Mecklenburg Brewery's Mecktoberfest—which won a silver medal at the Great American Beer Festival in 2012—is one of Charlotte's most highly anticipated seasonal beers. This märzen is more akin to the authentic German versions, which is to say it is not as sweet as some American attempts. It is an exceptionally clean, crisp beer with a rich maltiness and notes of toasted bread, balanced by the perfect amount of hop bitterness. For the full experience, attend the brewery's yearly Mecktoberfest celebration and quaff a liter of it under the tents.

which is just as authentic. It is exceptionally refreshing. The malts bring biscuit and cracker, the hops contribute lemon and a slightly herbal quality. In addition to those two, the brewery also brews several popular seasonals and has started brewing "Brauhaus Reserve" series beers that are most often on tap only at the brewery. You will occasionally even find some of their beers aged in bourbon barrels. After all, the *Reinheitsgebot* specifies what you can brew with, but not what you can age it in.

In early 2014, the brewery moved into a new space just down the road from the original brewery. The new brewery has a beautiful taproom and a large outdoor *Biergarten* under massive oak trees.

TRIPLE C BREWING

2900 Griffith St., Charlotte, NC 28203; (704) 372-3212; TripleCBrewing.com;
@TripleCBrew

Founded: 2012 **Founders:** Chris Harker, Chris and Christina Murphy **Brewer:** Scott
Kimball **Flagship Beer:** Light Rail Pale Ale **Year-Round Beers:** Light Rail Pale Ale,
Smoked Amber, Greenway IPA, Road to Nowhere Porter, Golden Boy, Baby Maker Double
IPA **Seasonals/Special Releases:** Hyzer Hefeweizen, 3C India Pale Ale, Urban Hop
Project, Cajun Stout, Sal's Paradise Saison, Imperial Smoked Amber, Up All Night Breakfast
Porter, Winter Ale **Tours:** Weds at 6:30 p.m. **Taproom:** Tues through Fri, 4 to 9 p.m.; Sat,
2 to 9 p.m.; Sun 12 to 6 p.m.

Just south of downtown in Charlotte's SouthEnd area is Triple C Brewing, which
opened its doors to the Queen City in 2012. Since that time, they have been a
popular watering hole for many who call this part of Charlotte home. The taproom
has a very clean, modern feel to it. The bar and tables were crafted from a 100-year-
old pine that was reclaimed from an old mill. Brick and pallet wood cover most of the
walls, save for an expansive window looking into the brewery where Scott Kimball
does his work.

The brewery delivered its first keg of **Light Rail Pale Ale** on the light rail itself,
taking it a few stops down to The Liberty. An easy-drinking beer with notes of

tangerine and pine, this has been one of the brewery's most popular beers since day one. It's one of a handful of hoppier beers that Triple C offers. The **3C IPA**—brewed with Citra, Centennial, and Chinook hops—has been met with much praise since they unveiled it. The humorously named **Baby Maker Double IPA** has a stronger malt backbone than most imperial IPAs, with a big sweetness and subtle nutty character. And the **Urban Hop Project** series of IPAs are brewed with fresh hops grown right at the brewery.

Smoked beers can be very polarizing, but Triple C's **Smoked Amber** has mass appeal thanks to Scott's deft hand with cherrywood-smoked malt, oats, and German chocolate wheat. It is a very food-friendly beer, and while Triple C does not have a kitchen, you can almost always find a food truck parked out beside the well-kept patio. Picnic tables under large orange umbrellas welcome eaters and drinkers alike, as well as their furry friends.

Beer Lover's Pick

Up All Night Breakfast Porter
Style: Imperial porter
ABV: 10 percent
Availability: On tap and in bottles
during the winter

If you're familiar with Widespread Panic's song "Up All Night," you will know where this beer got its name. It's a big imperial porter, brewed with coffee from Charlotte's Magnolia Coffee as well as honey, flaked oats, and lots of chocolate malt. It is also aged on oak chips, which imparts vanilla notes that pair well with the sharp roast and decadent sweetness of this beer.

THE UNKNOWN BREWING COMPANY

1327 S. Mint St., Charlotte, NC 28203; UnknownBrewing.com; @UnknownBrewing
Founded: 2013 **Founder:** Brad Shell **Brewer:** Dave Scott **Flagship Beer:** Over the Edge USPA **Year-Round Beers:** Over the Edge USPA, Head First Pale Ale, No Shame Wheat **Seasonals/Special Releases:** Pregame Session Ale, Open Road Hop Red, Ginger Wheat, Tele-Porter **Tours:** Check website **Taproom:** Weds through Fri, 4 to 10 p.m.; Sat and Sun, 12 to 8 p.m.

For founder Brad Shell, opening The Unknown Brewing Company was a dream almost 10 years in the making. As a 21-year-old working on the bottling line of Atlanta's SweetWater Brewing Company, Brad made a promise to himself that he would open his own brewery by the time he was 30. Scrawled on a bar napkin, it would become his life's mission as he went on to work for Terrapin Beer Co. in Georgia, Rogue Ales in Oregon, and Fish Brewery in Washington State.

When he turned 30, he had already left Washington for Charlotte, a city he thought would be a perfect fit for his vision. The idea behind his brewery's name is that everyone should frequently step into the unknown, whatever that unknown may be. Brad did just that when he built his brewery in a sprawling 25,000-square-foot building just three blocks south of Bank of America Stadium, home to the Carolina Panthers. It is a popular tailgating spot during football season and a great location in general, considering its proximity to the light rail and uptown Charlotte.

Throughout the taproom are the contrasting colors of gray and bright green, creating a fun space that reflects Brad's philosophy of doing things that stray a bit from the norm. Brad chose to start out with a large 30-barrel system in anticipation of growth years down the road. Coming out of the gate in 2013, Unknown offered three year-round beers: **Over the Edge USPA, Head First Pale Ale,** and **No Shame Wheat**. The latter's name suggests that no one should ever be ashamed for drinking a wheat beer, and those who drink this refreshing beer surely do so with pride. It finishes clean and is an ideal warm weather beer. Unknown Brewing will offer a wide variety of seasonal and small-batch beers, with plans to get into blending and barrel-aging down the road.

Over the Edge USPA

Style: India pale ale

ABV: 6.9 percent

Availability: On tap year-round

True to his contrarian nature, Brad refuses to call the Unknown Brewing Company's IPA an IPA, even if that's the style it most resembles. Over the Edge is instead called a USPA or "United States Pale Ale," which isn't a real style but does reflect Brad's notion that America has redefined the IPA category. Regardless of the name, you will find in this beer an assertive display of West Coast hops that contribute lots of pine and tangerine. Caramel malt makes itself known subtly on the finish.

Charlotte

Brewpubs

BESSEMER CITY BREWING AT WHISKEY MILL BAR & GRILL

201 W. Pennsylvania Ave., Bessemer City, NC 28016; (704) 629-2325; WhiskeyMill.com
Founded: 2013 **Founder:** Michael Croft **Brewer:** Chris Webber **Flagship Beer:** Lithium Pale Ale **Year-Round Beers:** Lithium Pale Ale **Seasonals/Special Releases:** Sir Henry Irish Red, Sir Henry's Mistress Vanilla Oak Bourbon Porter, Furnace Scotch Ale **Tours:** No **Taproom:** Mon through Thurs, 10:30 a.m. to 11 p.m.; Fri and Sat, 11 a.m. to 2 a.m.; Sun, 12 to 11 p.m.

Whiskey Mill Bar & Grill is located in downtown Bessemer City, and if you were to look at the Western-style building from the outside you might not expect craft beer to be served there, let alone brewed there. The bar sells its share of Bud, Miller, and Coors, make no mistake, but in 2013 owner Michael Croft and brewer Chris Webber started brewing a handful of house beers on a half-barrel brewing system in the back under the name Bessemer City Brewing. They specialize in styles from Ireland and the United Kingdom, as they think most of them are approachable enough that even people new to craft beer will appreciate them.

PHOTO BY AUTHOR

Their **Lithium Pale Ale** certainly fits that bill. The name is a reference to Bessemer City's reputation as a lithium-mining center. Of course, you won't find Lithium in this English pale ale, but rather notes of biscuit and a subtle hop bitterness. It is a mild and very drinkable beer that has already converted many of the bar's light lager drinkers. The taplist at Whiskey Mill still consists of many of those light lagers, but if Bessemer City's initial beers are any indication you could be seeing a shift here soon. The bar prides itself on educating consumers about their house-brewed beers and hopes to continue growing the brewery.

Sir Henry, named after Sir Henry Bessemer, is an Irish red ale that has a smooth malty sweetness and just a hint of toffee and toast. **Sir Henry's Mistress,** however, is much darker. This vanilla bourbon oak porter was brewed by some of Whiskey Mill's ladies, and it is a decadent display of coffee, chocolate, and vanilla, with a little bourbon sweetness coming through on the finish. Bessemer City has a storied history as an iron-smelting town, and that industry is paid tribute by the brewery's **Furnace,** a big Scotch ale. It has mild notes of chocolate and dark fruits like raisins and plums, with just a wisp of smoke coming through on the finish.

Whiskey Mill has an extensive food menu filled with appetizers, sandwiches, and massive burgers. They are very well known for their ribs and wings, as well as their Buzzard on a Stick, which is chicken that's been marinated for a full day in the bar's Black Jack sauce and then dry-rubbed with their house seasonings. You can enjoy the full menu inside the bar or outside on Whiskey Mill's spacious patio. The bar often features live bands, making it a popular hangout for many.

HEIST BREWERY

2909 N. Davidson St., #200, Charlotte, NC 28205; (704) 375-8260; HeistBrewery.com
@HeistBrewery
Founded: 2012 **Founder:** Kurt Hogan **Brewer:** Zach Hart **Flagship Beer:** I2PA
Year-Round Beers: I2PA, Premium Light Lager, Station #7 Red Ale, Oatmeal Stout, Hefeweizen, Pale Ale **Seasonals/Special Releases:** Kristalweizen, Peach Hefeweizen, Blueberry Blonde, Raspberry Porter, Maibock, Dubbel, Tripel, Himalayan Whiteout IPA, Black IPA

A lot of brewpubs—and restaurants, for that matter—make much about their inventive and creative approach to food. Heist Brewery actually puts it into practice with what they call "twisted American cuisine." In what other brewpub could you enjoy steak-and-papaya martinis? Lobster bisque poured into test tubes? Swirls of house-made, lemon-wasabi cotton candy wisped about a skewered shrimp?

These are all the brainchild of Rob Masone, who was the original chef at the Mash House Brewery and Chophouse in Fayetteville. If Rob laid the food foundation

for Mash House, Zach Hart did the same for its beers. The two both joined founder Kurt Hogan to build Heist Brewery in Charlotte's NoDa neighborhood, creating a beautiful space for food and beer lovers alike. In a banking town like Charlotte, not everyone could pull off a name like Heist. But for Kurt—whose grandmother's cousin was Lester Gillis, aka Baby Face Nelson—it is appropriate. Photos of mobsters are spread throughout the stylish and warm brewpub, a nod to Kurt's nefarious ancestor.

At Mash House, Zach Hart designed many of the beers that are still brewed there today. At Heist, he has continued brewing a variety of true-to-style offerings that complement the food without overpowering it. Very few craft brewers take on lagers, let alone light lagers, but Heist Brewery's **Premium Light Lager** is easy-drinking and the perfect "gateway" beer to those more accustomed to big beer. Named after the historic fire station just down the street, the **Station #7 Red Ale** has a caramel-like sweetness that pairs well with the brewpub's burgers. Flaked oats and nine other malts go into Heist's **Oatmeal Stout,** a rich beer with notes of espresso and bitter chocolate that is served from a nitro tap for a creamy mouthfeel. The **I2PA,** an imperial IPA with notes of pine and citrus, is the brewpub's most popular offering.

ROCK BOTTOM RESTAURANT & BREWERY

401 N. Tryon St., Charlotte, NC 28202; (704) 334-2739; RockBottom.com; @CLTRockBottom

Founded: 1997 **Founder:** Frank Day **Brewer:** Robb MacLeod **Flagship Beer:** Kölsch **Year-Round Beers:** Kölsch, White Ale, India Pale Ale, Red Ale, Specialty Dark **Seasonals/Special Releases:** Spring Lager, Belgian Style Ale, Summer Honey Ale, Rocktoberfest, Winter Tartan, Brewmaster's Choice

Rock Bottom Restaurant & Brewery came to uptown Charlotte in 1997, which makes it Charlotte's longest standing brewery. The location is one of many Rock Bottom breweries across the nation, and while ownership has changed hands over the years, they are all now owned by CraftWorks Restaurants & Breweries, Inc. (the same company that owns the Gordon Biersch chain, amongst others).

The Charlotte Rock Bottom has a prime location downtown at the intersection of Tryon and Seventh Street. An outside patio sweeps around the exterior of the building, with garage doors that pull up to reveal the inside. The restaurant has a very sleek and modern feel to it. There are several TVs at the bar, one of which displays a digital taplist of the beers that are currently on as well as a brief description and other stats.

For the most part, the beers offered at this Rock Bottom are the same you will find at other locations, all of them being very well made and stylistically accurate. The **White Ale** is a refreshing wheat beer brewed with orange peel and coriander. The **IPA** is a balanced take on the style, with restrained notes of pine and tangerine. The brewery does rotate through its Specialty Dark selection, and allows the brewers free rein to brew what they will for the Brewmaster's Choice tap. Rock Bottom boasts several popular seasonals, including the **Summer Honey Ale** and **Rocktoberfest.**

The brewpub has a large food menu, and almost everything on it is made from scratch. While the menu changes a bit seasonally, you can always expect a good mix of appetizers, burgers, steaks, and seafood entrees. Rock Bottom also offers a popular happy hour with specials on beer and food from 4 to 6:30 p.m. every weekday.

Beer Bars

CAROLINA BEER TEMPLE

131-1C Matthews Station St., Matthews, NC 28105; (704) 847-2337; CarolinaBeerTemple
.net; @NCBeerTemple
Draft Beers: 16 **Bottled/Canned Beers:** 400+

If you worship beer, you owe it to yourself to check out Carolina Beer Temple in downtown Matthews. The combination bottle shop and beer store is the brainchild of Rob Jacik and his wife, Megan, who have been huge fans of Belgian styles since visiting Belgium together. These styles are heavily showcased at Carolina Beer Temple, as are some a little closer to home. Of the 16 taps at Carolina Beer Temple, at least half are devoted to beers from North Carolina (with a good portion of those from Charlotte breweries). At least two taps—but usually more—are saved for Belgian styles.

The bottle shop has a small cooler with a handful of beers, and of course hundreds more on the shelves. In addition to the bar seating, there are a few tables, a couch, and even a small red throne, fit for beer royalty. Carolina Beer Temple frequently hosts brewery tap takeovers, with special discounts on beers and flights.

COMMON MARKET

2007 Commonwealth Ave., Charlotte, NC 28205; (704) 334-6209; CommonMarketIsGood
.com; @CommonMarket
Draft Beers: 15 **Bottled/Canned Beers:** 400+

Common Market in Plaza Midwood isn't just a beer bar or bottle shop, and it certainly isn't common. This eclectic Charlotte institution does indeed boast 15 taps and hundreds of bottles that can be enjoyed there or purchased to take home, but it also has a small deli, wine, coffee, old-school candy, and lots of gag gifts. It is a convenience store if convenience was never a consideration.

Don't let the tubs of tallboys fool you: Common Market has an extensive and well thought out draft and retail selection. You can enjoy the beers inside at the bar or at a handful of tables, outside in the "alleyway" or out front at the picnic tables. There are always a good selection of Charlotte and other NC beers to be had. The bar does free tastings every Wednesday night and many events throughout the year.

There is another Common Market in SouthEnd (1515 S. Tryon St.), and it has a similar vibe and selection, albeit with fewer taps. Both are worthy visits for any beer lover.

DUCKWORTH'S GRILL & TAPHOUSE

4435 Park Rd., Charlotte, NC 28209; (704) 527-5783; Duckworths.com; @DuckworthsPark

Draft Beers: 60 **Bottled/Canned Beers:** 20–30

Before opening the first Duckworth's, founder Rob Duckworth spent three days touring Philadelphia and eating nothing but cheesesteaks. He returned intent on replicating some of those great Philly icons in Charlotte, where his first restaurant would boast 18 cheesesteaks, fries, and ice cream. When the latter proved unpopular, he replaced the ice cream bar with 19 taps—and craft beer has been a heavy focus ever since.

An abundance of TVs makes Duckworth's an ideal spot to catch a game, but don't let the sports bar aspect fool you into thinking they don't take craft beer seriously. The Park Road location—one of four in the Charlotte area—boasts 60 taps and an extensive bottle list. With hundreds of options it can be difficult to choose, but Duckworth's does offer flights of most of their beers. You can also purchase bottles to go, and they usually have a cask beer on as well.

The cheesesteaks run the gamut from old to new school, with the latter camp featuring toppings like fried eggs or Buffalo chicken. The restaurant's wings and pizzas are popular menu options as well, and the kitchen is given creative liberty during many beer dinners and small-plate events throughout the year (pancake breakfasts with stout syrups, anyone?).

GOOD BOTTLE CO.

125 Remount Rd., Charlotte, NC 28203; (704) 527-1003; GoodBottleCo.com; @GoodBottleCo

Draft Beers: 12 **Bottled/Canned Beers:** 500+

Good Bottle Co. is a combination bottle shop and beer bar not far from Triple C Brewing in Charlotte's SouthEnd neighborhood. It has a clean and modern industrial feel to it, with lots of neutral colors that allow the beer to stand out all the more. Hundreds of bottles line the shelves, which are broken down by style and geography. Upon entering, there is a full rack devoted just to beers brewed in North Carolina.

Past all of these bottles and under a faux tin roof is a bar with a dozen drafts, and behind this is a map showing where each beer is brewed. The taps, too, often reflect a commitment to beers brewed in North Carolina. Owner Chris Hunt frequently drives to breweries that don't distribute to Charlotte to pick up special kegs, and it's not uncommon for some of these beers to be the only ones of their kind in the city. Good Bottle hosts a variety of tastings, tap takeovers and other events throughout the year, often for good causes. While there is no kitchen here, you can bring food in from surrounding restaurants.

GROWLERS POURHOUSE
3120 N. Davidson St., Charlotte, NC 28205; (704) 910-6566; GrowlersPourhouse.com; @GrowlersPH
Draft Beers: 14 **Bottled/Canned Beers:** 20+

Named twice as one of *Draft* magazine's top 100 beer bars in America, Growlers Pourhouse has 14 taps as well as an antique beer engine used to dispense cask ale. This small bar in the heart of Charlotte's NoDa neighborhood features a rotating selection of North Carolina craft beers as well as national brands. They also host a variety of events throughout the year, from beer dinners, to oyster roasts, to the bar's popular monthly "Beer Ed" series of educational beer topics.

In addition to their draft lineup, Growlers Pourhouse also has a small menu of "beer food," which includes oysters, housemade sausages and hot dogs, pretzels, hand-cut gravy fries, and sandwiches. The kitchen is open until midnight every night but Sunday, and Growlers is open until 2 a.m. every night of the week. For a NoDa pub crawl route that features Growlers Pourhouse, check the pub crawl section at the end of the Charlotte chapter.

THE LIBERTY
1812 South Blvd., Charlotte, NC 28203; (704) 332-8830; TheLibertyCharlotte.com; @TheLiberty
Draft Beers: 20 **Bottled/Canned Beers:** 50+

One look at The Liberty's beer-inspired decor and you know this is a place worthy of the "gastropub" moniker. An illuminated wall of yellow suds separates a portion of the restaurant, stacked kegs stand in as columns, and on walls built from pallets hang framed posters with poems about beer. Across one wall is a quote often misattributed to Ben Franklin: "Beer is proof that God loves us and wants us to be happy."

Mr. Franklin never actually said that (a similar quote was penned in reference to wine), but one look at The Liberty's menu and beer list is all you need to realize founder Matthew Pera wants us to be happy. Chef Tom Condron and his kitchen take great care in preparing a variety of salads and entrees, and their burgers are considered some of the best in Charlotte. The Crunch Burger features pimento cheese, bacon, and house-made potato chips piled atop freshly ground beef and sandwiched between brioche. It and the rest of the burgers are all exceptionally filling. If you are looking for something just a little lighter to accompany the beers, consider the house-made soft pretzels, which are served with beer cheese and spicy mustard.

QUEEN CITY Q
225 E. 6th St., Charlotte, NC 28202; (704) 334-8437; QueenCityQ.com; @theQclt
Draft Beers: 40+ **Bottled/Canned Beers:** 90+

Everyone has their opinions on which school of barbecue is right, but Queen City Q doesn't play favorites. The menu has something for everyone, with Texas brisket, St. Louis–style ribs, and slow-smoked pulled pork, along with a variety of sauces.

Queen City Q has become well known for its 'cue no matter the type, but they have also built a reputation upon having a great selection of craft beer. They usually have the largest selection of beers brewed in the Queen City, so if you want to try a wide variety of Charlotte's breweries, this is a perfect place. They rotate through their 40-plus taps often and offer frequent specials, making this one of uptown Charlotte's best places to grab a beer.

SALUD BEER SHOP
3306-B N. Davidson St., Charlotte, NC 28205; (704) 900-7767; SaludBeerShop.com; @SaludNODA
Draft Beers: 6 **Bottled/Canned Beers:** 400+

Salud Beer Shop is a great spot to buy bottles of craft beer to take home, but you'd be remiss not to grab a beer and stay for a while. Since opening in March of 2012, Salud Beer Shop has become a favorite neighborhood hangout for many NoDa residents. Owner Jason Glunt has six taps and stocks hundreds of bottles, which can be opened to enjoy right there on the couch or at the small bar.

This bar and bottle shop is proof that sometimes it's not about lengthy taplists, but about hanging out with good friends with a mutual appreciation for good beer. Often people will purchase bombers of beer and share them there with friends and strangers alike. There's an old-school Nintendo up front near the couch, and several classic games to enjoy while sipping a beer. Oh, and snap an obligatory selfie in front of the gold sunburst-style mirror in the bathroom while you're at it. It's a rite of passage.

VINTNER WINE MARKET

8128 Providence Rd., Charlotte, NC 28277; (704) 543-9909; VintnerWineMarketNC.com; @VintnerNC
Draft Beers: 16 **Bottled/Canned Beers:** 400+

Don't let the wine in the name fool you—Vintner Wine Market is one of Charlotte's better beer bars. Almost one half of this bar and bottle shop's selection is devoted to craft beer, and behind the granite bar are 16 taps with a heavy emphasis on local offerings. General manager Grant Denton takes great care in selecting those 16 drafts, rotating in Charlotte and other NC beers along with a few standards as well as more limited beers. There are a couple coolers full of bottles that are chilled as well that can be enjoyed at the bar or purchased to take home.

Grant also serves as Vintner's executive chef, and he can most often be found back in the small kitchen turning out a delicious assortment of sandwiches, flatbreads, cheese and charcuterie plates, and more. Enjoy said food at the bar, at the many tables, or outside on the patio.

Pub Crawl

Charlotte

The NoDa neighborhood is one of Charlotte's most fun, eclectic areas. Charlotte's Historic Arts District used to be little more than a collection of run-down buildings in a mill village, but then artists came in and with them a handful of studios and galleries, bringing new life to this area. Today, it is home to a great number of restaurants and bars, all in one of the city's funkiest and most walkable areas.

Heist Brewery, 2909 N. Davidson St., Ste. 200, Charlotte, NC 28205; (704) 375-8260; HeistBrewery.com. In a building that used to house an old mill, Heist Brewery has built a gorgeous space filled with reclaimed wood, painted brick, and probably the only bullet-riddled chandelier in all of Charlotte. Through an expansive glass wall in the main dining area, you can see the small copper brewhouse. Heist always keeps six beers on tap, which they call the "standard bandits," but head brewer Zach Hart also brews a variety of seasonals. The brewery has a full bar, too, where they mix up a variety of craft beer cocktails.

Leave Heist Brewery and head north down North Davidson into the heart of NoDa. After about a four-minute walk, you will find Growlers Pourhouse on your right where North Davidson intersects East 35th Street.

Growlers Pourhouse, 3120 N. Davidson St., Charlotte, NC 28205; (704) 910-6566; GrowlersPourhouse.com. Named as one of *Draft* magazine's top 100 beer bars in America, Growlers Pourhouse has 14 taps and an antique 1936 Gaskell & Chambers beer engine used to dispense cask ale. They also have a small menu of "beer food," which includes oysters, house-made sausages and hot dogs, pretzels, hand-cut gravy fries, and sandwiches.

Exit Growlers and continue heading north on North Davidson until the next intersection at East 36th Street (about a two-minute walk). Revolution Ale House is on the corner.

Revolution Ale House, 3228 N. Davidson St., Charlotte, NC 28205; (704) 333-4440; RevolutionAleHouse.com. If you have made it this far in the crawl without eating, Revolution Ale House is as good a place as any to do so. Their menu boasts a large selection of gourmet pizzas, including the popular Carolina Cyclops, a white pizza with ham, pancetta, roasted peppers, cheddar, provolone, and—the best part—a cracked egg at its center. There is no shortage of beers, either, as Revolution Ale House boasts 44 taps.

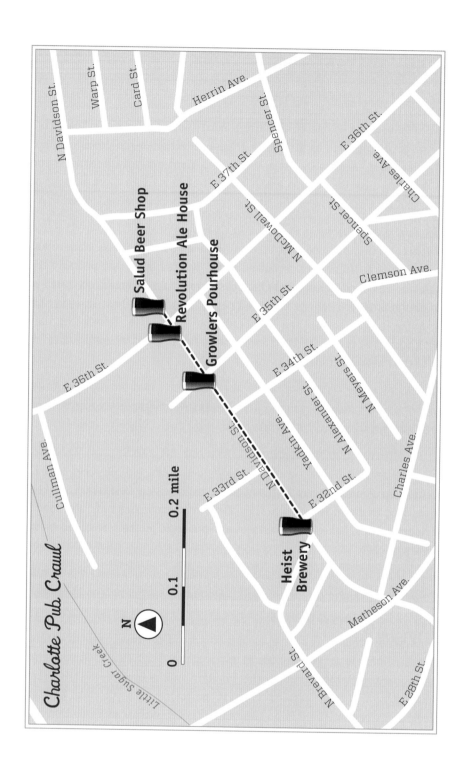

Charlotte Pub Crawl

Salud Beer Shop

Revolution Ale House

Growlers Pourhouse

Heist Brewery

N Davidson St.
Warp St.
Card St.
Herrin Ave.
Spencer St.
E 37th St.
E 36th St.
Charles Ave.
N McDowell St.
Spencer St.
Clemson Ave.
E 35th St.
E 34th St.
N Myers St.
E 36th St.
N Alexander St.
N Myers St.
Yadkin Ave.
Cullman Ave.
E 33rd St.
N Davidson St.
E 32nd St.
Charles Ave.
Matheson Ave.
N Brevard St.
E 28th St.
Little Sugar Creek

N

0   0.1   0.2 mile

Leave Revolution and cross over E. 36th Street, continuing down North Davidson in the direction you have been heading. Shortly after crossing, you will see Salud Beer Shop on your right.

Salud Beer Shop, 3306 N. Davidson St., Charlotte, NC 28205; (704) 900-7767; SaludBeerShop.com. Salud Beer Shop is the perfect spot to end the night. While they usually close between 10 and 11 p.m., it is not uncommon to find them staying open well into the night if there is a crowd. Here you can plunk down on a comfortable couch and play some old-school NES while enjoying the last of the evening's beers. Salud has six beers on tap and a large selection of bottled beers to choose from, and often you will find people purchasing large bottles and sharing them with friends and strangers alike. Of course, you can purchase beers to go at Salud as well.

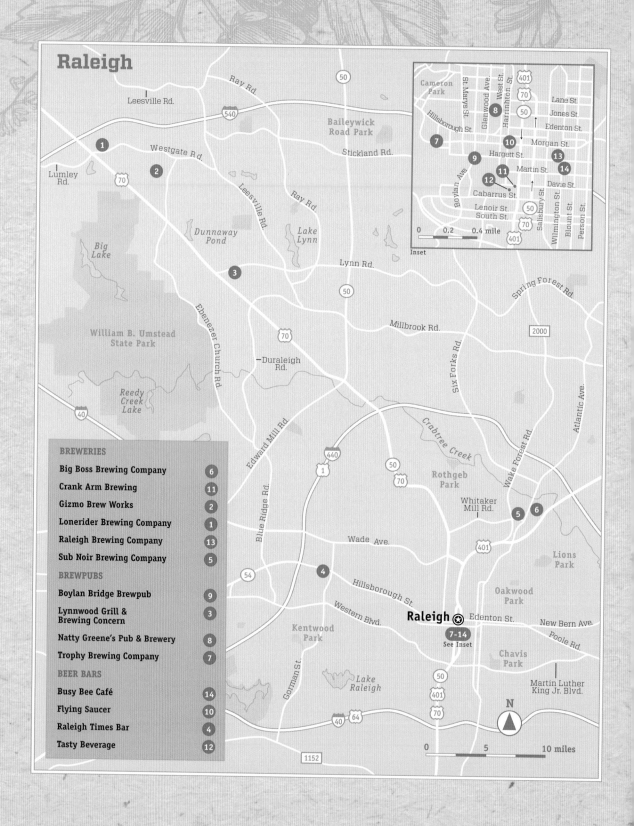

Raleigh

BREWERIES

Big Boss Brewing Company	6
Crank Arm Brewing	11
Gizmo Brew Works	2
Lonerider Brewing Company	1
Raleigh Brewing Company	13
Sub Noir Brewing Company	5

BREWPUBS

Boylan Bridge Brewpub	9
Lynnwood Grill & Brewing Concern	3
Natty Greene's Pub & Brewery	8
Trophy Brewing Company	7

BEER BARS

Busy Bee Café	14
Flying Saucer	10
Raleigh Times Bar	4
Tasty Beverage	12

Raleigh

The entire Research Triangle area is filled with breweries, but so many are located in Raleigh proper that the city demands its own section. From established breweries like Lonerider and Big Boss to new startups like Trophy and Crank Arm, the brewing scene in the capital city is one of North Carolina's finest.

Breweries

BIG BOSS BREWING COMPANY

1249 Wicker Dr., Raleigh, NC 27604; (919) 834-0045; BigBossBrewing.com; @BigBossBeer
Founded: 2007 **Founders:** Geoff Lamb, Brad Wynn **Brewer:** Brad Wynn **Flagship Beer:** Bad Penny Brown Ale **Year-Round Beers:** Bad Penny Brown Ale, Hell's Belle, Blanco Diablo, Angry Angel, High Roller **Seasonals/Special Releases:** Aces and Ates, The Countess, Big Operator, Monkey Bizz-ness, Sack Time, Harvest Time, D'Icer Dunkelweizen, Saucey Pants, Deuces Wild, Night Knight **Tours:** Second Sat of each month at 2 p.m. **Taproom:** Mon, 4 p.m. to 12 a.m.; Tues and Wed, 4 p.m. to 2 a.m.; Thurs, 3 p.m. to 2 a.m.; Fri and Sat, 2 p.m. to 2 a.m.

Large, hefty wooden doors with sledgehammer handles greet visitors to Big Boss Brewing Company, giving the impression you're about to enter a medieval dungeon instead of one of the Triangle's largest breweries.

While Big Boss hasn't been around since the dark ages, the building they call home does have a storied history of brewing. Since 1996, this building in an industrial section of Raleigh has held Tomcat Brewing, Pale Ale Brewery, Rock Creek Brewing, and Chesapeake Bay Brewing. When that last brewery closed in 2003, brewers Brad Wynn and Brian Baker started yet another operation in Edenton Brewery. In 2007, Geoff Lamb purchased a majority stake in the company and, along with Brad, redubbed the brewery Big Boss after one of Edenton's most popular beers.

Inside, a stairway bathed in burgundy leads to a taproom upstairs, with surrounding rooms containing games like pool, darts, and table tennis. Airplane nose panels hang around the dimly lit taproom. Here you will find most of the brewery's year-round beers and some seasonals, as well as small-batch beers or barrel-aged offerings that rarely make it outside of the taproom.

The brewery offers a diverse selection of year-round beers, including the **Bad Penny Brown Ale,** with its notes of coffee, toffee, and almonds, and the **Angry Angel,** a crisp ale in the German kölsch style that is the brewery's most easy-drinking beer. The **Harvest Time** pumpkin ale is one of the brewery's most popular seasonal offerings.

Beer Lover's Pick

Aces and Ates
Style: Coffee stout
ABV: 8 percent
Availability: On tap and in 12-ounce
bottles from Nov through Dec

Ten different malts are used in Aces and Ates, yet the most noticeable ingredient—both in the aroma and the taste—is the coffee. Most stouts have some degree of roast character, but this one has it in spades. The coffee is cold-brewed just down the road at Larry's Beans exclusively for Big Boss. When added to the base stout, you get a beer with a sharp roasted character, a subtle chocolate sweetness, and just a wisp of smoke on the finish. Like a good cup of coffee, this is one to sip and savor.

CRANK ARM BREWING

319 W. Davie St., Raleigh, NC 27601; CrankArmBrewing.com; @CrankArmBrew
Founded: 2013 **Founders:** Adam Eckhardt, Dylan Selinger, Michael Morris **Brewer:**
Michael Morris **Flagship Beer:** Rickshaw Rye IPA **Year-Round Beers:** Rickshaw Rye IPA,
White Wall Wit, Unicycle Single Hop Pale Ale, Uphill Climb, Flying Scotsman Scottish Ale
Seasonals/Special Releases: Holy Mole Smoke Porter, Eat Sleep Bike ESB, Reflector
Red, Motivator Stout **Tours:** N/A **Taproom:** Mon through Weds, 4 p.m. to midnight;
Thurs and Fri, 4 p.m. to 2 a.m.; Sat, 12 p.m. to 2 a.m.; Sun, 12 to 10 p.m.

There has always been a crossover between fans of beer and bikes, and nowhere is that more apparent than at Crank Arm Brewing in Raleigh. The brewery opened in 2013, but they had been building their brand with Crank Arm Rickshaw, the other portion of their business. Those rickshaws are parked inside the brewery for all to see, and if you end up overimbibing you can even buy a ride home.

The bike theme is also apparent in the design of the brewery, with frames, chain rings, wheels, and other bicycle pieces welded together to form artwork on the wall.

Raleigh

The flight holders are shaped like cranks. On Saturdays, cyclists meet up at the brewery for group rides, and the bike-savvy brewery employees can even offer basic tuneup services.

Past a blue-lit bar sits the seven-barrel J.V. Northwest brewhouse for all to see, separated not by glass but by an unobtrusive railing that features more of those welded bike pieces. Michael Morris, formerly a brewer at Natty Greene's and Big Boss in Raleigh, is the man behind the beers. He is one of three founders, the other two being Adam Eckhardt and Dylan Selinger.

The **White Wall Wit** is unique in that it relies on American hops—and not oft-used spices like coriander or orange peel—to impart the citrus notes one expects in the style. The brewery cycles (forgive the pun) through a variety of hops in their **Unicycle Single Hop Pale Ale** so as to showcase the unique flavors each imparts. One of Crank Arm's most popular seasonals is the **Holy Mole Smoke Porter,** which is brewed with smoked malt and aged on habanero peppers and cocoa nibs from Videri Chocolate Factory just around the corner.

There is no kitchen, but you can order or bring food in from area restaurants (and The Pit Authentic Barbecue is right across the street).

Rickshaw Rye IPA

Style: Rye IPA

ABV: 7 percent

Availability: On tap year-round

Rye makes up almost a quarter of Rickshaw Rye IPA's grain bill, imparting plenty of spice and pepperiness. The rest of that bill keeps the rye from overpowering the beer, lending notes of sweet caramel that help to balance everything out. Nugget and Zythos hops contribute herbal and fruit-forward notes and an assertive bitterness.

GIZMO BREW WORKS

5907 Triangle Dr., Raleigh, NC 27617; (919) 782-2099; GizmoBrewWorks.com; @Gizmo BrewWorks

Founded: 2013 **Founders:** Bryan Williams, Matt Santelli, Bryan Shaw, Elizabeth Morgan, Jeff Sgroi, Alwyn Smith **Brewer:** Tyler Cox **Flagship Beer:** N/A **Year-Round Beers:** Black Stiletto **Seasonals/Special Releases:** Palisade Wasp IPA, Raleigh Red, Alternating Current Altbier, Know Wonder Pale Ale, Born Again Brown **Tours:** Sat at 2 and 4 p.m. **Taproom:** Thurs, 4 to 8 p.m.; Fri, 4 to 10 p.m.; Sat, 12 to 10 p.m.

Gizmo Brew Works opened their doors in April of 2013, but beer has been brewed in their Umstead Industrial Park building years prior to that. Gizmo's six owners purchased the brewery from Ryan and Eric Roth, who had operated Roth Brewing in that building for almost three years prior to selling their brewery. They were all regulars who did not want to see their favorite watering hole go under, so they worked together to purchase the building and equipment. These six new owners come from different backgrounds, and yet all of them consider themselves to be "thinkers, tinkerers, makers, and inventors."

They soon got to work brewing their own beers on the same two-barrel system used by Roth Brewing. The guys (and gal) at Gizmo made some changes in the

Palisade Wasp IPA
Style: American India pale ale
ABV: 6.3 percent
Availability: Rotating

Gizmo Brew Works didn't play it safe when they brewed their first IPA. Instead, they decided to feature Palisade hops, which are usually used in a complementary role and not the focus of the beer. The Palisade Wasp IPA has more floral character and fewer citrus notes than most in the style. The bitterness is noticeable but not overpowering, and the beer finishes dry.

taproom, too. They repainted inside and knocked down a wall, greatly opening up the space. Four taps come out of a concrete wall behind the small bar. The taproom has a couple comfortable sofas—one red, the other a vintage leather model dotted with buttons. There are a couple plastic tables and a slew of rolling office chairs around them.

The brothers Roth brewed some excellent beers, however they all but eschewed hoppier styles. One of the first beers Gizmo unveiled was the **Palisade Wasp IPA,** a beer that was initially going to be a test batch using Palisade hops but was so well liked they had to brew it again. Due to the size of their brewing system, the folks at Gizmo want to constantly rotate the styles of beer they brew. While they don't want to be known for a flagship beer, they do want to have an IPA on at all times, even if it isn't the Palisade Wasp IPA. The **Black Stiletto Stout** is as close to a year-round beer as you will find at Gizmo, and it is a reworking of Roth Brewing's popular Dark Construct Stout. While they still brew on the same electric two-barrel system the Roth brothers used, the owners at Gizmo have plans to expand with a seven-barrel system and matching fermenters in 2014. There is no kitchen at Gizmo, but you can often find food trucks parked outside on the weekends.

LONERIDER BREWING COMPANY

8816 Gulf Ct., Ste. 100, Raleigh, NC 27617; (919) 442-8004; LoneriderBeer.com; @LoneriderBeer
Founded: 2009 **Founders:** Sumit Vohra, Mihir Patel, Steve Kramling **Brewers:** Galen Smith, David Nelson, David McComas **Flagship Beer:** Sweet Josie Brown Ale

Year-Round Beers: Sweet Josie Brown Ale, Shotgun Betty Hefeweizen, Peacemaker Pale Ale **Seasonals/Special Releases:** DeadEye Jack Porter, True Britt ESB, The Preacher Saison, Mad Doc Weizenbock, The Beer With No Name, Pistols at Dawn, The Hangman **Tours:** By appt (Loneriderbeer.com/tours) **Taproom:** Mon through Fri, 3 to 10 p.m.; Sat and Sun, 12 to 7 p.m.

Sumit Vohra, Mihir Patel, and Steve Kramling all worked together in the software industry. Mihir and Steve had been homebrewing for some time when Sumit joined their team, and it wasn't long before they—like so many homebrewers before them—began to entertain the idea of opening a brewery of their own. When Myrtle Beach's Mad Boar Brewery closed, the three bought their equipment and acquired some warehouse space not far from the Raleigh-Durham International Airport.

From the beginning, the three didn't want to brew beers for the masses—they wanted to do something different, to follow their own path. Before settling on the name Lonerider, they considered the name Outlaw Brewing Company. That outlaw mentality still lives on in their branding, as they say they are proud to make "ales for

DeadEye Jack
Style: English porter
ABV: 6 percent
Availability: Seasonal

Lonerider's DeadEye Jack is a porter in the English tradition, with a medium body, creamy mouthfeel, and notes of caramel, coffee, and chocolate. It has garnered several medals, including a silver from the Great American Beer Festival and golds from both the US Open Beer Championship and the Carolina Championship of Beer. The base beer is excellent, as are the occasional espresso and bourbon-infused variations.

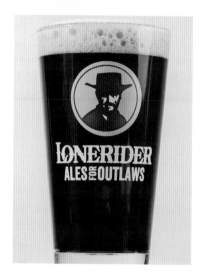

outlaws." In keeping with their Western theme, the taproom is called The Hideout. It is an enclosed space built onto the building with a bar and picnic tables inside.

Lonerider brews and bottles three year-round beers: **Shotgun Betty Hefeweizen, Sweet Josie Brown Ale,** and **Peacemaker Pale Ale.** Those three are all perfect examples of their respective styles, and in 2010 Sweet Josie took home a gold medal at the Great American Beer Festival. The brewery also releases a line of seasonals and a Most Wanted series of beers that find their way into 22-ounce bombers. In this latter series is the popular **Pistols at Dawn,** an American stout brewed with chocolate, coffee, oats, and lactose.

Ever since their first year, the brewery has offered homebrewers the chance to brew their beers on the big system as part of their "Brew It Forward" series. They split some of the profits between the winner of the competition as well as nonprofits and the North Carolina Brewers Guild. These beers are also bottled in 22-ounce bombers.

RALEIGH BREWING COMPANY

3709 Neil St., Raleigh, NC 27607; (919) 400-9086; RaleighBrewingCompany.com;
@RaleighBrewing

Founded: 2013 **Founders:** Kristie and Patrik Nystedt **Brewers:** John Federal, Alex
Smith **Flagship Beer:** House of Clay Rye IPA **Year-Round Beers:** House of Clay Rye
IPA, City of Blokes Bitter, Blatherskite Scottish Ale, Hell Yes Ma'am Belgian-Style Golden,
Hidden Pipe Porter, Uncommon Curiosity Lager **Seasonals/Special Releases:** No Love
Lost Wheat IPA, **Tours:** Every Sat at 3 p.m. **Taproom:** Mon through Thurs, 12 to 10 p.m.;
Fri and Sat, 12 p.m. to 12 a.m.; Sun, 12 to 6 p.m.

When you walk into Raleigh Brewing Company you have two choices, depending on whether you want to drink beer or brew it. If the former, make a beeline to the bar. If the latter, head to the right and visit Atlantic Brew Supply, the brewery's sister shop. Both businesses are owned by Kristie and Patrik Nystedt.

Beer Lover's Pick

Hidden Pipe Porter
Style: Porter
ABV: 6.5 percent
Availability: On tap year-round
The legend goes that Thomas Briggs
hid gold and silver in pipes and
buried them before the Union occupation of Raleigh in 1865. After
the Union left, he finally found his
coins and used them to construct
the four-story Briggs Hardware
building that stands tall in Raleigh
to this day. That's the rumor, at
least, but there's certainly treasure
in the Hidden Pipe Porter. Dig deep
enough and you'll find notes of
espresso, bitter dark chocolate, and
tobacco.

The homebrew shop was opened in 2012 while the Nystedts worked on the brewery, which opened in March of 2013. The red brick building that these businesses call home once held a cotton-manufacturing plant. There is chalkboard paint where wainscoting would normally be, allowing visitors to sign their names, doodle, and otherwise leave a record of their visit to the brewery. The brewery also boasts Pac-Man and Galaga arcade games.

The Nystedts have an appreciation for the area's rich history, and many of their beer names include historical references. The **House of Clay Rye IPA** is named after one of Shaw University's first buildings, which was built with red clay bricks made by the students themselves. Five different hops are thrown at a solid malt backbone, with a bit of rye adding a dry, peppery quality to the beer. The brewery's **City of Blokes Bitter** is proof positive that lower-alcohol beers can be very flavorful. It offers a sweet, toasted malt character with a subtle earthiness, and it does so while coming in at only 3.8 percent ABV.

No matter their occupation at the brewery, all employees eventually get to brew their own beer as part of Raleigh Brewing's employee beer release program. These beers are usually tapped on Tuesday nights. With the shop next door, it's only natural that the brewery has reached out to the local homebrew community as well. And if they're not brewing beer, they're likely brewing kombucha and root beer, both of which can be found at the taproom.

Outside their red brick building, the brewery has a few picnic tables and umbrellas for when the weather's warm. Food trucks are often parked outside as well. And if you show up early on a Sunday morning, don't be surprised to find a brewery full of people doing yoga before beer can even be served.

SUB NOIR BREWING COMPANY

2039 Progress Ct., Raleigh, NC 27608; (919) 480-2337; SubNoir.net; @Sub_Noir
Founded: 2012 **Founders:** Michael Stagner, Brennan Watson **Brewers:** Michael Stagner, Brennan Watson **Flagship Beer:** Hi-yo, Saison! **Year-Round Beers:** Hi-yo, Saison!, Stiff Upper Lip **Seasonals/Special Releases:** Zelda's Barleywine, Sarsaparilla Brown, Écru White IPA, The MFer, McLovin, Quentin's Reserve Root Beer Porter, Zee Count, Zeruda No Eru **Tours:** N/A **Taproom:** Fri, 6 p.m. to 12 a.m.; Sat, 2 to 8 p.m.

Sub Noir Brewing Company occupies a small, unassuming space among a strip of miscellaneous shops. With a 300-square-foot taproom and a 400-square-foot brewery behind it, Sub Noir is a nanobrewery in the truest sense of the word.

The taproom features a few small black tables and chairs, and the chalkboard wall lets drinkers know what is on tap at all times. Those beers are poured from a

modified chest freezer called a Keezer (a portmanteau of the words "kegerator" and "freezer"), the kind you might find in an advanced homebrewer's garage. On a barrel in the other corner of the taproom sits a TV that is connected to an old-school Nintendo, allowing visitors to play classic games like Duck Hunt or Zelda.

Michael Stagner and his wife Amy are such fans of that last game, in fact, that they named their daughter Zelda and brewed **Zelda's Barleywine** in her honor. Zelda's father, along with co-owner Brennan Watson, crafts these beers on a half-barrel SABCO system in the back. The small system doesn't allow Sub Noir to crank out the volume that some of their neighbors do, but it does allow them to experiment with a variety of ingredients with less consideration to money or time spent. This has resulted in fun styles like the **McLovin Spearmint Stout** and **Quentin's Reserve Root Beer Porter.**

The beers are fermented in 21-gallon conical fermenters that can be rolled into temperature-controlled upright freezers. It is a solution you won't find at many breweries, but one that does the job. As they continue to grow, the brewers would like to develop a sour program that would allow them to produce styles like Flanders Red Ales.

Just a few miles away from this small brewery, you can find Big Boss Brewing Company. That brewery is one of Raleigh's largest, and yet both of these breweries exemplify the same enthusiasm and commitment to quality. Visit Sub Noir to see the passion that inspires so many brewers to turn pro and, if you've got the time, pick up a Nintendo controller while you're at it.

Hi-yo, Saison!
Style: Saison
ABV: 6 percent
Availability: Year-round on tap

Because they're such a small operation, Sub Noir does not have a huge portfolio of beers that they cycle through. The Hi-yo, Saison!, however, is often on—and for good reason. This beer strikes that perfect balance between refreshment and complexity. Motueka hops—often referred to as "Belgian Saaz"—provide notes of dill and spice that pair well with the peppery Belgian yeast, and a crisp finish invites another sip.

Brewpubs

BOYLAN BRIDGE BREWPUB

201 S. Boylan Ave., Raleigh, NC 27603; (919) 803-8927; BoylanBridge.com; @BBBrewPub
Founded: 2009 **Founder:** Andrew Leager **Brewer:** Donovan Matthews **Flagship Beer:**
Endless Summer Ale **Year-Round Beers:** Endless Summer Ale, Rail Pale Ale, Gantlet
Golden Ale, Bruno Bitter, Pullman Porter, Southbound Stout, Trainspotter Scottish Ale,
Hopped Off the Tracks IPA **Seasonals/Special Releases:** Autumn Amber, Polar Bear
Winter Warmer

With its 20-foot ceilings and expansive 12,000 square feet of space, the basement of the three-story building at the corner of Boylan Avenue and Hargett Street seemed the perfect spot for architect Andrew Leager to build his woodworking business. When the landlord told him he would have to take the other two floors above it, however, Andrew had to think about ways to put those other areas to good use.

Andrew had been a homebrewer for many years, finding in it that same pleasure in skillfully crafting something from raw ingredients that he found in woodworking. He decided to add a kitchen and brewery above that gymnasium-size woodshop. It should come as no surprise that Andrew put his woodworking skills to work inside. A long piece of mahogany was used to construct a semicircular bar, and an old glass mezzanine matches its arc above it. The seven-barrel brewery is visible from the bar.

Outside, Andrew built a long wooden deck with a pergola where once there was a parking lot; it is so seamlessly integrated, you would think it was built when the original building was constructed. The result is a beer-garden type of atmosphere with several long tables that encourage conversation with friends new and old. The view of the Raleigh skyline from this deck is one of the best around.

The menu—food and beer alike—is filled with train-inspired names, given the tracks that curve just behind the building. The **Pullman Porter** drinks as easily as coffee with cream, and is just as soothing. No matter the time of year, the **Endless Summer** provides a light-bodied option with just a hint of bready malt and citrus.

LYNNWOOD GRILL & BREWING CONCERN

4821 Grove Barton Rd., Raleigh, NC 27613; (919) 785-0043; LynnwoodGrill.com; @LynnwoodGrill
Founded: 2013 **Founder:** Ted Dwyer **Brewer:** Bill Gerds **Flagship Beer:** Blonde Moment **Year-Round Beers:** Blonde Moment, Bill and Ted's Excellent Amber, Bad Leroy, Hop on Top IPA **Seasonals/Special Releases:** Helluva Hef, Czech Yourself

Just off the intersection of Lynn Road and Glenwood Avenue is Lynnwood Grill, a sports-bar-meets-brewpub located in a shopping center with a couple of big-box stores and a movie theater. From day one, founder Ted Dwyer planned the business as a brewpub but needed to wait on ordering the brewing equipment. Lynnwood Grill opened as a restaurant in 2011, and then started brewing in 2013.

At first glance, the restaurant doesn't seem all that different from most sports bars. There are a couple arcade games, and neon beer signs glow warmly on the walls. On one side of the restaurant, however, is a large glass window overlooking the 10-barrel, steam-fired brewery. And on the glass, a warning: "Please do not tap on glass, feed, or otherwise disturb brewmaster in natural habitat."

The man behind the glass—and the beer—is Bill Gerds, who formerly worked for Arbor Brewing Company and Cranker's Brewery in Michigan. At Lynnwood, Bill brews a variety of true-to-style, easy-drinking beers that pair well with the food served there. **Bad Leroy** is a near-perfect English brown ale, with more of the expected caramel and toffee notes than most examples. The **Czech Yourself** pilsner is a light, crisp lager that is the perfect gateway beer for drinkers that might be tempted to order a mass-market lager at the restaurant. With its generous additions of Amarillo and Cascade hops, **Bill and Ted's Excellent Amber** might be the least true to style—yet it's one of the brewpub's tastiest.

Of course, beer is only part of the reason to visit Lynnwood Grill. The food is affordable and made fresh in-house, with the pizzas being the most popular menu items. One fan's custom order was such a favorite with others that they added "The Russell" to the menu: It is a marinara-based pizza with grilled chicken, red onions, diced tomatoes, pineapple, jalapeños, and feta cheese. Whether you order food or beer, you can enjoy them inside, on the outdoor patio, or atop the fun rooftop patio with its own bar.

NATTY GREENE'S PUB & BREWERY

505 W. Jones St., Raleigh, NC 27603; (919) 232-2477; NattyGreenes.com; @Natty_Greenes

Founded: 2010 **Founders:** Chris Lester, Kayne Fisher **Brewers:** Sebastian Wolfrum, Mike Rollinson **Flagship Beer:** Buckshot Amber Ale **Year-Round Beers:** Buckshot Amber Ale, Southern Pale Ale, Wildflower Witbier, Guilford Golden Ale, General Stout **Seasonals/Special Releases:** Old Town Brown Ale, Swamp Fox Belgian Blonde, Elm Street English IPA, Freedom American IPA, Hessian Hefeweizen, Summerfest Dortmunder Lager, Red Nose Winter Ale, Cannonball Double IPA, Smokey Mountain Porter

Natty Greene's got its start in Greensboro, where they opened a small brewpub in a historic downtown building out of which they still operate today. A couple of years after opening that brewpub, they built a production brewery in Greensboro to help in distributing their beer into other accounts, whether on tap or in six-packs. The brand continued to grow, and in 2010 Natty Greene's opened another brewpub in the building that used to hold Raleigh's Southend Brewery.

While this brewpub doesn't have the history of the Greensboro location, it does share an aesthetic with the original Natty Greene's. Hardwood floors and lots of brick

create a comfortable feel, and there is a long bar with 12 taps behind it. And like the original pub, the draft selection is usually a mix of the brewery's core beers, a few seasonals, and small-batch beers that can only be found at the Raleigh location. Their year-round beers include classics like the **Buckshot Amber,** an easy-drinking amber ale with notes of toast, caramel, and a slight nuttiness. The other core beers include the brewery's pale ale, witbier, and golden; these are all refreshing, true-to-style beers, which explains why they have done so well in the six-pack format.

At the brewpub, Natty Greene's brewers can experiment a little more and brew much smaller batches than they do at the Greensboro production facility. Whether it's the popular **Smokey Mountain Porter** or a handful of pub-only IPAs, make sure you try these beers when visiting either the Raleigh or the Greensboro brewpub.

TROPHY BREWING COMPANY

827 W. Morgan St., Raleigh, NC 27603; TrophyBrewing.com; @TrophyBrewing
Founded: 2013 **Founders:** Chris Powers, David "Woody" Lockwood **Brewer:** Les Stewart
Flagship Beer: Best in Show **Year-Round Beer:** Best in Show **Seasonals/Special
Releases:** Next Best in Show, Biggest Flirt, Rose Gose, The King, Trophy Wife American
Pale Ale, Brandy Barrel Drausinus, 30 Fathoms, Peruvian Pecan Porter, Trophinator,
Slingshot Coffee Porter, Limbo Champ, Yellow Belt, Gold Rush

When Chris Powers and David "Woody" Lockwood were scouting locations for
their brewery, they found an old trophy shop that they thought would be
perfect. Instead of moving into the trophy shop's space, they ended up opening their
brewery in a small spot next to a convenience store and laundromat. The trophy
shop location didn't end up working out, but the name stuck.

When it came time to build out the taproom and brewery, the owners invited people from the community to bring in old trophies, which can be found throughout the brewpub. The tap handles are made from trophies, gleaming relics of past accomplishments now used to pour beers worthy of their own accolades. Those beers are brewed by Les Stewart, who was a homebrewer before signing on with Trophy. The entire establishment—from the brewery to the kitchen to the taproom and outdoor patio—is fairly tight, though not cramped. It is a small space, but that adds to the neighborhood feel.

The brewpub keeps five taps of their beers on at all times, most of them with trophy-inspired names. **Best in Show** is the brewery's flagship saison, which has notes of honeydew melon and lemon. **Trophy Wife** is a well-balanced American pale ale that pairs well with any number of the brewpub's pizzas. Because they brew on such a small system, the guys at Trophy can afford to experiment a bit and offer unique styles you don't often see elsewhere. The **Rose Gose** is a well-done example of the once obscure salty German wheat beer that is now making a comeback. At 3.8 percent, it is a perfectly refreshing beer well suited to Trophy's patio. For dessert, try **The King,** a beer that the banana-sandwich-loving Elvis Presley surely would have enjoyed. With this as his inspiration, Les brewed a Belgian dubbel—which already has notes of bread and banana—and then added peanut butter.

You can create your own pie or opt for one of several specialty pizzas on the menu. The Most Loyal has pesto as its base, with herb-roasted chicken, mozzarella, tomatoes, and honey atop it. On the spicier side, you have The Daredevil. Its fire-roasted tomato sauce is topped with ghost chile pepper salami, mozzarella, fresh jalapeños, caramelized onions, and Sriracha hot sauce.

Beer Bars

BUSY BEE CAFÉ

225 S. Wilmington St., Raleigh, NC 27601; BusyBeeRaleigh.com; @BusyBeerCafe
Draft Beers: 16 **Bottled/Canned Beers:** 100+

Chris Powers and David Lockwood—also the minds behind Raleigh's Trophy Brewing—had long talked about opening a restaurant that specialized in organic food and craft beer. They did just that in 2009, renovating a building that the original Busy Bee Café had occupied as early as 1913. That cafe closed in 1925, but Chris and David kept the name in a nod to the building's history.

Named one of America's 100 Best Beer Bars by *Draft* magazine, Busy Bee Café offers a dozen drafts downstairs and four more upstairs. The Busy Bee Café consists of three levels, the most scenic undoubtedly being the rooftop patio. There is seating outside in front of the building as well.

The restaurant also offers an extensive bottle selection that is broken down into categories like session, malt, hop, Belgian-style, vintage, wheat, wild/sour, and barrel-aged. Busy Bee Café usually has a cask beer on, and they host rare tappings, beer dinners, tastings, and other events just about every week.

In the kitchen, Chef David Mitchell prepares a lunch and dinner menu that changes frequently in accordance with the season and whatever local ingredients are available at the time. On it are accompanient and small plates, salads and dinner entrees, sandwiches and burgers. The towering burgers are a favorite here, especially the pimento burger. The fries are a good side, as they are with any burger, but you can also choose tater tots or fried green tomatoes (among other sides). Busy Bee Café serves a popular brunch from 11 a.m. to 3 p.m. on Saturday, Sunday, and Monday.

FLYING SAUCER

328 W. Morgan St., Raleigh, NC 27601; (919) 821-7469; BeerKnurd.com;
@FlyingSaucerRal
Draft Beers: 81 **Bottled/Canned Beers:** 250+

The Flying Saucer Draught Emporium—known as the Saucer to most—is a chain of beer bars that was founded in 1995 in Fort Worth, Texas. In the Carolinas, there are Flying Saucer locations in Columbia, SC, as well as Charlotte and Raleigh, NC.

The Raleigh location sits in a long, white-brick building in Raleigh's warehouse district. There is an outdoor patio, with plenty of tables underneath a green canopy. Inside, the walls are lined with hundreds of plates going all the way up to the ceiling. These plates are awarded to UFO club members upon consuming 200 unique beers. After doing so, they are immortalized in the Ring of Honor and get to put their custom plate on the wall with the others. It's a goal many of the Saucer's "beer knurds" aspire to, and it is made a little easier by the sheer diversity of beers the Saucer offers. The Raleigh location's 81 draft lineup boasts beers from all over the globe, so there is something for everyone.

The Saucer offers a menu of standard American pub fare like appetizers, sandwiches, and pizzas. There are a few options that are particularly well suited to their large beer selection, such as the Hungry Farmer. This plate allows you to choose from a variety of meats and cheeses, alongside each a recommendation of what beer style would pair best with that item.

RALEIGH TIMES BAR

14 E. Hargett St., Raleigh, NC 27601; (919) 833-0999; RaleighTimesBar.com;
@RaleighTimesBar
Draft Beers: 6 **Bottled/Canned Beers:** 100+

The Raleigh Times Bar is so named because it sits in a downtown building that was built in 1906 to house the *Raleigh Times,* a newspaper that put out its final edition in 1989. When the owners of the bar purchased the space, they worked hand-in-hand with Raleigh's Historic District Commission to ensure their design was in accordance with the old building, even if a bar is quite a bit different from a newspaper. The sign on the window was based on the gold-leaf sign that can be glimpsed

in a 1912 photograph. They purchased old volumes of the paper at a flea market, and many of these can be found hanging throughout the bar. The building has lots of painted brick, plaster and exposed beams and ductwork. In short, it has history.

The draft selection may be small, but the selection of craft beer in cans and bottles is extensive. For the most part, the beer menu is broken down by beer style, and around half of it is devoted to Belgians. The bar prides itself on its Belgian selections, and they have many big bottles that are ideal for sharing with the rest of your party (note that prices are naturally higher for these than retail).

The bar's food menu consists of new takes on classic pub favorites, with several salads, sandwiches, burgers, and larger plates. The chicken-fried pickles and BBQ pork nachos are perennial favorites among visitors. Enjoy them inside that building brimming with character, or on the rooftop patio for a beautiful view of Raleigh.

TASTY BEVERAGE
327 W. Davie St., #106, Raleigh, NC 27601; (919) 828-2789; TastyBeverageCo.com; @TastyBeverageCo
Draft Beers: 6 **Bottled/Canned Beers:** 500+

Tasty Beverage Company is a combination beer store and beer bar located in the Raleigh Depot. The bulk of the shop's business is devoted to its vast bottle selection that includes a great selection of beers from around the world, but there is a small tasting bar with six taps at the back. It is a clean, well-lighted place with a fun and modern feel. With only six on at a time, Tasty Beverage Co. is constantly rotating its taps for special events and tastings or simply to keep things fresh and interesting. On the right side of the building is a row of coolers, and these beers can be purchased for on-premise consumption as well.

Whether you are enjoying a beer there or looking for something to bring home, Tasty Beverage Company's employees are some of the most knowledgeable, helpful, and down-to-earth folks you will find.

Pub Crawl

Raleigh

There are some great bars in downtown Raleigh's Entertainment District, but if you are looking to walk from one excellent craft beer destination to another, head to the city's Warehouse District. This pub crawl will take you to one of the city's best beer bars, a combination bottle shop/bar, a legendary barbecue restaurant, and one of Raleigh's newest breweries.

Brewmasters Bar & Grill, 301 W. Martin St., Raleigh, NC 27601; (919) 836-9338; BrewmastersBarandGrill.com. The neon "restaurant" sign above the entrance to Brewmasters hints at its former heritage as a longtime Raleigh restaurant location. With 66 taps and abundance of North Carolina beer, Brewmasters Bar and Grill is a great place to start your pub crawl. The bar and restaurant is also well known for its pub fare and burgers in particular. You certainly wouldn't need it this early in a pub crawl, but The Hangover burger features avocado, bacon, pepperjack, a fried egg, and—get this—an aioli made from a Bloody Mary mix.

Leave Brewmasters by heading west down West Martin Street until you come to Commerce Place on your left. Follow that until you see The Pit Authentic Barbecue on your right. The total walk time is around three minutes.

The Pit Authentic Barbecue, 328 W. Davie St., Raleigh, NC 27601; (919) 890-4500; ThePit-Raleigh.com. Sure, it sounds great, but don't fret if you skipped out on The Hangover burger at Brewmasters. That's because the next stop, The Pit Authentic Barbecue, is a legend in the world of Carolina 'cue. The smell of woodfire and slow-cooked meat emanates for blocks around The Pit, and you could probably abandon the previous directions and simply follow your nose. As for the beer selection, you will find a dozen taps with some fine local options dispensed as 10-ounce, 20-ounce, or pitcher pours. The restaurant also has a bottle selection with large-format bottles listed as "Beers to Share."

To get to your next destination, you have only to leave The Pit and look across West Davie Street. You will see the Raleigh Depot, which Tasty Beverage Company calls home.

Tasty Beverage Company, 327 W. Davie St., Ste. 106, Raleigh, NC; (919) 828 2789; TastyBeverageCo.com. Upon first entering Tasty Beverage Company, you may be too

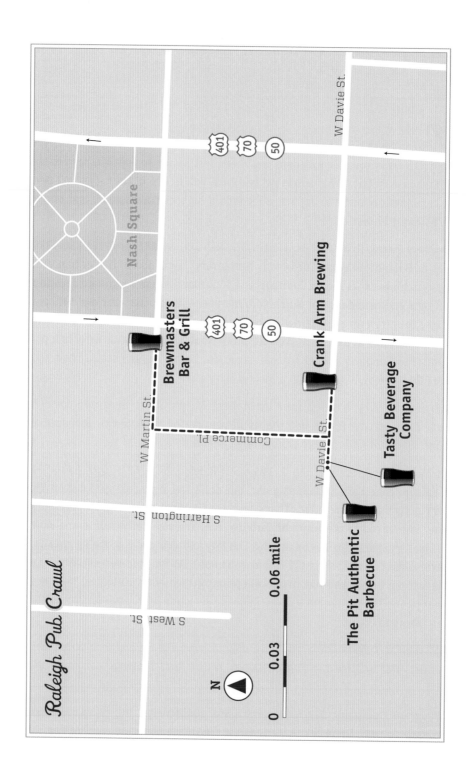

Raleigh Pub Crawl

Nash Square

Brewmasters Bar & Grill

Crank Arm Brewing

Tasty Beverage Company

The Pit Authentic Barbecue

W Davie St.

W Martin St.

Commerce Pl.

S Harrington St.

S West St.

W Davie St.

401 70 50

401 70 50

N

0   0.03   0.06 mile

awestruck by the thousands of bottles lining the shelves to even see the tasting bar and its six taps in the back. Once you regain your focus, head back there to see what is on. Though six taps pale in comparison to many bars these days, those six are always well thought out. There are cold beers in the cooler, too.

Leave Tasty Beverage Company and walk back to West Davie Street. Turn right and walk a couple hundred feet until you see Crank Arm Brewing on your right.

Crank Arm Brewing, 319 W. Davie St, Raleigh, NC 27601; CrankArmBrewing.com. Crank Arm Brewing was started by the guys behind Crank Arm Rickshaw, and you're likely to see several rickshaws in the brewery. The bike theme is prevalent throughout the brewery, with art fashioned from bike parts and flight holders shaped like cranks. A flight is a good way to go here, allowing you to try all of Crank Arm's beers without committing to so many pints at the end of a pub crawl. And if you've had too much, you just might be able to get a rickshaw ride home.

The Triangle

BREWERIES

Aviator Brewing Company — 16
Bombshell Beer Company — 15
Carolina Brewing Company — 14
Deep River Brewing Company — 19
Double Barley Brewing — 20
Fortnight Brewing Company — 13
Fullsteam Brewery — 7
Hosanna Brewing Company — 17
Mystery Brewing Company — 1
Starpoint Brewing Company — 6
Steel String Brewery — 2
Triangle Brewing Company — 10
White Rabbit Brewing Company — 18
White Street Brewing Company — 11

BREWPUBS

Bull City Burger & Brewery — 9
Carolina Brewery — 4
Carolina Brewery & Grill — 12
Top of the Hill Restaurant & Brewery — 5

BEER BARS

Beer Study — 3
Tyler's Taproom & Restaurant — 8

The Triangle

For as many breweries, brewpubs, and beer bars as you will find in Raleigh, you can find even more in the Research Triangle. The Triangle area is usually thought of as a region framed by Raleigh, Durham, and Chapel Hill. Those last two cities have some great beer destinations, as do smaller surrounding towns like Holly Springs, Fuquay-Varina, Clayton, Wake Forest, and many more.

Breweries

AVIATOR BREWING COMPANY

209 Technology Park Ln., Fuquay-Varina, NC 27526; (919) 567-2337; AviatorBrew.com; @AviatorBrew

Founded: 2008 **Founder:** Mark Doble **Brewers:** Mark Doble, Austin Brown, Justin Simo **Flagship Beer:** HogWild IPA **Year-Round Beers:** HogWild IPA, Devil's Tramping Ground Tripel, HotRod Red, Black Mamba Oatmeal Stout, Steamhead California Common, MadBeach American Wheat **Seasonals/Special Releases:** Saison de Aviator, Oktoberbeast, Frostnipper, Horsepower Double IPA **Tours:** Thurs and Fri at 6 p.m.; Sat, 4 to 6:30 p.m. **Taproom:** Thurs and Fri, 5 to 8 p.m.; Sat, 3 to 8 p.m.

The Aviator Brewing Company originally took flight inside a small airplane hangar at Triple W Airport in Fuquay-Varina. Founder Mark Doble rented the space when he moved to the town from Florida, where his family had their own brewpub. Mark wanted to avoid the restaurant side of the business, and after a cross-country

trek to pick up equipment, he soon assembled a brewery in that small hangar. Crowds seemed to form whenever Mark opened the hangar up for tastings, and in 2009 he opened the Aviator Tap House in a historic Varina train depot in downtown Fuquay-Varina. Across the street sits the Aviator SmokeHouse, which was opened in 2011. You can enjoy Aviator beers and the restaurant's food at either location.

In the years between opening those two businesses, Mark moved the brewery itself from the airport out to a much larger building down the road in an industrial park (the address and hours above are for the brewery itself, but do check out the Tap House and SmokeHouse downtown). This allowed the brewery a little breathing room as it continued to add tanks, a bottling system, and a canning line. In 2013, the brewery underwent another expansion to add an additional 12,000 square feet.

Beer Lover's Pick

Bourbon Barrel-Aged Black Mamba Stout
Style: Oatmeal stout
ABV: 6.5 percent
Availability: Seasonal
Molasses and roasted oats join seven different malts in Aviator's Black Mamba Oatmeal Stout, and if that's not enough the brewery also offers a bourbon barrel–aged version. The effect is mild, imparting subtle notes of vanilla and oak that work well with the bitter dark chocolate and coffee notes in the base beer. A bit of a warming, boozy quality is lent to the beer, yet it's a smooth stout that comes in a touch thinner than some big imperial versions.

With a name like Aviator Brewing Company, it should come as no surprise that aviation-related posters and even a pair of wings cover the taproom's walls. Many of Aviator's beers can be found on tap or in bottles and cans at the taproom, including the popular **HogWild IPA,** a crisp beer with pine and grapefruit notes that finishes dry on the palate. If Belgians are more your style, try the **Devil's Tramping Ground Tripel,** a beer that achieves its sweetness and 9.2 percent ABV partially from the use of candi sugar.

BOMBSHELL BEER COMPANY

120 Quantum Dr., Holly Springs, NC 27540; BombshellBeer.com; @BombshellBeer
Founded: 2013 **Founders:** Ellen Joyner, Jackie Hudspeth, Michelle Miniutti **Brewer:**
Stephen O'Neill **Flagship Beer:** Lost My Way IPA **Year-Round Beers:** Lost My Way IPA,
Polished Pilsner, Pick Up Line Porter, Perception Pale Ale **Seasonals/Special Releases:**
N/A **Tours:** N/A **Taproom:** Thurs and Fri, 4 to 9 p.m.; Sat, 12 to 7 p.m.

Whenever they were rained off of the golf course, Holly Springs residents Ellen Joyner, Michelle Miniutti, and Jackie Hudspeth would head over to Carolina Brewing Company, the brewery that has called Holly Springs home since 1995. It was there that their passion for craft beer was ignited; Ellen began homebrewing and then several years later Michelle joined her.

The three had experience in the business world—Ellen in marketing, Michelle in sales, and Jackie in fund-raising—but dreamed of doing something for themselves. In 2013, that dream came to fruition when they opened Bombshell Beer Company in Holly Springs, just down the road from the brewery that they spent so many rainy days in.

Lost My Way IPA
Style: India pale ale
ABV: 7.5 percent
Availability: On tap year-round
Bombshell Beer Company's Lost my Way IPA is exceptionally well balanced, with citrus hops lending just the right amount of bitterness against sweeter yet more subtle flavors of caramel and honey. It is a refreshing and easy drinking take on the style.

Like Carolina Brewing Company, Bombshell is located in a business park. The Bombshell building is home to a lab, a 1,400-square-foot tasting room and, of course, the brewery itself. At the helm of Bombshell's 15-barrel system is Stephen O'Neill, who was a head brewer at Church Brew Works in Pittsburgh before joining Bombshell for the chance to start something from the ground up. The brewery equipment is US steel, manufactured by Smart Machine Technologies in Stokesdale, NC.

Bombshell's core beers include their **Lost My Way IPA, Polished Pilsner, Pick Up Line Porter,** and **Perception Pale Ale.** You can enjoy them in the taproom or out back at the small patio that backs up to the woodline. Despite the female-centric name and being completely female-owned, the ladies want to ensure their beers appeal to men and women alike. One thing's for sure: They'll be spending a lot more days—rainy and otherwise—at the brewery.

CAROLINA BREWING COMPANY

140 Thomas Mill Rd., Holly Springs, NC 27540; (919) 557-2337; CarolinaBrew.com; @CarolinaBrewing

Founded: 1995 **Founders:** John Shuck, Greg Shuck, Joe Zonin **Brewer:** Mark Heath **Flagship Beer:** Carolina Pale Ale **Year-Round Beers:** Carolina Pale Ale, Carolina India Pale Ale, Carolina Nut Brown Ale **Seasonals/Special Releases:** Carolina Spring Bock, Carolina Summer Ale, Carolina Oktoberfest Lager, Carolina Winter Porter, Black Lager, Groundhog Day Imperial Stout, WIGGO! **Tours:** Sat at 1 p.m. **Taproom:** Mon through Thurs, 9 a.m. to 5 p.m.; Fri, 10 a.m. to 6 p.m.; Sat, 12 to 4 p.m.

Since 1995, Carolina Brewing Company has been brewing in a small business park in Holly Springs. They were one of the first tenants in the park, and the road leading to their brewery was not yet paved. That didn't matter to those eager to try beers from the county's first brewery, whose cars would kick up dust as they drove out to Carolina Brewing Company.

When Joe Zonin and brothers John and Greg Shuck decided to build a brewery, they were living in Seattle. Even in the early 1990s, though, Seattle had a developing beer culture, so the three looked for an area with a little less competition. They found that in Holly Springs, just south of Raleigh. It is there you can find their small tasting room, behind which sits a 20-barrel brewhouse, several fermenting

Carolina India Pale Ale
Style: India pale ale
ABV: 5.4 percent
Availability: Year-round in bottles and on tap

Introduced in 2005, Carolina Brewing's India Pale Ale offers a similar profile to their Pale Ale, but with more of that beer's citrus and pine flavors courtesy of Cascade and Crystal hops. It is brewed very much in the West Coast style, but with a more restrained hand than most these days. Like their pale ale and brown, it finishes very clean.

tanks, and a bottling line that puts out 100 bottles a minute. You can tour and enjoy samples for free each Saturday at 1 p.m.

The brewery's flagship **Carolina Pale Ale** is a well-balanced pale ale with notes of citrus and pine. It accounts for around 50 percent of the brewery's sales. The **Carolina Nut Brown Ale** is a quaffable English-style brown with notes of toffee and toast, with just enough hop bitterness to prevent it from being overly sweet. The beer's clean finish leaves you wanting more, and at 4.9 percent alcohol you need not worry as much about overindulging.

Much has changed since 1995, in both the craft beer industry on the whole and North Carolina in particular. In 2005, a full decade after they opened, the state's cap on alcohol by volume in beer was lifted from 6 percent to 15 percent. As a result, the brewery started brewing higher-gravity options, while still continuing production of their core beers that allowed them to sustain those dark times. Carolina Brewing has produced their popular **Carolina Oktoberfest Lager** and **Carolina Spring Bock** since 1998. And, for no particular reason other than that no other breweries do it, they brew a special beer for Groundhog Day and throw a party to celebrate everyone's favorite marmot.

The Triangle

DEEP RIVER BREWING COMPANY

700 W. Main St., Clayton, NC 27520; DeepRiverBrewing.com; @DeepRiverBruin
Founded: 2013 **Founders:** Paul and Lynn Auclair **Brewer:** Paul Auclair **Flagship Beer:**
Riverbank Rye-It **Year-Round Beers:** Riverbank Rye-It, Twisted River Wit, Backcountry
Black IPA **Seasonals/Special Releases:** Oxbow Pale Ale, Double D's Watermelon Lager,
Pumpkin Porter, 4042 Chocolate Stout, JoCo White Winter **Tours:** During open hours
Taproom: Thurs, 5 to 9 p.m.; Fri, 4 to 9 p.m.; Sat, 1 to 9 p.m.

Paul and Lynn Auclair broke ground when they opened Johnston County's first legal brewery in 2013, but Deep River Brewing Company has longstanding roots in an agrarian South. The 15,000-square-foot building they now call home once housed a cotton-spinning mill, and the weathered wood that covers the brewery's main wall and bar was taken from a dilapidated tobacco shed. Hanging above that bar is a row of mason jar lamps, in keeping with the brewery's rustic feel. All of this combines to create a beautiful and rural aesthetic in a building that is more than a century old.

Paul and Lynn take a lot of pride in Johnston Co. and its history. Where possible, they use local malt, hops, and other ingredients in Deep River's beers. **JoCo White Winter,** for example, is brewed with a blend of spices, toasted marshmallows, and locally grown sweet potatoes. The result is, not surprisingly, a beer that calls to mind those wonderful sweet potato casseroles that are so often served during the holidays. The **Double D's Watermelon Lager** sees local watermelons added to a crisp light lager base, a style that many craft brewers shy away from. The **4042 Chocolate Stout** is brewed with chocolates from local chocolatiers. It is thinner than most chocolate stouts but all the more drinkable for it. It took home a silver medal at the Carolinas Championship of Beer.

The brewery's **Twisted River Wit** has the citrus notes you would expect given the style, though in this case they are derived from the use of Cascade hops, a variety more commonly used in hop-forward styles like pale ales and IPAs. The popular **Riverbank Rye-It** is brewed with a generous portion of rye, resulting in an easy-drinking pale ale with a hint of peppery spice. There is no kitchen at Deep River Brewing Company, but there are often food trucks on hand.

Beer Lover's Pick

Backcountry Black IPA
Style: Black IPA
ABV: 7.9 percent
Availability: Year-round
Deep River Brewing Company's Backcountry Black IPA, like so many in this emerging style, comes across as a mix between a porter and an IPA. It has notes of roasted coffee and chocolate, which contrast with the bitterness and citrus character imparted through the use of five different types of hops. It finishes relatively dry, with a faint kiss of smoke.

DOUBLE BARLEY BREWING

3174 US Hwy. 70W, Smithfield, NC 27577; (919) 934-3433; DoubleBarleyBrewing.com
Founded: 2013 **Founders:** Larry and Cheryl Lane **Brewers:** Larry Lane, Mark Kirby
Flagship Beer: Wilma's Wandering EyePA **Year-Round Beers:** Wilma's Wandering
EyePA, Thrilla in Vanilla Porter, Revelation Pale Ale, Abby's Amber Ale, Double Dubbel,
Double Black IPA, Touché IPA, Steak Cake Stout, Sexy Rexy Red Rye **Seasonals/Special
Releases:** Sparkky's Coffee Chocolate Milk Stout, FFF Holiday Ale **Tours:** N/A **Taproom:**
Weds through Fri, 4 to 10 p.m.; Sat, 1 to 10 p.m.; Sun, 1 to 8 p.m.

For his 40th birthday, Cheryl Lane bought her husband Larry a homebrew kit. Like so many others, Larry quickly became immersed in his newfound hobby, and soon the Lane house was a popular spot for neighbors wanting to sample his beers. He enjoyed brewing so much and became so proficient at it that he and Cheryl decided to leave corporate America and start Double Barley Brewing.

The brewery in Smithfield may look industrial from the outside, but inside it is anything but. A 100-year-old barn provided much of the wood used throughout the taproom, including the multicolored tables made from ash, pecan, oak, and maple. Red tin from the barn's roof lines the walls of the tasting room, giving it a warm and rustic feel.

You can try a wide variety of beers inside the taproom, most of them big and bold. **Thrilla in Vanilla Porter** marries a sharp, roasty flavor with the sweet notes of bourbon-soaked vanilla beans. Another dark option is the brewery's **Double Black IPA,** which has notes of pine, chocolate, and roasted malt. The brewery doesn't have many beers you would classify as light in color or alcohol, however the **Sexy Rexy Red Rye Ale** was brewed with the beach in mind. This wheat beer uses a hefty portion of rye malt to provide just a hint of spice to this refreshing style.

On nice days, drinkers may prefer to enjoy these beers outside in the beer garden, which is secluded from the nearby highway with thick pallets that were once used by a logging company. The beer garden also has a stage for live music.

Beer Lover's Pick

Wilma's Wandering EyePA
Style: Double India pale ale
ABV: 12 percent
Availability: Year-round on tap
Not many breweries claim a 12 percent beer as their flagship, but Wilma's Wandering EyePA really does represent what Double Barley is all about. This imperial IPA is brewed with lots of Cascade and Centennial hops. The higher ABV is achieved, in part, from the California orange blossom honey used in the beer. The beer balances all of those West Coast hop notes—citrus, grapefruit, and pine—with a sweet but unobtrusive malt backbone.

FORTNIGHT BREWING COMPANY

1006 SW Maynard Rd., Cary, NC 27511; FortnightBrewing.com; @fortnightbeer
Founded: 2014 **Founders:** Stuart Arnold, David Wilkinson, Mo Mercado, David Gardner, Bob Greczyn, Will Greczyn **Brewer:** Derek Garman **Flagship Beer:** English Ale **Year-Round Beers:** English Ale, Porter, Hybrid IPA, Lager **Seasonals/Special Releases:** Summer Ale **Tours:** During open hours **Taproom:** Fri, 4 to 10 p.m.; Sat, 11 a.m. to 11 p.m., Sun, 12 to 6 p.m.

While most American craft breweries brew their take on styles that originated in England—India pale ale, stout, porter, etc.—very few brew them as they were brewed before they crossed the pond. Stuart Arnold is looking to change that. Fortnight Brewing isn't unique simply because they are brewing English ales—they are also Cary's first craft brewery. The name derives from the fact that it takes the average ale two weeks—or a fortnight—to ferment.

Many beers spend their fortnights aging in the fermenting tanks at Fortnight Brewing. Fortnight's **Porter** is, naturally, a more English take on the style; it is more earthy and less hoppy than most American examples. Of course, not all of Fortnight's beers are so blatantly British. Their **Hybrid IPA** is so named because it uses English malt and yeast as most English IPAs do, yet it is hopped with American varieties that sneak in just a hint of a West Coast IPA. The brewery brews other English styles with American ingredients as well. They have cask-conditioned beers on quite frequently, allowing beer lovers to compare pints poured in this traditional fashion versus those dispensed from the keg.

English Ale
Style: Bitter
ABV: 4 percent
Availability: On tap year-round
The base style of Fortnight Brewing's English Ale is a bitter, and yet most beer lovers know that the style is not bitter at all (at least in today's craft beer climate). Fortnight's example pours dark amber and drinks easily thanks to a light body and low ABV. It has notes of caramel and toast, making for an immensely sessionable beer and a great choice for a flagship.

While the beers are all mostly inspired by styles from England, the guys at Fortnight are committed to their local area. Whether that means holding fundraising events for local nonprofits or giving spent grain to area farmers, Fortnight Brewing has embraced Cary and their surrounding communities.

FULLSTEAM BREWERY

726 Rigsbee Ave., Durham, NC 27701; (919) 682-2337; Fullsteam.ag; @Fullsteam
Founded: 2010 **Founder:** Sean Lilly Wilson **Brewer:** Chris Davis **Flagship Beer:** Fullsteam Lager **Year-Round Beers:** El Toro Classic Cream Ale, Fullsteam Lager, Rocket Science NCIPA **Seasonals/Special Releases:** Hula Hoop IPA, Carver, Working Man's Lunch, Beasley's Honey White, Cack-a-lacky™ Ginger Pale Ale, Hogwash Hickory-Smoked Porter, Fearrington Summer, Summer Basil Farmhouse Ale, First Frost Winter Persimmon Ale, Fruitcake the Beer **Tours:** Check website **Taproom:** Mon through Thurs, 4 p.m. to midnight; Fri, 4 p.m. to 2 a.m.; Sat, 12 p.m. to 2 a.m.; Sun, 12 p.m. to midnight

Fullsteam Brewery didn't open its doors until 2010, but Sean Lilly Wilson had his hands in North Carolina's beer culture many years before that. He was instrumental in leading the state's Pop the Cap movement, which when passed in 2005 raised the NC's ABV cap from 6 percent to 15 percent. Now he's continuing to represent the state well at Fullsteam, where their mission is to "create distinctly Southern beer that celebrates the culinary and agricultural traditions of the South."

Fullsteam's three year-round beers that make up the brewery's American Progress series are all styles that are indigenous to America, but with a Southern spin. Their **El Toro Classic Cream Ale** uses locally grown and malted barley, as well as local corn grits. Just a bit of sweet corn flavor comes through, but the grits are primarily used as a fermentable and to give the beer a lighter body. The **Fullsteam Lager** is actually a steam beer, meaning it is brewed with a lager yeast but fermented at ale temperatures. The result is a hybrid style, crisp and clean like a lager but with floral and pear-like notes you might expect in an ale. And while the IPA was born across the pond, American examples—like Fullsteam's **Rocket Science NCIPA**—are a style all their own.

Southern cuisine inspires many of the brewery's beers: **Working Man's Lunch** is likened to an RC Cola and Moonpie; **Hogwash** is brewed with malt smoked by hand at the brewery; **Beasley's Honey White** was designed to complement fried chicken; and **Carver** is brewed with 250 pounds of sweet potatoes per batch.

A backwards white "F" on a massive red door marks the entrance to the tavern, the inside of which is modeled after a German beer garden. If you can't find suitable conversation amid the long orange tables (you can!), try your hand at the

The Common Good
Style: Kentucky common
ABV: 6 percent
Availability: Seasonal

Fullsteam's The Common Good was inspired by the Kentucky common, an obscure, low-alcohol dark beer usually brewed with a sour-mash process similar to those used by Kentucky distillers. Full-steam's take on the style is brewed with grits, barley and rye grown in NC, and with apple pommace from Foggy Ridge Cider in Virginia. Finally, it is quick-aged in barrels that once held Maker's Mark bourbon. It is a refreshing and yet complex blend of sweet and sour, the beer world's answer to the Manhattan cocktail.

pinball machines or arcade games, or spend your time taking in all of the quirky little details and decorations throughout the tavern. The brewery hosts a variety of events, including screenings of movies that are so bad they're good.

HOSANNA BREWING COMPANY

2912 N. Main St., Ste. 100, Fuquay-Varina, NC 27603; (919) 376-5911; HosannaBrewing .com;
Founded: 2013 **Founder:** Charles Ryder **Brewer:** Charles Ryder **Flagship Beer:** Pale Ale **Year-Round Beers:** Pale Ale, Citrus IPA, Chocolate Stout, Oatmeal Stout **Seasonals/Special Releases:** Lite It Up Ale, Summer Ale, Saison, Belgian Tripel, Hefeweizen, Mr. Dunkel Dunkelweizen, Belgian Tripel, Porter **Tours:** No **Taproom:** Mon through Wed, 3 to 10 p.m.; Thurs and Fri, 2 to 11 p.m.; Sat, 12 p.m. to 12 a.m.

Charles Ryder had been homebrewing for years, but stopped brewing because he was focusing so much of his time on his online business. Like so many that enter the brewing industry, Charles found that his day job paid the bills but didn't

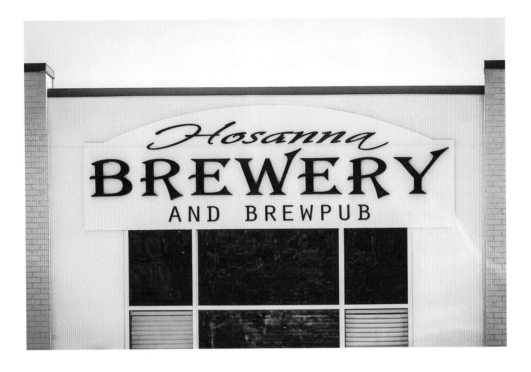

really excite him. He did a lot of soul-searching and praying, thinking about what he might do that could provide him with joy and at the same time give back to the community.

He woke up one morning with a single word resounding his head: Hosanna. He didn't know what it meant at the time, but would later find that it could be interpreted as "a cry to God for salvation." Charles knew then that he would open a brewery. With a name like Hosanna, he is not shy about tying together his brewery and his faith: for him, the two go hand-in-hand. Regardless of his patrons' religious views, though, he simply wants Hosanna to be a place you can come and have a conversation. The tasting room has comfortable couches that give it the feel of a coffee shop. The bar has three sides, so you can see and converse with your fellow drinkers. The brewery frequently has live music in the taproom, and food trucks are often parked outside.

On a five-barrel system in the back of the brewery, Charles brews a variety of beers. Most are fairly sessionable in nature, such as the hoppy **Summer Ale** or the quenching **Pale Ale.** The **Belgian Tripel** is one of the brewery's biggest beers, and it contains notes of banana and honey. Those looking for something lower in alcohol might consider the refreshing and sessionable **Lite It Up Ale.**

Oatmeal Stout

Style: Oatmeal stout

ABV: 6 percent

Availability: On tap year-round

Hosanna's Oatmeal Stout is sweet and has a bitter roastiness to it. It drinks very easily and has a lighter body than many other oatmeal stouts. With notes of espresso, it's the perfect choice to enjoy in Hosanna's coffeehouse-like atmosphere.

MYSTERY BREWING COMPANY

230 S. Nash St., Hillsborough, NC 27278; (919) 245-1325; MysteryBrewing.com; @MysteryBrewing

Founded: 2010 **Founder:** Erik Lars Myers **Brewers:** Erik Lars Myers, Chris Shields

Flagship Beer: N/A **Year-Round Beers:** N/A **Seasonals/Special Releases:** Gentlemen's Preference, Langhorne Rye Wit, Pickwick Mild Ale, Ballantrae Scottish 60, Queen Anne's Revenge, Lockwood's Retreat, Fantine, Hornigold English IPA, Beatrix, Evangeline, Rosaline, Annabel, St. Stephen's Green, Papa Bois, Thornfield's End, Six Impossible Things, Humboldt German ESB, Litwos Grodziske, Batch #1, Fawkes **Tours:** Last Fri of the month **Taproom:** Mon and Tues, 4 to 10 p.m.; Weds and Thurs, 4 p.m. to 12 a.m.; Fri, 2 p.m. to 12 a.m.; Sat, 12 p.m. to 12 a.m.; Sun, 12 to 10 p.m.

So, what's the mystery? It's a question Erik Lars Myers, founder of Mystery Brewing Company, gets quite often. As early as 12th-century London, the word was used to refer to the "art and craft of a trade," which included brewers. Being someone who appreciates that brewing is both an art and science, Erik felt it a fitting name for his brewery. His own talents as a brewer were not a mystery to many, however, as Erik's Kickstarter campaign to help fund the brewery earned over $44,000 from people who believed in him. That wasn't all he needed to build the brewery, of course, but it provided him with a good start and also earned him the distinction of being one of the first crowd-funded breweries ever.

He used those funds, as well as investments from his partners, to build a brewery in Hillsborough's historic Eno River Cotton Mill (also known as the Hillsborough Business Center). He opened his doors at 437 Dimmocks Mill Road in February of 2012. The next year, he opened the Mystery Brewing Public House just around the corner, and this building effectively serves as the brewery's taproom (the brewery itself is only open for tours on the last Friday of the month; you can purchase tickets on their website). It is a fun space often filled with regulars who spend their time at the bar, playing shuffleboard and other games, or out back on the spacious patio.

Mystery Brewing keeps a variety of their beers on at the Public House, as well as a few guest taps. The brewery is unique in that they do not have a flagship or any year-round beers, but instead rotate through four beers per season, which fall into the categories of a session beer, a hop-forward beer, a saison, and a stout. Take the latter, for instance: In the spring, Mystery brews **St. Stephen's Green,** a dry Irish stout. In the summer, they brew **Papa Bois,** a citrus foreign extra stout brewed with

Queen Anne's Revenge
Style: Carolinian dark
ABV: 5.8 percent
Availability: On tap in the spring

Mystery Brewing's spring hop-forward beer is Queen Anne's Revenge, which the brewery calls a Carolinian dark ale. It's a play on Cascadian dark ale, or what some call a black IPA (neither term makes perfect sense, since not all hops come from the Pacific Northwest and black pale ale is a contradiction in terms). Queen Anne's Revenge stands apart from today's heavily hopped black IPAs in its restrained use of English hops, namely Fuggle and East Kent Goldings. These add an earthy quality that works well with the chocolate malt, creating a smooth beer that defies style conventions.

lemongrass and lemon peel. When fall comes, there's **Thornfield's End,** a smoked rye stout, and winter brings **Six Impossible Things,** a chocolate breakfast stout. This same effort to brew beers reflective of these seasons applies to the session, hop-forward, and saison beers as well. The brewery also offers more limited beers and one-offs through its Novella series and barrel program.

The name for **Six Impossible Things,** like so many other Mystery beers, is a literary reference (in this case to Lewis Carroll's *Through the Looking-Glass*). Erik has a degree in theater and performance art, and his wife, Sarah, is an English professor. Other beer names allude to authors, characters, or works of literature.

STARPOINT BREWING COMPANY

Private brewery, not open to the public; StarpointBrewing.com; @StarpointBrewin
Founded: 2012 **Founder:** Tim Harper **Brewer:** Tim Harper **Flagship Beer:** Surfin'
Buddha **Year-Round Beers:** Surfin' Buddha IPA, Mornin' Wood DIPA, DUH! DIPA
Seasonals/Special Releases: Instant Karma Porter, Ginger Porter, Piedmont Harvest
Ale, Olde North State Oktoberfest, Ball Don't Lie Kellerbier, Chapel Pils, Booghi Sattva
Tours: No **Taproom:** No

Tim Harper was an established homebrewer when he first tried Russian River's Pliny the Elder, one of the country's most sought after double IPAs. He spent the next three years trying to craft something similar to it. Once he got close he started entering local homebrew competitions, where he took home several medals. This, along with much cajoling from family and friends, encouraged Tim to build his own brewery.

He didn't have to go far to find a location. On his wooded property in Carrboro, Tim built a garage-style building and filled it with a three-barrel brew system and a few six-barrel fermenting tanks. Because it's on his property, the brewery is considered production-only and not open to visitors (aside from the occasional deer, or the butterflies that light in the puddles of wort pooling outside the building's

DUH!
Style: Double India pale ale
ABV: 8 percent
Availability: Year-round in bottles and on tap

Double IPAs are a dime a dozen, but Starpoint's DUH! stands out from the pack in its use of both rye and wheat. The rye provides its trademark spiciness, and the wheat, according to Tim, "gives the hop oils something to hold onto." Of course, the hops are the showcase here, and they are legion. The combination of Columbus, Simcoe, Centennial, Amarillo, and Citra hops provide the beer with a slick mouthfeel and an assault of resinous pine. Despite the abundance of hops, the beer is easy drinking and has a clean finish.

doors). Though you can't visit Starpoint Brewing, you can find the beer on tap and in bottles around the Triangle area.

Given Tim's affinity for Pliny the Elder, it should come as no surprise that some of his most popular beers are on the hoppier side. Of the brewery's IPAs, **Surfin' Buddha** is the most balanced and approachable, with more citrus and tropical fruit notes than bitterness. **Mornin' Wood DIPA** is a little closer to Pliny, with piney hops standing up well against the candy-like sweetness from a maltier backbone than the Buddha.

While IPAs are their specialty, Starpoint brews a variety of other styles. The **Instant Karma Porter** is an easy-drinking porter with notes of chocolate and roast. There's enough of a vanilla presence that you'd think it was brewed with the bean, but that actually comes from the American oak spirals the beer is aged on. For the holidays, Starpoint brews a variation of it called **Ginger Porter** using four pounds of grated ginger. College basketball is wildly popular in nearby Chapel Hill, and Starpoint's **Ball Don't Lie Kellerbier** is a great choice while watching a game.

STEEL STRING BREWERY

106A S. Greensboro St., Carrboro, NC 27510; (919) 240-7215; SteelStringBrewery.com; @SteelStringBrew

Founded: 2013 **Founders:** Cody Maltais, Andrew Scharfenberg, Eric Knight, Will Isley **Brewer:** Will Isley **Flagship Beer:** Rubber Room Session Ale **Year-Round Beers:** Rubber Room Session Ale, Big Mon India Pale Ale **Seasonals/Special Releases:** Hiphopopotomus Farmhouse IPA, Sue Black Saison, Manzanita Black IPA, Little Sadie Farmhouse Ale, Cryin Holy IIPA, Adventure Amber, Exile Hefeweizen **Tours:** No **Taproom:** Mon through Sat, 12 p.m. to 2 a.m.; Sun, 12 to 10 p.m.

When Will Isley and Cody Maltais played bluegrass at Milltown in Carrboro, they never would have imagined that the two craft beers a week they received from the bar would lead them to start their own brewery, let alone one just a few blocks away. But that's exactly what happened.

The two so enjoyed their craft beers at Milltown that Will started homebrewing with his friend, Andrew Scharfenberg. The three decided to open a brewery and

Rubber Room Session Ale
Style: American pale ale
ABV: 4.7 percent
Availability: Year-round on tap

Steel String designed their taproom to be the kind of place at which you would want to sit and share a few beers over many hours, and their flagship Rubber Room Session Ale is the perfect beer to do just that. Named after an acoustic studio in Chapel Hill, this beer is brewed with rye grown in NC and Motueka hops grown in New Zealand. The result is a crisp, medium-bodied beer with a little pepper from the rye and citrus notes from the hops.

brought on Eric Knight—another musician—as the fourth founder. With three of the four founders being musicians, it seemed natural that they would draw on their shared passion when naming the brewery.

When naming themselves, they opted for titles that spoke to the craft beer revolution: Cody is the financial czar, Andrew is the logistic czar, Eric is the hoopla czar, and Will is the brew czar. The bold orange-and-red mural in the taproom marries this proletariat mindset with their love of beer and bluegrass. Below it sits a steel-colored concrete bar, its curves mimicking those of a guitar. Quilts made from old grain bags hang on the wall opposite.

The four czars have created a unique and fun taproom they want the community to enjoy, and that's even reflected in their beers. Most of their beers are of lower ABV, allowing drinkers to have more beers than they would were they higher in alcohol. Most also fall into one of two camps—hoppy or yeasty. Will wants the hops or yeast used to be the focus of the beer, and so Steel String brews several IPAs and saisons. **Big Mon India Pale Ale,** for example, balances a West Coast hop presence with a subtle caramel malt profile. With **Sue Black Saison,** though, you have a beer that balances the tart and peppery farmhouse notes with a little roast—think of a porter fermented with a saison yeast. This beer also uses cold-pressed coffee from their neighbors at Carrboro Coffee Roasters.

TRIANGLE BREWING COMPANY

918 Pearl St., Durham, NC 27701; 919-683-2337; TriangleBrewery.com; @TriangleBrewing
Founded: 2007 **Founders:** Rick Tufts and Andrew Miller **Brewer:** Rick Tufts **Flagship Beer:** Belgian Golden Ale **Year-Round Beers:** Belgian Golden Ale, White Ale, India Pale Ale **Seasonals/Special Releases:** Imperial Amber Ale, Habanero Pale Ale, Sour Bourbon-Aged Abbey Dubbel, Best of Both Worlds Stout, Lambic, Best Bitter, Farmhouse Ale, Belgian-Style Abbey Dubbel, Winter Stout **Tours:** Sat at 1:30 p.m. **Taproom:** Sat, 1 to 3:30 p.m.

The industrial building that Triangle Brewing Company occupies was built in the 1950s. When high school buddies Rick Tufts and Andrew Miller built the brewery in 2007, they heard tales of human remains found in a bag in the clay of the building's basement. Not wanting to anger any lingering spirit, they felt it best to give him a name. They dubbed him Rufus. And because Rufus means "red" in Latin, they crafted a big, red **Imperial Amber** as the first in the Rufus Reserve series.

Other Rufus Reserve beers include a **Sour Bourbon-Aged Abbey Dubbel** that displays sweet and sour notes over a Belgian base. If spicy is more your game, seek out the **Habanero Pale Ale**—this 5 percent ABV pale ale is immensely drinkable, despite the addition of locally grown habanero peppers. Of course, Triangle does more than just brew beers in honor of Rufus. The brewery cans and distributes three year-round beers across the Carolinas. The brewery's refreshing **White Ale** is another take on a traditional Belgian style, made all their own by the use of locally grown white and red wheat as well as coriander and orange peel.

In November of 2013, Rick and Andrew opened Triangle Brewing

Company Pint and Plate at 802 West Main Street. They don't brew here, but you can find a dozen drafts of their beers as well as a cask ale. This is an ideal place to try a full range of their beers, since the brewery itself is only open for tours from 1–3 p.m. on Saturdays (and it's not uncommon to see people waiting in line for them to open the gates beforehand). For just $3, you can sample the brewery's beers and go on a tour of the brewery. The inside is sparse, with a few benches and cornhole boards placed near pallets of cans and glassware, but the crowd and tour make for a fun experience. If you happen to see an employee slipping some beer down one of the drains in the floor, well, just remember Rufus.

Beer Lover's Pick

Belgian Golden Ale
Style: Belgian golden strong ale
ABV: 8 percent
Availability: Year-round on tap
and in cans
The Belgian Golden Ale is an untraditional choice for a flagship, but the beer—which has notes of sweet malt, bananas, honey, and pear—accounts for nearly half of the brewery's sales. The cans make this one a great beer for the great outdoors; just remember that, at 8 percent, it's no session ale.

WHITE RABBIT BREWING COMPANY

219 Fish Dr., Angier, NC 27501; (919) 527-2739; WhiteRabbitBrewery.com;
@WhiteRabbitBeer

Founded: 2012 **Founders:** Kenneth Ostraco, Anthony DiBona **Brewers:** Kenneth
Ostraco, Anthony DiBona **Flagship Beer:** Alice's Blonde Ale **Year-Round Beers:**
Alice's Blonde Ale, Gryphon's Lager, Drink Me Cream Ale, Absolom's Ale, Pale in the Park,
Queen's Red Ale, Dubbel Trouble, Jabberwocky Trippel, Rabbit's Nutbrown Ale, 10/6ths IPA
Seasonals/Special Releases: Cheshire Pumpkin Ale, Dunkin Dormouse Oktoberfest Ale,
Tea Party Vanilla Bourbon Porter **Tours:** Fri from 6 to 7 p.m. and 7 to 8 p.m.; Sat from 3
to 4 p.m. and 5 to 6 p.m. (reservations requested) **Taproom:** Thurs, 6 to 10 p.m.; Fri, 6
to 11 p.m.; Sat, 4 to 11 p.m.

Homebrewers for many years, Kenneth Ostraco and Anthony DiBona were planning to open a brewery together but were struggling with the name. Then, one
night while pushing through some paperwork, Jefferson Airplane's "White Rabbit"
came on and Kenneth went down the rabbit hole with it. The result is a small
brewery in Angier themed after *Alice's Adventures in Wonderland*. Sir John Tenniel's
classic illustrations, now in the public domain, serve as the starting point for the
brewery's branding.

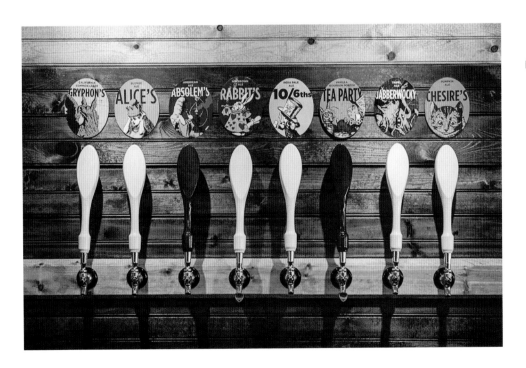

Tea Party Vanilla Bourbon Porter
Style: Porter
ABV: 9.1 percent
Availability: Limited
This robust porter is aged with vanilla beans and wood chips that have been bathed in Jack Daniel's whiskey, but neither the vanilla or whiskey overpowers the beer. Rather, these flavors work in union with the roasty and milk chocolate flavors of the porter. Would the Mad Hatter have made more or less sense had he enjoyed this instead of tea?

The brewery's lineup of beers is as diverse as Lewis Carroll's cast of characters. You might be wondering why their **Jabberwocky Trippel** shares its name with that writer's "nonsense poem," until you realize that, at 11.3 percent ABV, too many pints of it will soon have you making up words and feeling "all mimsy" yourself. The beer provides most of the trademark tripel flavors, including banana and a soft maltiness. Not all of the brewery's beers are so high in ABV, though; the **10/6ths IPA** is intentionally brewed with subtlety in mind, and it hits its mark: With very little bitterness and rounded notes of apricot and melon, this beer is quite different from most India pale ales. In *Alice's Adventures in Wonderland*, the Gryphon is a cross between an eagle and a lion; at White Rabbit Brewery, **Gryphon's Lager** is actually a California Common, or a cross between a lager and an ale. This hybrid style uses a lager yeast, but is fermented at higher temperatures. The result is a smooth, crisp beer with subtle toasted malt flavors.

The taproom itself is small but comfortable, with white wicker chairs and a table perched upon barrels. Photos of regulars line the bathroom walls. You can drop by for a pint or flight at the tasting room, or schedule a tour.

WHITE STREET BREWING COMPANY

218 S. White St., Wake Forest, NC 27587; (919) 647-9439; WhiteStreetBrewing.com; @WhiteStreetBrew

Founded: 2012 **Founders:** Dino and Tina Radosta **Brewers:** Ian VanGundy, Chris Bivins **Flagship Beer:** Kölsch **Year-Round Beers:** Kölsch, Scottish Ale, Imperial Pale Ale, Black IPA **Seasonals/Special Releases:** Baltic Porter, Altbier, Wee Heavy, Brown IPA, Centennial IPA, Abbey, Hoppy Wheat, Witbier, Belgian Singel **Tours:** Last Sat of the month; RSVP on website **Taproom:** Mon through Thu, 4 to 10 p.m.; Fri, 2 p.m. to 12 a.m.; Sat, 12 p.m. to 12 a.m.; Sun, 12 to 10 p.m.

White Street Brewing Company is located in historic downtown Wake Forest, in a building that served as a car dealership in the 1930s. Having renovated two other buildings in Wake Forest, co-founder Dino Radosta saw the potential of this charming brick building and opened the brewery in 2012. The brewery is located in the back corner of the building, separated from the rest of the tasting room by only a half wall. In the front of the building is a beautiful bar built of glossy red oak with a couple of dartboards to the left of it and a brick wall with a chalkboard

to the right. The brick walls are covered in white paint, with bits of crimson coming through after all these years. The space is simple yet sophisticated, a great spot in which to enjoy White Street's beers.

The brewery's flagship **Kölsch** is a crisp and refreshing beer with a soft maltiness and notes of apples and freshly cut grass. It is the sort of beer that can appeal to seasoned beer lovers as well as those new to craft beer. The **Black IPA** strikes the perfect balance between roast and citrus hop flavors, leaving a bitterness that lingers on after the sip. White Street's **Baltic Porter** is one of the brewery's most popular seasonals. Sweet milk chocolate, plums, and figs marry perfectly with just a touch of roast in this fall release.

There are a few TVs, and bands often play in the brewery. While there is no kitchen at White Street, you can bring food in from nearby restaurants. Food trucks are also parked outside occasionally.

Beer Lover's Pick

Scottish Ale
Style: Scottish ale
ABV: 4.5 percent
Availability: On tap year-round
In comparison to White Street Brewing's seasonal Wee Heavy, their Scottish Ale might be considered Wee Light—not in flavor, but in terms of ABV. It bears a similar profile to its bigger brother, with notes of sweet malt, figs, and just a bit of smoke. At 4.5 percent, this one proves that sessionable beers need only be light in alcohol, not color or flavor.

Brewpubs

BULL CITY BURGER & BREWERY

107 E. Parrish St., Durham, NC 27701; (919) 680-2333; BullCityBurgerandBrewery.com; @BullCityBurger

Founded: 2011 **Founder:** Seth Gross **Brewers:** Seth Gross, Luke Studer, Shadoe Stewart **Flagship Beer:** Bryant Bridge Gateway Golden Ale **Year-Round Beers:** Bryant Bridge Gateway Golden Ale, Parrish Street Pale Ale **Seasonals/Special Releases:** 27701 Durham Mild, Boars Russian Imperial Stout, Bull's IPA, Honeycutt Milk Stout, Littlen Horny, Olden Horney, Malbourne Maibock, Pigmeat Markham Smoked Rye Ale, Pro Bono Publico Porter, Rattelade RyePA, Rogers Lager, Viola Weiss, W.E.B. Du Bois Saison

If you visit Bull City Burger & Brewery frequently enough, you're bound to learn something. The tables are marked with labels telling of the old family farmhouses that once held the wood before it underwent "reinbarnation." The beers, too, often contain references to people or places in the area. And the brewpub's "Professional Hop Doctorate" program (yes, Ph.D.) encourages you to sample the 50 or so beers that they cycle through, many of which also take their names from local names of note.

The Ph.D. program introduces drinkers to a range of beer styles, but most have one thing in common: balance. Before founding Bull City Burger & Brewery, owner Seth Gross spent time as a sommelier, chef, and brewer at Goose Island's brewpub in Chicago. Whether in food or fermentables, Seth believes in using quality ingredients in harmony, where no one aspect of the dish or drink overwhelms the other. Many of his beers are "session beers"—that is, they're low enough in alcohol that one could enjoy a few in one sitting without overdoing it. The brewpub's two year-round beers are **Parrish Street Pale Ale,** a true-to-style pale of the maltier British variety, and **Bryant Bridge Gateway Golden Ale,** a floral, sweet, and light-bodied beer that most anyone could appreciate. At just 3.5 percent ABV, the **27701 Durham Mild** offers earthy and milk chocolate notes in a beer that is light in alcohol but not in flavor or color.

Because they are so well balanced, many of Bull City's beers pair well with the food, which is also crafted with a focus on fresh, local ingredients. As you might expect, the burgers—made with NC pasture-raised beef—are among the most popular items. Choose from one of the four specialty burgers, or build your own with add-ons like pickled veggies, triple-fermented sauerkraut, or bacon marmalade. All of these are made in-house, as are the buns between which they're sandwiched. If you don't eat meat, the Veggie Burger is just as highly regarded.

The brewpub doesn't bottle its beers, but you can take home a six-pack of their own hot sauce, spicy beer mustard, or beer-and-bacon barbecue sauce in 12-ounce jars. See their recipe for **Soft Rye Pretzels with Beer Cheese Spread** on p. 306.

CAROLINA BREWERY

460 W. Franklin St., Chapel Hill, NC 27516; (919) 942-1800; CarolinaBrewery.com; @CBreweryBeer
Founded: 1995 **Founder:** Robert Poitras **Brewers:** Jon Connolly, Nate Williams
Flagship Beer: Sky Blue Golden Ale **Year-Round Beers:** Sky Blue Golden Ale, Copperline Amber Ale, Flagship IPA, Firecracker Pale Ale, Genuine Oatmeal Porter
Seasonals/Special Releases: Bullpen Pale Ale, Black IPA, Super Saaz Imperial Pilsner, To Hell 'n' Bock, Saison and On, Maibock, West End Wheat, Circle City Wheat, Myth Perpetuator Double IPA, Franklin St. Lager, Tripel, Jumpin' Bean Coffee Stout, Old Familiar Barley Wine, Old North State Stout

If you're not watching the Tar Heels play in the Dean Smith Center, you might consider pulling up a barstool at Carolina Brewery. The Carolina-blue sign perched above a small patio space on Franklin Street should be the first hint that this brewpub proudly backs the home team, as do the crowds that fill in on any game days.

Founded in 1995, Carolina Brewery in Chapel Hill is one of the state's oldest brewpubs. The Pittsboro location opened in 2007, and the additional brewing capacity has allowed the Chapel Hill location to produce more one-offs and small-batch beers. Their five year-round beers are all very popular, especially the **Sky Blue Golden Ale.** This kölsch-style beer is light in body, with subtle notes of bread and lemon. It took home a bronze medal at the Great American Beer Festival in 2012. In 2006, the brewery's **Flagship IPA** won a gold medal at that same festival. The **Oatmeal Porter** has a great creamy milk chocolate quality to it, and if you're feeling especially decadent the brewery offers a float using that beer as the base.

That would be a fine choice for dessert, but what to have before that? Carolina Brewery offers an extensive menu full of contemporary American cuisine, and they use local produce and meats when they can. The Tar Heel Burger is covered in chili, onions, coleslaw, and mustard—all ingredients that define the Carolina-style burger. Like all of the brewery's sandwiches and burgers, it is served between bread from Pittsboro Bread Shop. The menu also features several seasonal specials.

CAROLINA BREWERY & GRILL

120 Lowes Dr., Ste. 100, Pittsboro, NC 27312; (919) 545-2330; CarolinaBrewery.com;
@CBreweryBeer

Founded: 2007 **Founder:** Robert Poitras **Brewers:** Jon Connolly, Nate Williams
Flagship Beer: Sky Blue Golden Ale **Year-Round Beers:** Sky Blue Golden Ale,
Copperline Amber Ale, Flagship IPA, Firecracker Pale Ale, Genuine Oatmeal Porter
Seasonals/Special Releases: Bullpen Pale Ale, Black IPA, Super Saaz Imperial Pilsner,
To Hell 'n' Bock, Saison and On, Maibock, West End Wheat, Circle City Wheat, Myth
Perpetuator Double IPA, Franklin St. Lager, Tripel, Jumpin' Bean Coffee Stout, Old Familiar
Barley Wine, Old North State Stout

As they started to gain wholesale accounts and distribute their beers outside of the Chapel Hill brewpub, it became clear to founder Robert Poitras and brewmaster Jon Connolly that they were going to need more space if they were serious about getting their beer across the Carolinas. In 2007, a dozen years after they had opened their doors on Franklin Street, the two opened another location in Pittsboro.

The new 9,000-square-foot brewery and additional tanks allowed Carolina Brewery to expand and grow wholesale accounts not just in North and South Carolina, but in Georgia, Tennessee, and Virginia as well. It can be seen behind glass inside the brewpub, which shares a food and beer menu with the original location (see the previous entry). Tours of the Pittsboro brewery take place at 5 p.m. every Saturday. There is a long bar and plenty of seating inside, and bands often play live music at the brewpub. Outside, there is a nice patio that includes a grain silo and several aluminum planters. In an adjacent space called "The Hop Shop," fans of the brewery can pick up merchandise as well as breakfast and Counter Culture Coffee before the brewery is open.

TOP OF THE HILL RESTAURANT & BREWERY

100 E. Franklin St., Third Fl., Chapel Hill, NC 27514; (919) 929-8676; TheTopoftheHill
.com; @TheTopoftheHill

Founded: 1996 **Founder:** Scott Maitland **Brewers:** Aaron Caracci and Chris Atkins
Flagship Beer: Kenan Lager **Year-Round Beers:** Kenan Lager, Old Well White, Ram's
Head IPA **Seasonals/Special Releases:** Blue Ridge Blueberry Wheat, Plott Hound Pale
Ale, Frank Graham Porter

Top of the Hill itself, with its rooftop patio and prime location at the "top of the hill" on Franklin Street, is tough to miss. Its entrance, however, is a little less noticeable. A side door on the street brings you to an elevator, which whisks you up to the restaurant and brewery. The doors open to reveal a peanut-shaped bar with a modern feel, and the glass-encased brewery is visible on the right. Several tables

surround the bar, but the best seat in the house is outside on the rooftop patio that overlooks Franklin Street. The Back Bar's brick walls are covered in chalk graffiti, and if you want to play darts, foosball, or just catch a game on TV, this is the place to be. This bar also contains an English-style cask.

Wherever you sit, you will always be able to enjoy three year-round beers—the Kenan Lager, Old Well White, and Ram's Head IPA—as well as several other seasonals. The **Kenan Lager** may not be the craft beer geek's favorite, but it's perfectly true-to-style and a great gateway beer for those accustomed to mass-market lagers. The **Old Well White,** named for the iconic landmark at the heart of UNC Chapel Hill, is a refreshing wheat beer brewed with the traditional coriander and orange peel. It is served with an orange slice, just as the **Blueridge Blueberry Wheat**—the brewery's most popular seasonal—is served with actual blueberries in the glass. To celebrate its arrival, Top of the Hill holds a celebration and tosses a blue ball off the roof. Another popular seasonal is the **Frank Graham Porter,** an earthy and dry English take on the style that is served on a nitrogen tap for an added creaminess.

The food menu is an eclectic one, offering a variety of entrees and appetizers. One of the more beer-friendly choices is the Lizard Chips, jalapeño and pickle slices that are battered in Kenan Lager and then fried to a crisp and served with a chipotle ranch dressing.

Beer Bars

BEER STUDY

106A N. Graham St., Chapel Hill, NC 27516; (919) 240-5423; BeerStudy.com; @BeerStudy
Draft Beers: 12 **Bottled/Canned Beers:** 300

Leave it to a bottle shop and bar in Chapel Hill to call itself "Beer Study" and, make no mistake, students of beer could learn a thing or two while poring over the dozen taps or hundreds of bottles. It is a long and dimly lit place, with most of the lighting coming from shop lights clamped to black shelving. Another light, behind the bar, illuminates a large wooden sign with "Beer Study" painted in bright, script.

One of the things that sets this bar apart from its competitors is its selection of drafts and bottles not typically available in Chapel Hill. These rarities—beers from breweries like Black Mountain's Pisgah Brewing or Charlotte's NoDa Brewing—are more often than not picked up by co-owner JD Schlick himself before being brought back to Beer Study. Lovers of more local libations need not worry, however, as Beer Study does a great job in stocking beers brewed closer to home (like bottles from nearby Starpoint Brewing, for instance).

TYLER'S TAPROOM & RESTAURANT

324 Blackwell St., Durham, NC 27701; (919) 433-0345; TylersTaproom.com
Draft Beers: 70 **Bottled/Canned Beers:** 100+

Of the four Tyler's Taproom locations in the Triangle, the Durham location is perhaps the most scenic. The American Tobacco Historic District that sits beside the Durham Bulls athletic park was once a cigarette factory, turning out millions of Lucky Strike cigarettes every year. Today, its million-square-foot campus is home to many restaurants, shops, a theater, Durham Performing Arts Center, and more. It is a fun mix of old Durham and new Durham.

Tyler's Taproom sits in the shadow of the Lucky Strike water tower, under which snakes a manmade canal. You can hear the water cascading through the canal from Tyler's patio and beer garden, which contains several long tables underneath strings of lights. Inside, drinkers will find a warm environment perfectly suited for conversation or taking in a game. Some of the tables include taps that you can use to pour your own pint. At the back of the taproom is the Speakeasy, which boasts another bar as well as billiard tables, foosball, a jukebox, and arcade games. A punching machine usually attracts a few swings, especially from patrons enjoying the bar's extensive draft list.

The restaurant puts its own unique stamp on traditional pub sandwiches, wraps, and burgers. The Pim Burger is built from such Southern staples as pimento cheese, smoked bacon, and fried green tomatoes. Get Tyler's famous garlic fries alongside it, and you've now had two of the bar's most celebrated menu items.

The taproom is a worthy destination by itself, as well as a nice spot to grab a beer and food before or after a concert or Durham Bulls game. Just be aware that it can fill up quickly during game days.

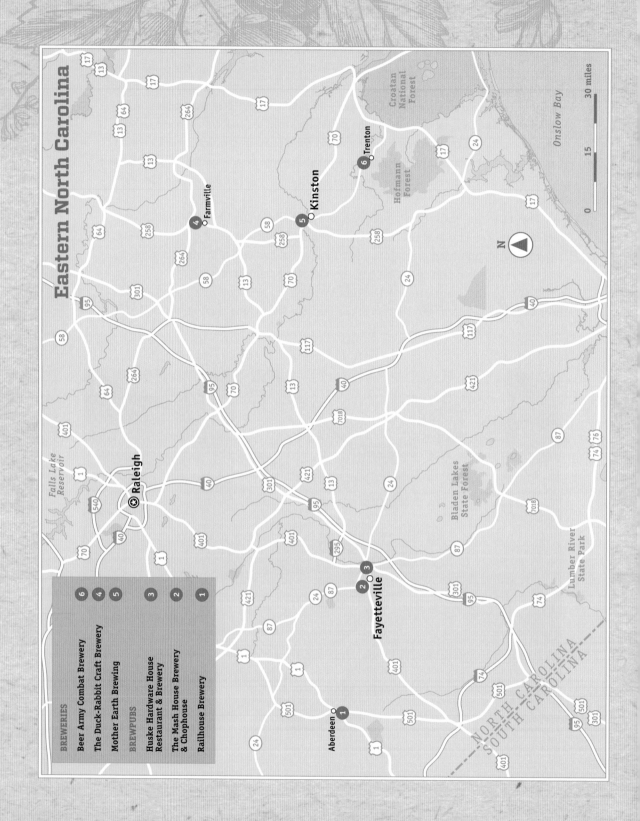

Eastern North Carolina

BREWERIES

6	Beer Army Combat Brewery
4	The Duck-Rabbit Craft Brewery
5	Mother Earth Brewing

BREWPUBS

3	Huske Hardware House Restaurant & Brewery
2	The Mash House Brewery & Chophouse
1	Railhouse Brewery

Raleigh

Fayetteville

Kinston

Farmville

Trenton

Aberdeen

NORTH CAROLINA
SOUTH CAROLINA

Croatan National Forest

Hofmann Forest

Onslow Bay

Falls Lake Reservoir

Bladen Lakes State Forest

Lumber River State Park

N

0   15   30 miles

Eastern North Carolina

The miles that stretch between Raleigh and the North Carolina coast make for beautiful country, filled with dense and dark forests that give way to sandhills before meeting the Atlantic. Thanks to newer breweries like Beer Army and established breweries like Duck-Rabbit and Mother Earth—as well as a couple of great brewpubs in Huske Hardware House and The Mash House—this area is no longer just a stop along the way to the coast, but rather an up-and-coming beer scene all its own.

Breweries

BEER ARMY COMBAT BREWERY

134 Industrial Park Dr., Trenton, NC 28585; (252) 448-1000; BeerArmy.com; @BeerArmy
Founded: 2013 **Founder:** Dustin Canestorp **Brewers:** Jeff Brungard, Matt John
Flagship Beer: Heroes Never Die IPA **Year-Round Beers:** Heroes Never Die IPA, Fire in
the Hole Irish Red Ale, Battle of Brock's Mill Smoked Porter, Angels Belgian-Style Blonde
Seasonals/Special Releases: Coastal Guardian, X-3134 Mild Ale, X-3129 Pilsner **Tours:**
Sat at 3 p.m. **Taproom:** Fri, 4 to 10 p.m.; Sat, 2 to 10 p.m.

When active-duty Marine Corps Major Dustin Canestorp returned from Iraq, he spent many nights playing poker and serving his homebrew to his friends and fellow soldiers. These brothers in beer soon become the "Beer Army," and not long after this they were helping to organize events like the Brew Bern Beer Fest and Jolly Skull Beer Fest. At these festivals, the Beer Army raised awareness of craft beer in an area where there was not much of a culture, and they also raised money for a variety of charities.

Battle of Brock's Mill
Style: Smoked porter
ABV: 5.5 percent
Availability: On tap year-round

The Battle of Brock's Mill Smoked Porter pours a dark brown with a dense white head. Intermingling with the standard notes of chocolate and coffee is a smoky quality that is distinct, but not overpowering. This 5.5 percent porter is on the milder side of smoked beers, making it a very food-friendly take on the style. A portion of this beer's sales go toward preserving Trenton's Brock Mill, which was built in the 1700s.

In 2011, they opened the Beer Army Outpost in New Bern. This bar and bottle shop boasts a beer engine, 16 taps and more than 600 bottles of beer. Through their work at the festivals, the Beer Army planted the seeds for a craft beer culture that they would see continue to grow at the Outpost. Two years after that, Dustin saw his full vision realized when the Beer Army Combat Brewery opened in Trenton in April of 2013.

Manning the brewhouse is Jeff Brungard, who after 28 years of active duty in the Marine Corps went on to attend Chicago's Siebel Institute and Germany's Doemens Academy. In the 10,500-square-foot warehouse, he and assistant brewer Matt John brew four year-round beers and several one-offs in the Range 35 series. **Angels** is a very true-to-style Belgian blonde, with a light mouthfeel and floral, fruity notes from the Belgian yeast. **Fire in the Hole,** an appropriately named red ale, has notes of caramel, toffee, and roasted hazelnuts. Those looking for more of a hop bite should try **Heroes Never Die IPA,** a maltier-than-most example that finishes clean.

From its humble beginnings at a poker table, the Beer Army has continued to grow. Even in the small town of Trenton, it is clear they will continue their mission of raising awareness not just for local craft beer, but also for area charities.

THE DUCK-RABBIT CRAFT BREWERY

4519 W. Pine St., Farmville, NC 27828; (252) 753-7745; DuckRabbitBrewery.com;
@DuckRabbitBrew
Founded: 2004 **Founder:** Paul Philippon **Brewers:** Will Pardon, Tim Clapper **Flagship Beer:** Milk Stout **Year-Round Beers:** Amber Ale, Milk Stout, Porter, Brown Ale
Seasonals/Special Releases: Hoppy Bunny, Wee Heavy, Baltic Porter, Rabid Duck, Schwarzbier, Märzen, Duck-Rabbator, Barleywine **Tours:** Fri at 3 p.m. **Taproom:** Fri, 3 to 9 p.m.

Do you see the duck or the rabbit? That's the question posed by former philosophy professor Paul Philippon, who traded in teaching for brewing when he founded The Duck-Rabbit Craft Brewery in 2004. The inspiration for the name and ambiguous logo comes from Ludwig Wittgenstein's *Philosophical Investigations*.

Though the logo might be a bit ambiguous, the brewery's mission is anything but—they are the "dark beer specialists." You might think that would be limiting, but the brewery manages to produce a diverse portfolio of dark beers that run the gamut from their **Amber Ale** to their **Rabid Duck** Russian imperial stout. The

brewery's most hoppy option is the **Hoppy Bunny,** an American black ale with citrus, pine and herbal characteristics alongside the roasted flavors that characterize so many of Duck-Rabbit's beers. Their **Baltic Porter** is a big, complex beer that layers flavors of molasses, plum, coffee, and chocolate atop each other. It is a fantastic beer, as is the very limited bourbon barrel-aged variant.

The brewery is located in an industrial section of Farmville. A picnic table and cornhole boards stand out front. Inside is a very small tasting room, with just a couple tables and a few feet of bar space. As the framed medals on the wall behind the bar show, the brewery is more concerned with brewing great beers and getting them to market than building a lavish taproom—and who could argue with that philosophy? Whether you see the duck or the rabbit, you can find the brewery's six-packs across the East Coast in North Carolina, South Carolina, Georgia, Tennessee, Virginia, and Pennsylvania.

Beer Lover's Pick

Milk Stout
Style: Milk stout
ABV: 5.7 percent
Availability: On tap and in
    bottles year-round

Leave it to the "dark beer specialists" to have a milk stout as their flagship, and one taste of it shows why this one is so popular. The "milk" portion of the stout comes from the addition of lactose, which adds a cream-like sweetness. Pair that with the sharply roasted character, and you have a bold-yet-balanced stout that can be enjoyed with a dessert or as a dessert in and of itself.

MOTHER EARTH BREWING

311 N. Heritage St., Kinston, NC 28501; (252) 208-2437; MotherEarthBrewing.com; @MotherEarthBrew

Founded: 2009 **Founders:** Stephen Hill, Trent Mooring **Brewer:** Josh Brewer **Flagship Beer:** Sisters of the Moon IPA **Year-Round Beers:** Sisters of the Moon IPA, Endless River Kölsch, Second Wind Pale Ale, Sunny Haze Hefeweizen, Weeping Willow Wit, Dark Cloud Munich-Style Dunkel Lager **Seasonals/Special Releases:** Tripel Overhead, Tripel Overhead (Bourbon Barrel Aged), Old Neighborhood Oatmeal Porter, Silent Night, Windowpane Series **Tours:** Tues through Fri, hourly from 10 a.m. to 5 p.m.; Sat, hourly from 1 to 8 p.m. **Taproom:** Tues through Thurs, 4 to 10 p.m.; Fri, 2 to 10 p.m.; Sat, 1 to 9 p.m.

When you are born in Kinston, raised in Kinston, and ultimately start a business in Kinston, it's perfectly acceptable to incorporate a slide from your childhood playground into your business.

That's a day at the office for Stephen Hill, who cofounded Mother Earth Brewing with his son-in-law, Trent Mooring. The slide spirals down from the employee offices and into the room that holds the canning line, which is used to package the popular **Sunny Haze Hefeweizen** and **Second Wind Pale Ale.** It's a nostalgic nod to the town Stephen—and later Trent—grew up in. The two of them and head brewer Josh Brewer added many fun touches to the brewery, which is now an anchor in downtown Kinston. In renovating the old brick building, they ensured that they lived up to their brewery's name. The solar panels sitting atop the brewery and tasting room

are just one of the brewery's many sustainability initiatives. In 2013, the company was the first brewery to receive the LEED® Gold certification status from the United States Green Building Council. To achieve this, Mother Earth had to undertake steps to lower operating costs, reduce waste, conserve energy, and reduce emissions.

The brewery and tasting room are some of the most visually pleasing in the state. The taproom has a modern feel, with blue light running down both sides of the bar. Floor-to-ceiling curtains line two of the walls, with paintings lining another. There is a beautiful patio behind this tasting room, with lots of green plants and outdoor furniture done in red and white. Inside or out, you can enjoy the brewery's year-round offerings as well as the occasional one-off or small batch beer. **Dark Cloud,** a soothing Munich-style dark lager with notes of dark, toasted bread, won a bronze medal at the 2012 Great American Beer Festival. The **Endless River Kölsch** is a crisp take on this hybrid style, with notes of lemon, toasted cracker, and grassy hops. The fall seasonal **Old Neighborhood Oatmeal Porter** is a smooth, creamy amalgamation of coffee, chocolate, and dark fruit flavors, and its label is a testament to the Kinston neighborhoods Stephen and Trent love so dearly.

Beer Lover's Pick

Silent Night
Style: Imperial stout
ABV: 9 percent
Availability: Winter seasonal
As surely as Christmas itself comes every year, so too does Silent Night, Mother Earth's bourbon barrel–aged imperial stout. This corked-and-caged treat is brewed with coffee from Counter Culture in Durham. It is a rich and full-bodied beer, with complex flavors of molasses, espresso, dark chocolate, and raisins. The brewery holds a release party at the taproom every year, but you can also find this one at better bottle shops across North Carolina.

Brewpubs

HUSKE HARDWARE HOUSE RESTAURANT & BREWERY

405 Hay St., Fayetteville, NC 28301; (910) 437-9905; HuskeHardware.com; @HuskHardware

Founded: 1996 **Founders:** Josh and Tonia Collins **Brewer:** Mark Fesche **Flagship Beer:** Level-Headed German Blonde **Year-Round Beers:** Level-Headed German Blonde, Ale Yeah Pale Ale, Kill-a-Man Irish Red, Farmhouse Ale, Sledgehammer Stout **Seasonals/Special Releases:** The Bleached Blonde, Watermelon Wheat, Jack's Honey Badger, Consecrator Grand Cru

Huske Hardware House gets its name from Benjamin Huske, who built the historic Fayetteville hardware store in 1903. Aside from the name, there are still some hints at the building's former purpose, such as the antique tools placed throughout the brewpub.

The similarities end there, though. From the front door, you can see the color-changing lights reflecting off of the brewpub's tanks at the back of the building. Two large projector screens hang on the wall above it, and a long bar runs down the right-side wall. A mezzanine provides a second level that runs along the brewery's perimeter. From one side of this mezzanine, you can look down on the six brite tanks that are hidden behind the bar on the main level.

One of the brewpub's most popular offerings is the **Level-Headed German Blonde,** a kölsch-style beer with just a hint of breadiness and the slightest bit of fruit. On the other end of the spectrum is the **Sledgehammer Stout**, it of the dry variety that so many associate with Guinness. Huske's is as creamy as that classic example, but with more of a roasted quality and notes of espresso. Fans of both of these beers can opt for **The Hammered Blonde,** which is the blonde poured over the stout. One of the brewery's most popular seasonals is the **Watermelon Wheat.** Brewed with 140 pounds of watermelons per batch, this refreshing wheat beer has an authentic melon flavor without venturing into too-sweet territory, as so many fruit beers are wont to do.

The brewpub has a full kitchen, with a portion of the menu devoted to UK pub fare, including fish-and-chips, shepherd's pie, and bangers and mash. Certified Angus beef is used in all of Huske's steak and burger dishes.

THE MASH HOUSE BREWERY & CHOPHOUSE

4150 Sycamore Dairy Rd., Fayetteville, NC 28303; (910) 867-9223; TheMashHouse.com; @MashHouseNC

Founded: 2000 **Founder:** Dean Ogan **Brewer:** Reuben Stocks **Flagship Beer:** Natural Blonde **Year-Round Beers:** Natural Blonde, Hefeweizen, Irish Red, India Pale Ale, Brown Porter, Stout **Seasonals/Special Releases:** Apricot IPA, Cherry Porter, Peach Hefeweizen, Watermelon Blonde, Strawberry Blonde, Jack'd Up Stout, Kristalweizen, Schwarzbier, Wee Heavy

In 2000, Fayetteville's Cross Creek Brewing Company became The Mash House Brewery & Chophouse. This mix of a brewery, steakhouse, and fine-dining restaurant was the brainchild of Dean Ogan, owner of Rocky Top Hospitality. It would seem that Dean's vision was a sound one, as The Mash House has been turning out excellent beers and food ever since (though it is now owned by a different restaurant group). From the outside, a tall silo is the only indication that there is a brewery in the otherwise nondescript building. The inside is dimly lit and elegant, with some tables showing their glossy wood surfaces and others covered by white linen. There is a bar, and through the glass behind it is the brewery's copper brewhouse.

The brewery's initial lineup of beers was designed by Zach Hart, who was a brewer with Cross Creek before the changeover to The Mash House. Zach stayed on, and most of his beers have remained unchanged throughout the years. When he left to help start Heist Brewery in Charlotte, Reuben Stocks became The Mash House's head brewer. Reuben has brewed a few beers that are all his own, while at the same time continuing to brew The Mash House's popular year-round and seasonal offerings. The **Natural Blonde** is the best-selling beer in the house, though it is actually a light lager and not a blonde ale. It is crisp and clean, and serves as a good base for some of the fruit beers Reuben does as well. The **Brown Porter** has notes of coffee, dark bread, and milk chocolate. Despite some of those sweet notes, it finishes dry.

If you are looking for a beer to pair with the many steaks on the menu, look no further than the **Irish Red,** a beer with caramel, roast and earthy flavors that work well with seared and caramelized cuts of beef.

Of course, those are the kinds of dishes that The Mash House specializes in. Besides the steaks and chops, the brewpub offers several popular appetizers, burgers, pizzas, and other entrees.

RAILHOUSE BREWERY

105 E. South St., Aberdeen, NC 28315; (910) 783-5280; RailhouseBrew.com; @RailhouseBrew
Founded: 2010 **Founders:** Brian Evitts, Mike Ratkowski **Brewers:** Brian Evitts, Chris Griffin **Flagship Beer:** Mastiff Oatmeal Stout **Year-Round Beers:** Mastiff Oatmeal Stout, KA-BAR Brown Ale, FCA IPA, Vanilla Porter, Pineland Pale Ale **Seasonals/Special Releases:** Beergasm Barleywine, English Ale, Honey Wheat

Flags from all of the armed forces are displayed proudly throughout the Railhouse Brewery in Aberdeen, which was itself founded by two veterans: Brian Evitts served in the US Navy, and Mike Ratkowski served in the US Army. All of the flags were donated by active military members. The brewery in historic Aberdeen is not far

from several military bases, with the distances in between covered in vast stretches of pine forests.

Brian started brewing in December of 2010, and then two years later he and Mike built the taproom (before this, sampling was done in the brewery itself). In 2013, they added a full kitchen that turns out burgers, sandwiches, and other bar fare. After 11 p.m., the menu shifts to all things fried: cheese curds, french fries, mushrooms, onion rings, and jalapeño poppers.

Beer Lover's Pick

Mastiff Oatmeal Stout
Style: Oatmeal stout
ABV: 6.5 percent
Availability: Year-round on tap and in bottles

Don't let the name fool you—Mastiff Oatmeal Stout is a light-bodied version of a full-bodied style, more bark than bite. This is not to say it isn't flavorful, but the roasted oat and coffee notes you expect from the style go down smoothly thanks to a lighter-than-usual body, which is by design. Railhouse wants Mastiff to satisfy your stout cravings, while at the same time not filling you up with a big, thick beer.

You can pair these foods with four year-round beers and several seasonal selections. Railhouse's **Vanilla Porter,** brewed with vodka-soaked vanilla beans, is as close as you will come to an ice cream-less beer float. It is smooth and creamy, and a coffee-like roastiness keeps the vanilla from becoming cloyingly sweet. The brewery has an agreement with KA-BAR knives, and the tap handle for the **KA-BAR Brown Ale** features the knife that is so widely used by the Marine Corps. The beer has mild chocolate flavors and a subtle nuttiness. In addition to their own beer, a variety of guest taps—most of them from fellow NC breweries—round out the taproom's 16 draft lines.

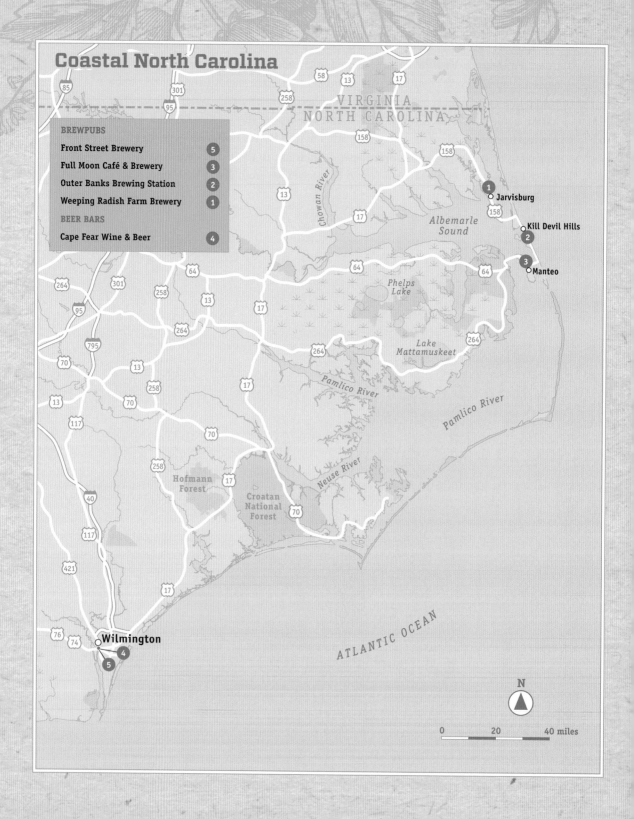

Coastal North Carolina

BREWPUBS
Front Street Brewery — 5
Full Moon Café & Brewery — 3
Outer Banks Brewing Station — 2
Weeping Radish Farm Brewery — 1
BEER BARS
Cape Fear Wine & Beer — 4

VIRGINIA
NORTH CAROLINA

Jarvisburg — 1
Kill Devil Hills — 2
Manteo — 3

Albemarle Sound
Chowan River
Phelps Lake
Lake Mattamuskeet
Pamlico River
Pamlico River
Neuse River
Hofmann Forest
Croatan National Forest

Wilmington — 4, 5

ATLANTIC OCEAN

N

0   20   40 miles

Coastal North Carolina

The North Carolina coast stretches for more than 300 miles. While this area is not as brewery-rich as the rest of the state, that does not mean it is lacking in good beer. From the Outer Banks down to Wilmington, the North Carolina coast features a handful of brewpubs producing great food and beer in one of the state's most picturesque regions.

Brewpubs

FRONT STREET BREWERY

9 N. Front St., Wilmington, NC 28401; (910) 251-1935; FrontStreetBrewery.com; @FSBrewery

Founded: 1995 **Founder:** Tom Harris **Brewer:** Kevin Kozak **Flagship Beer:** Coastal Kölsch **Year-Round Beers:** Coastal Kölsch, Riptide Raspberry Wheat, Amberjack ESB, Port City IPA, Dram Tree Scottish Ale **Seasonals/Special Releases:** Spring Brew Biere de Mars, Major Reilly's Irish Red Ale, Black River Oatmeal Stout, Corncob Cream Ale, Oktoberfest, Swamp Lager Schwarzbier, St. Stan's Baltic Porter, Tiny Tim's Christmas Porter

In a building dating from 1865, and just a block away from Wilmington's riverfront area, is Front Street Brewery. The brewpub itself entered the historic building in 1995, at a time when craft breweries were popping up all over the country. They weathered the first wave of brewery closings at the turn of the century, and continue to excel due to their exceptional food and craft beers.

Head brewer Kevin Kozak's 10-barrel copper brewhouse can be seen as soon as you step into the building. Of the brewpub's 10 taps, five are devoted to the flagships and five to seasonals. The one thing almost all of these beers have in common is that they are brewed perfectly to style. The **Coastal Kölsch** is a crisp and refreshing take on the German style, with just a hint of fruitiness from the ale yeast. For fruit beer fans, the **Riptide Raspberry Wheat** offers another light and quenching beer that is perfect when sitting out front people-watching on Front Street in the summer.

The **Spring Brew,** a *bière de mars,* won gold at the World Beer Cup in 2012. Every fall, Front Street brews **St. Stan's Baltic Porter** for a yearly Polish festival that features Polish food and drink. It is fermented with lager yeast, resulting in a smooth porter with lots of chocolate and minimal roast. The brewpub's **Dram Tree Scottish Ale**—the strongest of their year-round offerings—offers a rich taste of chocolate malt, caramel, earthiness, and dark fruit. That beer is used in the brewery's Brew-B-Q sauce, which is also available for purchase in 22-ounce bottles (beer mustard and buffalo sauce are available as well).

That Brew-B-Q sauce is slathered upon the brewpub's ribs, which are one of their more popular menu items. The pulled chicken nachos are another, topped with slow-cooked chicken and the usual nacho accoutrements. Want something more appropriate for the coastal setting? Try their shrimp grits (and be sure to check out a recipe for this dish in this book's "In The Kitchen" section, p. 302). The prices for food and beer alike are more than fair, and Front Street always offers a 10-ounce mug of the day for just $1.99.

FULL MOON CAFÉ & BREWERY

208 Queen Elizabeth St., Manteo, NC 27954; (252) 473-6666; TheFullMoonCafe.com
Founded: 2011 **Founders:** Paul Charron, Sharon Enoch **Brewer:** Owen Sullivan
Flagship Beer: Lost Colony Nut Brown Ale **Year-Round Beers:** Lost Colony Nut Brown
Ale, Charon Stout, Devil's Own English IPA, Vitamin O ESB, Baltimore Blonde, Paddy
Wagon Irish Red Ale, Manteo Porter, Stone of Destiny Scottish Ale **Seasonals/Special
Releases:** Holy Hand Grenade Imperial Stout, Headless Hessian Pumpkin Ale, Holiday
Porter

Full Moon Café & Brewery is one of a handful of businesses located at the Manteo
waterfront near Roanoke Island. The cafe portion of the business has been
around since 1995, and in April of 2011 founders Paul Charron and Sharon Enoch
decided to start a brewery when the adjoining building next door became available.

Into that small space they put a two-barrel system and a few two-barrel fermenters. Around all of this, they added a table and a small copper bar. The brewing side of Full Moon Café was born. Brewer Owen Sullivan brews up British styles almost exclusively. In fact, the best-selling **Baltimore Blonde** isn't really a blonde, but a lighter take on an English bitter. The **Vitamin O ESB** is an incredibly well-balanced beer that has just enough hop bitterness to complement the toasted, biscuit malt base. With a lighter body and 4.1 percent ABV, **Charon Stout** is a great example of a dry Irish stout, with notes of medium roast coffee and a lingering yet subtle smokiness. The **Stone of Destiny,** a Scotch ale, has notes of sweet figs and plums with a slight alcohol twinge.

If the small bar inside the brewery is full, the cafe and brewery has patio seating outside. Given their proximity to the water, it should come as no surprise that some of the most popular menu items at Full Moon Café & Brewery are seafood dishes. The shrimp 'n grits, shrimp and crab enchiladas, and fish-'n-chips are favorites among those who stop into this quaint brewpub.

OUTER BANKS BREWING STATION

600 S. Croatan Hwy., Kill Devil Hills, NC 27948; (252) 449-2739; OBBrewing.com; @OBXBrew

Founded: 2001 **Founders:** Aubrey Davis, Eric Reece **Brewers:** Scott Meyer, Adam Ball **Flagship Beer:** Ölsch **Year-Round Beers:** Ölsch, Lemongrass Wheat, Intergalactic IPA, Captain's Porter **Seasonals/Special Releases:** Moondog ESB, Santa's Little Sledgehammer

Wind rushes from the Atlantic Ocean and through Kill Devil Hills. It's the wind that the Wright brothers flew on when they became "first in flight." It's the wind that so many pitch kites into from the sandy dunes of Kill Devil Hills, where they soar high above, dots of color in the sky. And it's the wind that allows the Outer Banks Brewing Station—the nation's first wind-powered brewpub—to brew its beer.

The wind turbine that harnesses this energy towers nearly 100 feet above the ground. It sounds like a small plane and calls to mind the Wright memorial just half a mile down the road. Below it is the tall, skinny building that Aubrey Davis and Eric Reece built in 2001 in the same style as the Kill Devil Hills lifesaving station.

Eric and Scott Meyer worked together at Bison Brewing Company and also at a winery in California. Eric knew Scott would be perfect as the brewmaster for the Outer Banks Brewing Station. After hiking and camping his way down 30 miles of beach, Scott Meyer knew exactly what sort of beer "fit" the Outer Banks. He brewed **Ölsch**—his take on the German kölsch style—in 2001, long before the style

caught on with beer geeks looking for a more flavorful alternative to light lagers. The brewpub's popular **Lemongrass Wheat** is just as refreshing, as the strong lemongrass flavor works well with the banana and bubblegum notes derived from the Hefeweizen yeast.

These are popular styles for summer, when so many flock to the Outer Banks. The "backyard" of the brewery is a beautiful, well-landscaped space with picnic tables and a ship playground for kids to play on while their parents enjoy a beer. A tiki bar serves beer, ice cream, and slushies—and if those aren't sweet enough for you, consider the desserts made by Eric's wife Karen, a trained pastry chef.

WEEPING RADISH FARM BREWERY

6810 Caratoke Hwy., Jarvisburg, NC 27947; (252) 491-5205; WeepingRadish.com; @WeepingRadish

Founded: 1986 **Founder:** Uli Bennewitz **Brewer:** Nickodemus Williams **Flagship Beer:** Black Radish Schwarzbier **Year-Round Beers:** Black Radish Schwarzbier, OBX Kölsch, Corolla Gold, IPA 25, Weizen **Seasonals/Special Releases:** Fest, Radler

There are many North Carolina breweries listed in this book, and none of them would be here today without the work of Uli Bennewitz. Uli worked tirelessly to change the laws so that breweries could open up in North Carolina. After the law passed, he opened Weeping Radish Farm Brewery in Manteo in 1986.

Fourteen years later, the floor beneath Uli's brewpub fell through. Rather than rebuild, he constructed a 20,000-square-foot building in Jarvisburg to house his restaurant and brewery. He also added a butchery in this new building. A German immigrant, Uli is committed to locally grown food and *Reinheitsgebot*-compliant beer (brewed only with barley, hops, water, and yeast). With goats out front, cornfields all around, and a building painted to resemble a barn, Weeping Radish is a farm brewery in the truest sense of the phrase.

The brewpub's **OBX Kölsch** is a popular seller, in part because it's a light beer in an area people often visit during warm months, and in part because it has those three trendy letters on the label. As popular as this beer is, though, their **Black Radish** is even more popular. This schwarzbier has subtle notes of roast and brown bread, and it drinks smoothly with a crisp finish.

All of the beers are milder examples of their respective styles, which makes them more approachable to the many tourists who visit during the summer. The beers also go well with the brewpub's menu, which includes traditional German fare as well as

burgers, wraps, and more. An on-premise butchery means you're getting the freshest cuts of meat, most of which come from animals raised on nearby farms. Grab a flight of beers and a sausage sampler to enjoy the full Weeping Radish experience.

Beer Bar

CAPE FEAR WINE & BEER
139 N. Front St., Wilmington, NC 28401; (910) 763-3377; CapeFearWineandBeer.net;
@CapeFearBeer
Draft Beers: 19 **Bottled/Canned Beers:** 300+

Located just a block away from the Cape Fear river is Cape Fear Wine & Beer, a bar and bottle shop that has called the Port City home since 2003. The Valhalla sign outside on the front patio hints at the Viking theme inside the dimly lit bar, which also has a punk-meets-Irish pub sort of feel.

Of the bar's 19 taps, five can be found in the "Connoisseur's Cabinet," a small, wooden box filled with five bottles of beer. Yes, you read that right: This custom setup actually taps bottles and keeps them carbonated for up to two weeks. This allows patrons the luxury of having a sample or glass of these beers without committing to a large bottle. The bar also keeps one cask ale on at all times, and on Thursday they infuse beers using a Randall.

Behind the bar is a row of coolers filled with around 300 bottles of beer, which can be enjoyed at the bar or purchased to go. The bar has a pool table and a couple of arcade games, along with a few cozy tables and booths. Cape Fear and Wine is a great spot for locals and tourists alike, and they host a variety of events aimed at raising funds for charity.

Coastal North Carolina

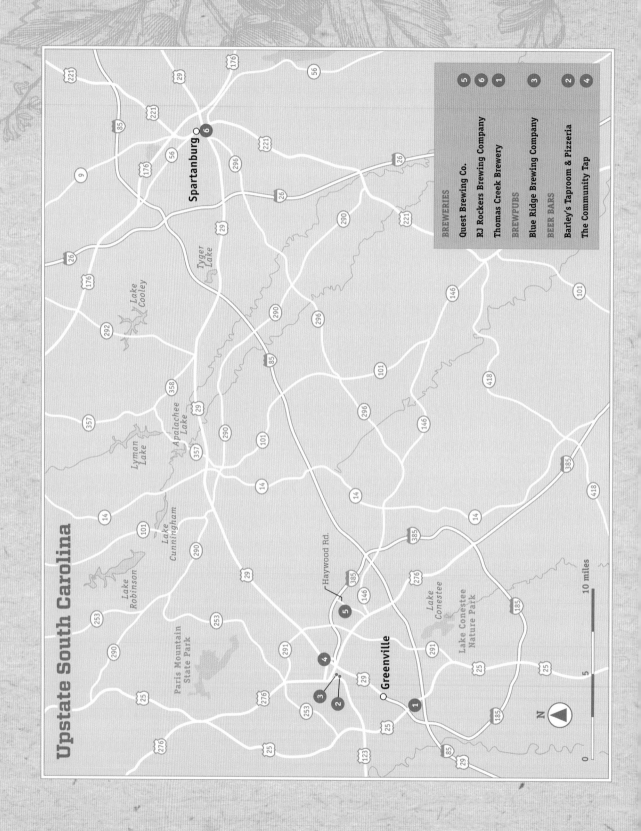

Upstate South Carolina

Spartanburg

Greenville

Haywood Rd.

Tyger Lake

Lake Cooley

Apalachee Lake

Lyman Lake

Lake Cunningham

Lake Robinson

Paris Mountain State Park

Lake Conestee

Lake Conestee Nature Park

BREWERIES
Quest Brewing Co. 5
RJ Rockers Brewing Company 6
Thomas Creek Brewery 1

BREWPUBS
Blue Ridge Brewing Company 3

BEER BARS
Barley's Taproom & Pizzeria 2
The Community Tap 4

N

0   5   10 miles

Upstate South Carolina

Upstate South Carolina offers something for everyone: a vibrant arts community, exciting downtowns in Greenville and Spartanburg, and beautiful parks and trails in the shadow of the Blue Ridge Mountains. Oh, and beer. New breweries and bars are popping up in an area that has long enjoyed favorites from established breweries like RJ Rockers and Thomas Creek Brewery, which continue to grow.

Breweries

QUEST BREWING CO.

55 Airview Dr., Greenville, SC 29607; (864) 272-6232; QuestBrewing.com; @QuestBrewing
Founded: 2013 **Founders:** Don Richardson, Andrew Watts **Brewer:** Don Richardson
Flagship Beer: Ellida IPA **Year-Round Beers:** Ellida IPA, Smoking Mirror Porter, Kaldi
Coffee Stout, Golden Fleece Belgian Pale Ale **Seasonals/Special Releases:** Dry-Hopped
Golden Fleece, Barrel-Aged Ellida IPA, Kermesse Pumpkin Saison, Pecan Porter **Tours:** Sat
at 1, 2, 3, and 4 p.m. **Taproom:** Tues and Wed, 4 to 8 p.m.; Thurs and Fri, 4 to 9 p.m.;
Sat, 12 to 9 p.m.

Spend enough time at Quest Brewing, and you're apt to learn a little mythology. The brewery's refreshing and sessionable **Golden Fleece Belgian Pale Ale,** brewed with coriander and grains of paradise, is named after that elusive fleece sought after by Jason and the Argonauts. The **Ellida IPA,** a well-hopped West Coast take on the style with a clean finish, is named after a Viking dragon ship of legend.

The **Smoking Mirror Porter,** which employs just a kiss of peat-smoked malt, is a reference to the Aztec god Tezcatlipoca, who was often depicted with a smoking mirror of obsidian on his chest. And the **Kaldi Coffee Stout,** so the legend goes, is named after the Ethiopian goat-herder who discovered the coffee plant.

If you're a coffee drinker, thank Kaldi. And if you're a beer drinker in Greenville, thank Andrew Watts and Don Richardson, two men who have undertaken a journey of their own to bring great beer to the upstate while using sustainable and low-impact brewing practices. Every hero has his origin story, and these two are no different. For Andrew, the beer journey started when he began drinking craft beer and homebrewing a decade prior to meeting Don Richardson in 2012. During his own quest, Don has served as a brewer at Colorado's Boulder Beer Company and Cottonwood Brewery in Boone. When Carolina Beer and Beverage purchased Cottonwood, Don brewed there as well.

The two both intended to bring a brewery to Greenville, and after hearing one another's plan they realized they shared a similar vision. Soon, they were working together to turn a nondescript, 5,300-square-foot building near Greenville's

Beer Lover's Pick

Kaldi Coffee Imperial Stout
Style: Imperial stout
ABV: 8 percent
Availability: Year-round on tap
Kaldi is brewed with local coffee from West End Coffee Company, and you can tell just from the aroma. In addition to the obvious coffee taste, Kaldi also contains notes of dark chocolate, molasses, and a distinct maple syrup quality. The sweetness balances well with the coffee's roastiness, resulting in a beer equivalent to a mocha.

downtown airport into a brewery. Inside, they built a taproom with rich wood from floor to ceiling and an indoor stage for live music. Posters featuring the art for the brewery's four "Legendary Series" beers hang on the walls. Behind the taproom is the 25-barrel brewery, which can be glimpsed through a large glass window. The wood-wrapped mash tun and hot liquor tanks, which were purchased from Big Boss Brewing in Raleigh, are particularly eye-catching. Before opening, they laid down new sod out back to build "Quest Field," a green stretch of grass sitting in front of a small outdoor stage.

Quest's core beers are nailed down, but they will be experimenting with seasonals and limited releases. Their journey is now under way, their story unfolding with each pint pulled.

RJ ROCKERS BREWING COMPANY
226-A W. Main St., Spartanburg, SC 29302; (864) 585-8224; RJRockers.com; @RJRockers
Founded: 1997 **Founder:** Mark Johnsen **Brewers:** Mark Johnsen, Robby Hayes, Taylor White **Flagship Beer:** Patriot Pale Ale **Year-Round Beers:** Patriot Pale Ale, Light Rock Ale, Bald Eagle Brown Ale, Day Drinker IPA, Bell Ringer Ale, Honey Amber **Seasonals/ Special Releases:** Son of a Peach, Fish Paralyzer, Good Boy Stout, Rockers Red Glare, Strawbeery Wheat, Oso Blanco Belgian White, Black Perle Dark IPA, Buckwheat After Dark, Gruntled Pumpkin, The First Snow Ale **Tours:** Thurs from 5 to 7 p.m.; Sat from 12 to 4 p.m. **Taproom:** Thurs and Fri, 5 to 7 p.m.; Sat, 12 to 4 p.m.

A drive down I-85 through South Carolina is an assault in all things peach. "Pull over," the bright billboards implore. "Try a peach milk shake, or peach jam! Perhaps a peach pie, or some peach salsa? Peach cider?" And that's saying nothing of the derriere-shaped peach water tower that moons all who pass by.

It should come as no surprise then, that in this peach-pregnant portion of the state, you can find a peach beer, too. And while the summer seasonal **Son of a Peach** is the best-known beer at RJ Rockers Brewing Company, it's not the only one that's being produced in the 46,000-square-foot building in downtown Spartanburg. The brewery has a small bar inside the large warehouse-style building where you can enjoy a wide range of beers. Downstairs is the brewery's packaging equipment, where so many RJ Rockers beers are bottled before being shipped out across the region. The brewery prides itself on its sustainability initiatives, which include 10 solar panels that can be seen on their roof.

Even though it's called **Light Rock Pale Ale,** that beer is the brewery's take on a kölsch. It is a refreshing beer with just a touch of citrus hops and bready malt. The **Patriot Pale Ale** is truer to the pale ale style, as it displays a more prominent hoppiness in balance with the beer's caramel malt backbone. **Bell Ringer** defies style conventions, leaving the brewery to call it an "Imperial ESB." One of RJ Rockers' most popular seasonal beers—and their highest-alcohol beer to date—is the **Black Perle,** a dark IPA brewed with lots of the German Perle hops. It has notes of cocoa powder, medium-roast coffee, and pine.

RJ Rockers holds tours and tastes every Thursday and Saturday. For just $5, you get a tour of the brewery, a pint glass, and four 4-ounce samples of beer. They also offer "Hoppy Hour" specials from 5 to 7 p.m. every Friday, and on one Friday a month they feature live music from 5 to 8 p.m. as part of their "Rock on the Dock" series. See their recipe for **Brown Sugar & Son of a Peach Salmon** on p. 309.

Beer Lover's Pick

Son of a Peach
Style: Fruit beer
ABV: 6 percent
Availability: Spring and summer, on tap and in bottles
At its base, RJ Rockers Son of
a Peach is a wheat beer brewed
with a copious amount of South
Carolina peaches. The peach is
anything but subtle, but to its
credit this beer does not venture
into the too-sweet territory so
common of fruit beers. Wheat
and biscuity malt flavors pair
well with the tartness of the
peach, combining to create a
refreshing beer that many seek
out during the warmer months.

THOMAS CREEK BREWERY

2054 Piedmont Hwy., Greenville, SC 29605; (864) 605-1166; ThomasCreekBeer.com;
@ThomasCreekBeer

Founded: 1998 **Founders:** Bill Davis, Tom Davis **Brewer:** Tom Davis **Flagship Beer:**
River Falls Red Ale **Year-Round Beers:** River Falls Red Ale, Deepwater Doppelbock,
Appalachian Amber, Pumphouse Porter, Class Five IPA, Up the Creek Extreme IPA, Dockside
Pilsner, Pumphouse Porter **Seasonals/Special Releases:** Chocolate Orange IPA, Banana
Split Chocolate Stout, Conduplico Immundus Monachus, Stillwater Vanilla Cream Ale,
Octoberfest, Coffee Oatmeal Stout, Pumpkin Ale, Dirty Monk **Tours:** By appt **Taproom:**
Mon through Fri, 8 a.m. to 6 p.m.; Sat, 10 a.m. to 6 p.m.

Open since 1998, Thomas Creek Brewery is one of South Carolina's oldest production breweries. Prior to opening their doors, the father and son team of Bill and Tom Davis had been leasing brewing equipment under the Thomas Creek name to a variety of brewpubs, including a restaurant called Henni's, where Tom was brewing at the time. He had learned much there, and so when Henni's left the brewing business, Tom and his father decided to start brewing under the Thomas Creek name.

They built a large building right off of Highway 20 to house their production brewery, where they brew and bottle a wide range of year-round and seasonal beers. The **River Falls Red Ale** is the brewery's flagship, and this Irish-style red features sweet caramel malts with just a bit of toasted character coming through. While that one is true to style, Thomas Creek's Atypical Series allows Tom to experiment a bit more. The brewery's **Banana Split Chocolate Stout** is a chocolate stout that gets its distinct banana notes from a Belgian yeast, not actual bananas themselves. The brewery's **Up the Creek** is a 12.5 percent monster of a beer that blurs the line between a double IPA and a barleywine. It was brewed in 2007 with the expectation that South Carolina's Pop the Cap campaign would lift the state's ABV cap on beer from 5 percent to 17.5 percent, and it did. This slow sipper of a beer is now available year-round.

In 2013, Thomas Creek broke ground on a 10,000-square-foot expansion that included a new brewing facility and several large fermenters that will enable Thomas Creek to meet demand in markets both new and old. They also took this time to add a new taproom and an outdoor patio for guests. One of the most popular events at the brewery is their cask night, which takes place on the last Tuesday of each month and features casks of Thomas Creek beers filled with interesting and creative additions.

Because there was no homebrew supply store in the area when they opened, many homebrewers would ask if they could buy malt, hops, and brewing equipment from Thomas Creek. As a result, they started selling equipment, and you can find a large range of ingredients and equipment at Thomas Creek.

Beer Lover's Pick

Castaway Chocolate Orange IPA
Style: India pale ale
ABV: 7.5 percent
Availability: On tap and in 12 ounce bottles year-round

As you might imagine given its name, this is not your typical IPA. It pours a dark amber color thanks to the use of chocolate wheat and black patent malts, and it actually tastes subtly of chocolate due to the addition of cocoa nibs. Orange peel and a bevy of hops lend the beer its citrus and pine notes.

Brewpub

BLUE RIDGE BREWING COMPANY

217 N. Main St., Greenville SC 29601; (864) 232-4677; BlueRidgeBrewing.com;
@BlueRidgeBrewCo

Founded: 1995 **Founder:** Bob Hiller **Brewer:** Dana Dickinson **Flagship Beer:** Rainbow Trout ESB **Year-Round Beers:** Kurli Blonde Ale, Rainbow Trout ESB, Colonel Paris Pale Ale, XXX Total Eclipse Stout **Seasonals/Special Releases:** Boltcutter IPA, Blood Orange Honey Saison, Monster Mash Milk Chocolate Stout, Black Honey Imperial Stout, Hurricane Hefeweizen, Little Willie Barleywine

Blue Ridge Brewing Company was one of the first new businesses to open up on Greenville's Main Street when downtown redevelopment started. Now this fun stretch of downtown abounds with diverse storefronts, restaurants, and businesses.

You might feel close to the brewhouse as you walk by the brewpub's front windows, behind which the tanks stand visible to all who pass. Once inside, though, you can take a seat at a table just feet away from a fermenter, an excess blowoff hose bubbling beside your feet. On the tables, schematics for the brewing equipment are

sketched out in blue ink. Above the bar, grotesque faces adorn the mugs that give the brewpub's "Ugly Mug Club" its name.

Of the brewpub's four year-round beers, the **Rainbow Trout ESB**—a dead-on take of the ESB style with its floral hops and biscuity malt—is the bestseller. The **Colonel Paris Pale Ale** is a maltier, sweeter version of the typical American pale ale. Lighter in body than those two is the **Kurli Blonde Ale,** which has floral notes and practically no bitterness. On the darker end of the spectrum is **XXX Total Eclipse Stout,** a beer that they bill as a "Caribbean stout." Coffee, chocolate, and licorice combine and culminate with a dry, roasty finish.

If that last beer sounds familiar, chances are you've visited Foothills Brewing, whose stout once shared the same name. Foothills formerly operated under "The Foothills Brewing Concern," though now that is only true of Blue Ridge. The stout is quite food-friendly, especially with the wild game sampler, which includes duck, venison, rabbit, and game sausage. The spent grains of the stout are used to create apple beignets from scratch, and the finished beer is reduced down to create a sweet caramel sauce in which to dip them.

Beer Bars

BARLEY'S TAPROOM & PIZZERIA

25 W. Washington St., Greenville, SC 29601; (864) 232-3706; BarleysGville.com;
@BarleysGville
Draft Beers: 72 **Bottled/Canned Beers:** 200+

Barley's Taproom in Asheville has been a haven for beer geeks in the Southeast since they opened in 1994. Two years after that location opened, a second Barley's opened up in downtown Greenville. Barley's Greenville has much in common with the Asheville location, including excellent pizzas, dart lanes, and pool tables and an exhaustive beer selection split between upstairs and downstairs bars.

There are 39 taps downstairs on the main level, and another 33 at the upstairs bar brings the total number of draft beers to 72. Water filter housings are screwed

into the wood beside many of the taps, serving as makeshift Randall devices that the taproom uses to infuse beers with special ingredients. The taproom frequently holds special beer events, tastings, or pint nights. In 2012, Barley's sold so much from Stone Brewing that they beat out 360 other beer bars across the nation to receive the title of Stone Brewing Company's Most Arrogant Bar in America. But don't let that fool you: The bartenders are incredibly humble and take great pride in guiding beer lovers through the beer menus and making recommendations.

THE COMMUNITY TAP

215 Wade Hampton Blvd., Greenville, SC 29609; (864) 631-2525; TheCommunityTap.com; @CommunityTap

Draft Beers: 12 **Bottled/Canned Beers:** 500+

Since 2010, The Community Tap has provided Greenville beer lovers with an extensive selection of beer, both bottled and draft. The drafts are more often dispensed into growlers, as The Community Tap is primarily a bottle shop. They do have a tasting room with several tables, however, or you could simply have a pint while perusing their impressive selection of beer. A dozen beers are kept on tap all times, and The Community Tap rotates through lots of well-known national brands as well as South Carolina favorites like Greenville's own Quest Brewing or Thomas Creek Brewery. They hold tastings just about every week as well as other special events, like their own craft beer festival.

The Midlands

BREWERIES
Benford Brewing Company — 3
Conquest Brewing Company — 9

BREWPUBS
Aiken Brewing Company — 10
Hunter–Gatherer Brewery & Alehouse — 7
Old Mill Brewpub — 4

BEER BARS
Flying Saucer — 6
Grapevine Wine Bar — 1
The Kraken Gastropub — 8
Millstone Pizza & Taphouse — 2
World of Beer–The Vista — 5

The Midlands

South Carolina's upstate and coast get a lot of well-deserved love, but plenty of great breweries, brewpubs and beer bars call the middle of the state home, too. From Columbia and surrounding towns like Aiken and Lexington up to Rock Hill near the state's border, the Midlands have a distinct and developing beer scene all their own.

Breweries

BENFORD BREWING COMPANY

2271 Boxcar Rd., Lancaster, SC, 29720; (803) 416-8422; BenfordBrewing.com
Founded: 2013 **Founder:** Bryan O'Neal **Brewer:** Bryan O'Neal **Flagship Beer:** O'Neal's Special Oatmeal Oyster Stout (O'SOO Stout) **Year-Round Beers:** O'SOO Stout, Smoked O'Hickory Brown Ale, Irish Honey Ale **Seasonals/Special Releases:** Barrel Aged O'SOO Stout, Riverside Red, World's Problem Solver IPA **Tours:** No **Taproom:** Open on occasion. For updates, check Facebook.com/BoxcarBrewery.

Bryan O'Neal has worked in the swimming pool industry since he was 15 years old, and today he owns a high-end pool-building company that has built pools for Carolina Panthers players and NASCAR drivers. Rest assured he knows a thing or two about water chemistry.

He also knows how to turn good water into good beer. The land on which he lives in Lancaster, SC, is home to three springs. Not long after he and his wife purchased the home, Bryan built a pool. Beside it, he tore down the old well house and erected a tiki bar in its place. And then later still, he built a large steel building to house his pool company's office, materials, and equipment.

Bryan didn't stop there. After homebrewing for several years, he decided to build himself a brewery, with no intentions of "going pro." He fashioned a brew system from 55-gallon drums and ran the gas and electrical components himself. He built two rolling, 110-gallon conical fermenters that he could wheel in and out of a cooled fermentation room, which he also built himself. He hadn't planned to build Lancaster's first craft brewery, but that's eventually what happened. He already had the building and practically no overhead, so he assumed very little risk in forming Benford Brewing.

Bryan found a great deal on an old cooler, the kind you might see holding cans of soda in an old gas station. He installed it above his office in the building and built stairs leading up to it so that he could store kegs in his new cold room.

Beer Lover's Pick

O'SOO Oyster Stout
Style: Oyster stout
ABV: 5.5 percent
Availability: On tap year-round
The abbreviation O'SOO stands for O'Neal's Special Oatmeal Oyster Stout, and a sip is all that is needed to see why this one is oh so popular. True to its name, it is brewed with oysters, which impart a brininess that works well with the stout's chocolate notes. O'SOO Stout has a creamy mouthfeel and a dry finish.

The brewery's **Smoked O'Hickory Brown Ale** employs malt that's been smoked over wood from a pecan tree that fell on Bryan's property. It is a fuller-bodied brown ale than most, with enough smoke to know it's there, but not enough that it's over-powering. The **Irish Honey Ale** is brewed using honey malt and oatmeal, for a sweet, smooth, and easy-drinking alternative to some of Bryan's darker beers.

You can find these beers around Lancaster, Fort Mill, and Rock Hill, but if you can catch Bryan on a day he's got the brewery open, I think you'll be impressed by the innovative way he has built the brewery—even if Bryan is quick to call it "red-neck brewing."

CONQUEST BREWING COMPANY

947 S. Stadium Rd., Bay 1, Columbia, SC 29201; (803) 712-3063; ConquestBrewing.com; @ConquestBrewing

Founded: 2013 **Founders:** Joseph Ackerman, Matthew Ellisor **Brewers:** Joseph Ackerman, Matthew Ellisor **Flagship Beer:** Sacred Heart IPA **Year-Round Beers:** Sacred Heart IPA, Artemis Blonde, Medusa Stout, Warrior Heart IPA **Seasonals/Special Releases:** Garnet Ale, Der Alte Fritz, The Finisher, Brutus Imperial Stout, Seven Seas Pale Ale, Sacred Heartier, Bipolar High Roller **Tours:** No **Taproom:** Wed through Fri, 5 to 9 p.m.; Sat, 12 to 4 p.m. and 5 to 9 p.m.; Sun, 1 to 4 p.m.

The garnet-colored paint that coats the walls of Conquest Brewing's taproom is well familiar to anyone who has seen the University of South Carolina Gamecocks play at Williams-Brice Stadium, which is just a couple blocks away from the brewery. Conquest's slogan is "History is written by the victor," and if their early success is any indication they will be doing a lot of writing.

Cofounded by Joseph Ackerman and Matthew Ellisor, Conquest brought a pro-duction brewery to a city sorely in need of one. They brew on a 3-barrel system in a space large enough to accommodate future expansion. The taproom itself is fairly small, with room enough for a couple of tables and a bar. On the far wall of the taproom are the brewery's sword tap handles, which are fashioned from real-life daggers.

They work well with the brewery's medieval image, as do the names of the beers themselves. **Artemis Blonde,** the brewery's lightest offering, offers up notes of sweet honey, a bit of biscuit, and a subtle yeastiness that lingers. The **Medusa Stout** abounds with light-roasted coffee and milk chocolate flavors, and at 5.2 per-cent ABV it's a little lower in alcohol than most others in its style. The **Sacred Heart IPA** is a decidedly East Coast take on the style, meaning it is well balanced and has a sturdy caramel malt backbone as well as notes of mango and pineapple. In addition

PHOTO BY AUTHOR

Warrior Heart IPA
Style: India pale ale
ABV: 7.2 percent
Availability: On tap year-round

If Conquest Brewing's Sacred Heart doesn't satisfying your craving for hops, look to Warrior Heart, its West Coast cousin. The name is appropriate, since this iteration is brewed with twice the amount of Warrior hops that are in Sacred Heart. The result is a much more bitter offering, yet with that bitterness comes notes of pineapple, orange, and grapefruit. It finishes a little drier than Sacred Heart and boasts 98 IBUs (international bitterness units).

PHOTO BY AUTHOR

to household hop names like Citra, Centennial, and Warrior, Sacred Heart also features a new variety called Belma.

The brewery's biggest beer is undoubtedly **The Finisher,** a massive imperial stout that undergoes three fermentations—one using Champagne yeast—on its way to 17.5 percent ABV. Brown sugar and honey bring a little sweetness to a beer meant for sipping and savoring.

Brewpubs

AIKEN BREWING COMPANY

140 Laurens St. SW, Aiken, SC 29801; (803) 502-0707; AikenBrewingCompany.com; @AikenBrewCo

Founded: 1997 **Founder:** Dan Beavers **Brewer:** Randy Doucet **Flagship Beer:** Thoroughbred Red **Year-Round Beer:** Thoroughbred Red **Seasonals/Special Releases:** Honey Wheat, Kölsch, Cream Ale, Nut Brown Ale, Czech Pilsner, English IPA, Oktoberfest, Jenny's Cream 500, Randy's Grand Cru, Carolina Pale Ale, West Coast Pale Ale, Olde Aiken Ale, Saison

The year 1997 was a big one for Aiken, SC. That was the year the National Civic League awarded the city with the All-America City Award, which is given to only 10 communities each year. It was also the year the Aiken Brewing Company opened its doors.

Until you are upon it, the building—which once housed a feed 'n seed, furniture store, and sporting goods shop—blends in with the rest of the businesses on Lauren Street, home to a strip of shops and restaurants in downtown Aiken. Look closely through the glass windows at the front of the building, however, and you'll see the seven-barrel brewhouse on one side and a row of fermenters in the other. Inside, the brick walls and thick wooden beams seem particularly well suited to a brewpub, and provide that comfortable, well-worn feel so many old establishments have. It is hard to imagine that where once there was grain for animals, now there is grain for ales.

The brewpub's flagship and only true year-round beer is the **Thoroughbred Red,** which won a silver medal at the Great American Beer Festival in 2001 and a gold in 2003. Its name is a reference to the well-known equestrian community in Aiken, which is also home to the Aiken Thoroughbred Racing Hall of Fame and Museum. The rest of the taps will vary among a wide range of styles, but the brewpub usually devotes one tap to a pale ale, one to a dark beer and one to a specialty. The man behind the beers, head brewer Randy Doucet, has been working at the brewpub since just a few months after it opened in 1997.

Upstairs, the brewpub has another bar and dining area complete with a pool table and shuffleboard. It is here that Randy hosts area homebrew club meetings to talk shop with other brewers. Often the brewpub will have live music in this room.

The brewpub has full lunch and dinner menus. The Big Tony, a bacon cheeseburger wrapped in a flour tortilla, is especially popular. And if you're reasonably close to Aiken, you'll want to sign up for the brewpub's mug club. There are many perks, chief among them that members get a full 20-ounce pour of each beer ordered rather than the standard 16-ounce pint.

HUNTER-GATHERER BREWERY & ALEHOUSE

900 Main St., Columbia, SC 29201; (803) 748-0540; HunterGathererBrewery.com; @HGBrewery

Founded: 1995 **Founder:** Kevin Varner **Brewer:** Kevin Varner **Flagship Beer:** Pale Ale
Year-Round Beers: Pale Ale, Wheat, ESB **Seasonals/Special Releases:** Porter, Plain X Stout, Black Patent Ale, Wry Old Bastard

A couple of blocks from South Carolina's capitol building sits the Hunter-Gatherer Brewery & Alehouse, one of the state's oldest brewpubs. Kevin Varner, a native South Carolinian, opened the brewpub in 1995 after the state passed a law allowing brewpubs in 1994. The law's passage was enough to call the native son home from Seattle, where he was working as a brewer at Hale's Ales.

The taproom has an eclectic and warm ambience. A stuffed spotted dog from Africa stands guard in a window, and African spears and shields grace a wall next to it. Casting a soft light over everything are long, antique iron lights sourced from an old church. And behind the bar is the 10-barrel system upon which Kevin brews. There is no wall or glass separating the brewhouse and the bar, only a curved set of shelves holding a selection of liquors.

PHOTO BY AUTHOR

On the night Hunter-Gatherer opened, an older gentleman ordered four full pints of each of the beers at the same time. After downing those, he had a glass of every wine they offered, and then a few more drinks before walking home. Kevin asked an employee to follow him to make sure he was okay. He did, and though they didn't see him after that, the man did inspire the brewpub's **Wry Old Bastard,** a wee heavy brewed with rye.

That one's only available during the holidays, but at any time throughout the year you can expect the brewpub to have their **Wheat, Pale Ale,** and **ESB** on tap, as well as one or two seasonals or rotating beers. Kevin focuses on drinkable, consistent and true-to-style British beers, and his draft lineup hasn't changed much since opening in 1995. Naturally, beer finds its way into a few of the dishes, like the **ESB Pimento Cheese Spread** (see recipe on p. 302) and beer-braised chicken thighs. Hunter-Gatherer's menu consists of several different sandwiches, pizzas, and other entrees, and the brewpub is as well known for its cuisine as it is its beer.

OLD MILL BREWPUB

711 E. Main St., Lexington, SC 29072; (803) 785-2337; OldMillBrewpub.net; @OldMillBrewpub

Founded: 2013 **Founders:** John and Kelly Clinger **Brewer:** Matt Rodgers **Flagship Beer:** N/A **Year-Round Beers:** N/A **Seasonals/Special Releases:** 12 Mile Oatmeal Porter, Indigo Double IPA, Spinning Jenny, Bine Climber IPA

When it was newly built just before the turn of the 19th century, the Lexington mill was a sprawling, state-of-the-art cotton manufacturing plant that derived all of its power from the mill pond behind it. More than a century later, the

PHOTO BY AUTHOR

building now known as "Lexington's Old Mill" houses a variety of shops, restaurants and studios, all of which still use the scenic pond out back for hydroelectric power.

One of the mill's newest businesses is turning that power into beer. The Old Mill Brewpub sits in the back of the complex, with a long patio overlooking the pond (which more resembles a small lake). Inside, the old stone walls, exposed copper ductwork and thick wood rafters overhead lend a lot of character to the restaurant. A small bar in the brewpub boasts 24 drafts and more bottles, but you would be doing yourself a disservice not to have a beer brewed in-house on the 3.5-barrel brewhouse in the corner of the brewpub.

Brewer Matt Rodgers previously worked just down the street at Keg Cowboy, an area homebrew store and bar where he also taught homebrewing classes. He has continued to lead such classes at Old Mill Brewpub, where attendees get to learn more about the beer-making process out back by the water. Matt brews a range of beers at Old Mill with an emphasis on seasonal selections. He owns a hop farm in Camden, SC, and frequently brings in locally grown hops to use in his beers. Like Mystery Brewing in Hillsborough, NC, Matt prefers to brew seasonal beers instead of committing himself to a flagship or other year-round beers.

Visitors to this mill made modern can tour its shops, grab a cup of coffee, and even rent paddle boards. The brewpub's patrons are apt to do the latter, and frequently host pub runs and Olympic-style "Brewpub Games."

Beer Bars

FLYING SAUCER

931 Senate St., Columbia, SC 29201; (803) 933-9997; BeerKnurd.com; @FlyingSaucerCol
Draft Beers: 80+ **Bottled/Canned Beers:** 150+

The Flying Saucer Draught Emporium—known as the Saucer to most—is a chain of beer bars that was founded in 1995 in Fort Worth, Texas. In the Carolinas, there are Flying Saucer locations in Columbia, SC, as well as Charlotte and Raleigh, NC.

The Columbia Saucer is one of many bars in a vibrant section of downtown Columbia called the Congaree Vista. As at every other Saucer, the walls are covered with plates from victorious UFO club members who have consumed 200 unique beers at the location, thus securing them a place in the Ring of Honor. The bar has an open beer hall feel to it inside. Outside, there is a small patio with several tables and chairs.

PHOTO BY AUTHOR

With more than 80 taps, the Columbia Saucer is able to carry a wide variety of national and regional breweries, as well as local favorites like Columbia's own Conquest Brewing. On the food menu, you will find standard bar cuisine like sandwiches, appetizers, and pizzas. The pretzels and brats are popular, as is the spicy beer cheese soup.

GRAPEVINE WINE BAR

1012 Market St., #105, Fort Mill, SC 29708; (803) 802-9989; MyGrapevineOnline.com; @GrapevineWine
Draft Beers: 12 **Bottled/Canned Beers:** 400+

Located in Fort Mill's charming Baxter Village, Grapevine Wine Bar is a combination bottle shop and beer and wine bar. They have a dozen taps behind the bar, which usually include popular national and local beers. The bar is not far from the border, and they frequently tap beers from Charlotte breweries as well as South Carolina favorites like Quest and Westbrook.

In addition to enjoying beers by the glass, you can also take home growler fills of the dozen beers that are on tap (unless noted). The bar often hosts guest bartending events for charity. They also host Saturday Beer Samplers about every two weeks, which allow people to purchase six 6-ounce pours, usually of a certain style or theme, for $12. Every March, Grapevine Wine holds the Beertopia beer festival in their parking lot. It is an excellent event, and you can find out more about it in this book's section on beer festivals.

THE KRAKEN GASTROPUB

2910 Rosewood Dr., Ste. 1, Columbia, SC 29205; (803) 955-7408; TheKrakenPub .com
Draft Beers: 30 **Bottled/Canned Beers:** 50+

On the bottom floor of a non-descript building in Columbia's Rosewood neighborhood is The Kraken Gastropub, a restaurant whose food menu and taplist are as interesting as the name itself. The bar has 30 well-curated taps—many of which are from the Carolinas—and countless more

PHOTO BY AUTHOR

bottles and cans. It is not uncommon to find $2 specials, and these are quality, craft beers—not those that are usually found in bars at that price point.

As impressive as the beer selection is, it is rivaled by a creative menu peppered with as many locally grown ingredients as possible. Both the small plates and bar menus are ever-changing, with other unique entrees being featured almost on a nightly basis. Some dishes, like truffle *frites,* poutine and the smoked wings, stay on pretty regularly, but don't count on dishes like Sriracha peanut butter glazed doughnuts to be on at all times. The patio out back overlooks the parking lot, their neighbor—a gas station—to the right. But with a diverse beer list and some of the most inspired food in Columbia, who needs a view?

MILLSTONE PIZZA & TAPHOUSE

121 Caldwell St., Ste. 103, Rock Hill, SC 29730; (803) 980-2337; MillstonePizzaandTap .com; @MillstonePizza
Draft Beers: 40 **Bottled/Canned Beers:** 25+

Pizza and beer both encompass many different ingredients and flavors, and yet no matter how they are prepared the two can almost always be combined into a perfect pairing. Nowhere is that more evident than at Millstone Pizza & Taphouse in Rock Hill.

When childhood friends Brendan Kuhlkin and David Clapp decided to open a pizzeria together, they figured touring the best pizza places in New York and Chicago was as good a market research as any. They put much of that research into practice in building Millstone Pizza & Taphouse. The wood-fired oven is the pizzeria's heart, and the 40 taps of craft beer its soul. In addition to a good mix of popular national beers, you will also find several taps devoted to South Carolina breweries like Benford Brewing, RJ Rockers Brewing, and Thomas Creek Brewery. Every first and third Sunday, the folks at Millstone host an hour-long Beer 101 class in which they discuss different beer styles, breweries, and more.

There is a pizza for just about any taste, including gluten-free and vegetarian options. One good example of the latter is the Classic Margherita, topped with the trademark basil and mozzarella you would expect. On the other end of the spectrum is the Meat Pizza, which features pepperoni, meatballs, Italian sausage, and prosciutto.

WORLD OF BEER—THE VISTA
902 Gervais St., Columbia, SC 29201; (803) 509-6020; WOBusa.com; @WOBTheVista
Draft Beers: 60 **Bottled/Canned Beers:** 500

Located in The Vista, downtown Columbia's World of Beer location offers an extensive beer selection on draft and in bottles. The draft menu features a good smattering of beers from both North and South Carolina, while coolers behind the bar contain a veritable United Nations of beer, with examples from all over the globe. Even the most seasoned beer geeks will always be able to find something new to try.

Like many bars these days, World of Beer offers a loyalty club in which faithful imbibers can earn perks like shirts, mugs, plaques, gift cards, and discounts. They frequently feature local breweries and hold special events, including pint nights and Randall infusions. Several televisions are in place for those wanting to watch the game.

PHOTO BY AUTHOR

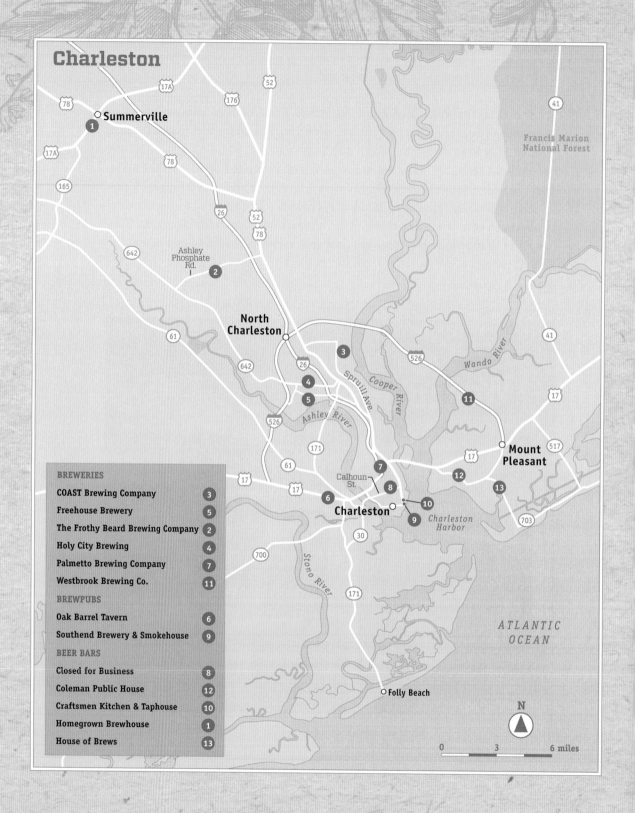

Charleston

78
17A
176
52
78
17A
165
26
52
78
642
Ashley Phosphate Rd.
2
61
North Charleston
642
26
3
526
4
5
Spruill Ave.
Cooper River
Wando River
526
41
Ashley River
11
171
61
17
7
Calhoun St.
12
8
17
17
Mount Pleasant
517
6
10
13
703
Charleston
9
Charleston Harbor
30
700
Stono River
171
41

78
Summerville
1

41
Francis Marion National Forest

○ Folly Beach

ATLANTIC OCEAN

N

0   3   6 miles

Charleston

In the shadow of so many steeples is South Carolina's oldest city, one where palm trees rise above cobblestone streets and antebellum architecture still stands. Charleston is one of the most enchanting cities in the country, and many are the reasons that thousands of people visit the city each year.

Locals and visitors alike will find no shortage of good beer in downtown Charleston proper, but the area's beer scene is made even richer by the many breweries, brewpubs, and beer bars in the North Charleston and Mount Pleasant areas.

Breweries

COAST BREWING COMPANY

1250 N. 2nd St., North Charleston, SC 29405; (843) 343-4727; CoastBrewing.com;
@COASTbrewing
Founded: 2007 **Founders:** David Merritt, Jaime Tenny **Brewers:** David Merritt, Michael
Davis **Flagship Beer:** 32/50 Kölsch **Year-Round Beers:** 32/50 Kölsch, HopArt IPA
Seasonals/Special Releases: Blackbeerd Imperial Stout, Barrel-Aged Blackbeerd,
Rye Knot Brown Ale, Boy King, Dave Brown, Bulls Bay Oyster Stout, Dead Arm Pale Ale,
ALTerior Motive, Event Horizon Cascadian Dark Ale **Tours:** During open hours **Taproom:**
Thurs, 4 to 7 p.m.; Sat, 11 a.m to 2 p.m.

A Charleston native, David Merritt got his start homebrewing in 1996 before moving on to work at Southend Brewing and Palmetto Brewing Company. He would spend eight years at Palmetto before he and his wife, Jaime Tenny, ventured out to build their own brewery. Before doing so, however, Jaime helped lead the state's Pop the Cap campaign to raise the maximum ABV allowed in beer from 5 percent to 17.5 percent ABV.

Shortly after that legislation passed, the husband-and-wife team opened COAST Brewing Company in North Charleston's old naval shipyard in 2007. Jaime still serves

Boy King
Style: Imperial India pale ale
ABV: 9.7 percent
Availability: Limited release in
    bottles and on tap

The Boy King was crowned the
minute it was released upon the
Charleston beer scene, and ever since
its appearance has been anxiously
anticipated by both locals and the
many beer lovers who drive hours
for a pint, a growler, or a bottle.
This double IPA is brewed with Citra,
Chinook, Nugget, Cascade, Centennial, and Columbus hops, the sum of
which combine to provide assertive
flavors of grapefruit, mango, and tangerine. It lacks the syrupy sweetness
of some double IPAs, instead opting

for a slightly thinner approach that makes its 9.7 percent ABV surprisingly drinkable.

as president of the South Carolina Brewers Association, and she also handles all
operations for the brewery. David handles the brewing side of things. For most of
COAST's history, he was brewing on a small seven-barrel system that they picked up
from a brewpub that closed in Macon, Georgia. This small system didn't allow them
enough capacity, and in late 2013 they expanded to a 30-barrel brewhouse to keep
up with the demand.

    The brewery's flagship **32/50 Kölsch** proved popular from day one. It is a light
and refreshing beer perfect for the Charleston heat, with soft floral and grassy notes.
HopArt IPA is their other year-round beer, a well-balanced and citrusy India pale
ale that they have brewed from the beginning. Outside of those two, the brewery
produces a range of seasonals every year as well as the occasional one-off here and
there. The **Blackbeerd Imperial Stout** is one of the finest of the style, with notes

of molasses, espresso, and bitter dark chocolate. It comes in at 9.3 percent ABV, but it is so smooth you would never guess it.

One of the things Jaime and David are most proud of is their commitment to using organic ingredients exclusively. They also run their brewhouse off of waste feedstock biodiesel, and take great pains to reduce their own waste whenever possible.

FREEHOUSE BREWERY

2895 Pringle St., Ste. B, Charleston, SC 29405; FreehouseBrewery.com
Founded: 2013 **Founder:** Arthur Lucas **Brewers:** Arthur Lucas, Devon Hamilton
Flagship Beer: Ashley Farmhouse Ale **Year-Round Beers:** Ashley Farmhouse Ale, Green Door IPA, Bridgetown Stout **Seasonals/Special Releases:** Forgotten Port Strong Brown, Lucky Oyster Stout **Tours:** N/A **Taproom:** Thurs through Fri, 3:30 to 6:30 p.m.; Sat, 1 to 5 p.m.

Arthur Lucas was "across the pond" when he first became intrigued by the pub scene. In the UK, a pub that was required to sell a certain amount of a brewery's beers—thus limiting their available selection—was called a tied house. A pub that

Ashley Farmhouse Ale

Style: Saison

ABV: 5.4 percent

Availability: On tap year-round

Farmhouse ales and saisons are among Arthur's favorite styles, and it shows in the Ashley Farmhouse Ale. This one manages to be both refreshing and complex, with bright bursts of lemon and a rye-like spiciness on the backend.

maintained full control of their selection and sold whatever they wanted without getting involved with the breweries was called a free house.

So it was then that Arthur, many years later, came to the name Freehouse Brewery. His location wasn't across the pond, mind you, but across the Ashley River—or at least right by it. The view is one of the most scenic of all the Charleston breweries. The taproom itself isn't quite as picturesque, and in truth it is more of a tasting bar with a deck than it is a true taproom. The majority of the building is dominated by the 15-barrel brewhouse and a handful of fermenters. For Arthur, it's all about the beer.

Of course, someone operating a free house would stay true to his own vision. Arthur's vision is a portfolio of sessionable beers crafted from organic ingredients. The **Green Door IPA,** for example, uses hops from an organic hop farmer co-op in Oregon. It is more expensive and far more work to use organic ingredients (especially hops), but it is something Arthur feels passionately about. Freehouse Brewery's **Bridgetown Stout,** named for the capital of Barbados, is unique in that it is a tropical stout. Tropical stouts are a subcategory of foreign extra stouts, and they typically exhibit more fruity esters than the latter. Freehouse's derives these from the use of a Belgian yeast, and these notes work very well in conjunction with the beer's subtle roast and sweetness. You might not be able to enjoy it in Barbados, but Freehouse Brewery's deck overlooking the Ashley River could be the next best thing.

THE FROTHY BEARD BREWING COMPANY

7358 B Peppermill Pkwy., North Charleston, SC 29418; (843) 793-2970; FrothyBeard.com; @FrothyBeard

Founded: 2013 **Founders:** Michael Biondi, Steve McCauley, Joseph Siconolfi **Brewers:** Michael Biondi, Steve McCauley, Joseph Siconolfi **Flagship Beer:** Photuris Pale Ale **Year-Round Beers:** Photuris Pale Ale, Never Winter Wheat **Seasonals/Special Releases:** Out at Third Tripel, Zingiber Pale Ale, Great White Wit, Smokey the Ambear, Peppermint Porter, Tides of Galway Irish Red, Boardslide Rye, Sergeant Sandias Surprise Watermelon Wheat, SIPA Sour IPA **Tours:** During open hours **Taproom:** Wed through Fri, 5 to 9 p.m.; Sat, 11 a.m. to 2 p.m.

Michael Biondi, Steve McCauley, and Joseph "Joey" Siconolfi have been homebrewing since 2006, and friends since well before that. The trio left upstate SC in 2008 for Charleston, where their shared home was soon overrun with homebrewing equipment, beers bubbling around every corner.

The three couldn't (responsibly) drink all of the beer they brewed, so they would host tasting parties that would draw as many as 100 people to their home. At these parties, they would pair six unique beers with six different foods, often prepared by

chefs working in Charleston's culinary scene. In addition to just being a great time, these tasting parties also helped the guys figure out which of their beers they would brew when they opened their own brewery, which they did in March of 2013.

Some of their homebrewing equipment made its way into the small, garage-like brewery and taproom in North Charleston, where it shares space with tables both picnic and Ping-Pong. They still use a few older chest freezers and a kegerator, and they upgraded to a 1.5-barrel system that makes them one of the state's smallest breweries. The smaller system allows the guys at Frothy Beard to brew a large variety of beers, just as they did in their homebrewing days.

The **Smokey the Ambear** is a summer seasonal brewed with a healthy portion of peat-smoked malt that lends a very distinct note of earthy smoke (and it's especially tasty served alongside some Carolina 'cue). A more approachable beer would be the **Never Winter Wheat,** a true-to-style wheat beer that is an ideal choice in a city that is usually warm enough to demand such styles. Of course, the name of that beer is just a little exaggerated, as cooler weather does creep into Charleston occasionally. When that happens, consider opting for the brewery's popular **Peppermint Porter.**

Beer Lover's Pick

Zingiber Pale Ale
Style: Pale ale
ABV: 5.3 percent
Availability: On-tap during the fall

Some of the hops in the Zingiber Pale Ale were pulled in favor of using three pounds of fresh ginger during the boil, resulting in a very aromatic and slightly spicy yet refreshing beer. The guys at Frothy Beard are no strangers to creating food-friendly beers, and this one would make a perfect pairing for sushi or other Asian cuisine.

HOLY CITY BREWING

4155 C Dorchester Rd., North Charleston, SC 29405; (843) 225-5623; HolyCityBrewing
.com; @HolyCityBrewing

Founded: 2011 **Founders:** Joel Carl, Sean Nemitz, Mac Minaudo, Chris Brown **Brewers:**
Chris Brown, Tim Bettencourt **Flagship Beer:** Pluff Mud Porter **Year-Round Beers:**
Pluff Mud Porter, Holy City Pilsner, Slanted Porch Pale Ale **Seasonals/Special Releases:**
Vienna Lager, Shiftee, Graveyard Shiftee, Pecan Dream, Bowens Island Oyster Stout,
Lowcountry Dark Ale, Smoked Märzen, Collision Stout, Washout Wheat, Fishbowl Series
Tours: Throughout taproom hours **Taproom:** Mon and Tue, 4 to 6 p.m.; Wed through Fri,
3 to 8 p.m.; Sat 12 to 8 p.m.; Sun 12 to 4 p.m.

With its surreal, rust-colored mural of Charleston, Holy City Brewing stands
out like a sore thumb in an otherwise nondescript section of metal-skinned
warehouse space. The 4,000-square-foot building was originally purchased by Mac
Minaudo, who had planned to use it to start up a biodiesel refining business, as
that's what he was doing in Asheville before moving to Charleston.

Pluff Mud Porter

Style: American porter

ABV: 5.5 percent

Availability: On tap and in bottles year-round

Just around a year after they had opened, Holy City Brewing received a gold medal in the brown porter category at the 2012 Great American Beer Festival for their Pluff Mud Porter. It is a smooth, medium-bodied beer with notes of chocolate and coffee that prove refreshing even in the sometime sweltering clime of Charleston. The dry finish and low ABV invite a second pint. The base Pluff Mud is available all year, but also keep an eye out for limited batches like the Baltic version or Notorious PIG, which is Pluff Mud brewed with forty pounds of bacon and wood chips that have been soaked in the bacon grease.

He decided to let his three friends use a quarter of that space to start a small brewery. Chris Brown had worked as a brewer at Gordon Biersch in Atlanta, and Joel Carl and Sean Nemitz had been operating a Charleston rickshaw company and homebrewing when they weren't pedaling around town (for more rickshaw and beer parallels, see the section on Crank Arm Brewing, p. 137). Those two were willing to leave their jobs for the brewery, and in the end the same was true for Mac—he scrubbed the biodiesel plans and partnered with his three friends to open Holy City Brewing in July of 2011.

The brewery has brewed a wide variety of beers in the years since, including a few year-round beers and lots of seasonals and one-offs. During his time at Gordon Biersch, Chris learned what it takes to craft fine examples of German styles, and you will see his own take on some of those at Holy City. The **Smoked Märzen,** with its perfect balance of sweet and smokey flavors, is not unlike those famed beers of Bamberg. The **Holy City Pilsner** is dry and crisp with just a bit of biscuit to it; it is hopped with traditional German Magnum, Hallertau, and Mittelfrüh varities, but more abundantly than most Bohemian pilsners.

Make no mistake, though—Holy City is not bound by any one culture's styles or brewing philosophy. Their **Pecan Dream,** a brown ale brewed with 150 pounds of home-roasted pecans, surely wouldn't fly with the *Reinheitsgebot*. The **Washout Wheat** would, on the other hand, since it relies solely on hefeweizen yeast to impart notes of banana and clove.

PALMETTO BREWING COMPANY

289 Huger St., Charleston, SC 29403; (843) 937-0903; PalmettoBrewingCo.com; @PalmettoBrewing
Founded: 1994 **Founders:** Ed Falkenstein, Louis Bruce **Brewer:** Ed Falkenstein
Flagship Beer: Amber **Year-Round Beers:** Amber, Pale Ale, Charleston Lager, Espresso Porter **Seasonals/Special Releases:** Aftershock, A.M. Wood, Ghost Rider, Hop Harvest IPA, Ginger Slap, Chocolate Bock, Watermelon Wheat **Tours:** Check website **Taproom:** Check website

Just off I-26, sandwiched between two buildings, is Charleston's oldest brewery. Not only does it predate Charleston's current crop of brewers, but the name was used by Palmetto Brewery long before Prohibition closed their doors. The name was resurrected in 1994 by Ed Falkenstein and Louis Bruce, two longtime friends whose shared interest in windsurfing carried them west on a trip from Charleston to Oregon. There, they visited Full Sail Brewery and wondered why Charleston didn't have a brewery producing such flavorful beers. Soon, they would open South Carolina's first production brewery since prohibition.

The first beer Palmetto brewed was their **Amber,** a malty sweet lager with subtle enough hints of toffee and caramel that it could serve as an appropriate gateway to those new to craft beer (as many were in the early '90s). The **Charleston Lager** is equally approachable, a Czech pilsner with a light breadiness and just a hint of spicy hops. Palmetto has brewed a porter for quite some time, but when they started adding cold-brewed coffee from their next-door neighbors at Charleston Coffee Roasters, the **Espresso Porter** was born. It has a smooth coffee flavor with a prominent roastiness and some chocolate notes to round off those sharp edges.

Until the state's pint bill passed in 2013, Palmetto Brewing Company had focused almost exclusively on satisfying their many accounts around Charleston, and the taproom itself was an afterthought. When the pint bill allowed drinkers to

enjoy beers at the brewery, however, they began to turn their space into one beer lovers could visit for beers, rather than simply for tours during odd hours. They have transformed what used to be a loading space in front of the brewery into a nice courtyard with a brightly colored mural painted across the wall they share with the coffee company. Inside they have a taproom, with painted palm fronds serving as tap handles and historical paintings and drawings of the old Palmetto Brewery gracing the walls.

Aftershock
Style: California common
ABV: 5.8 percent
Availability: Seasonal

After a devastating earthquake hit Charleston in 1886, the original Palmetto Brewery brewed its take on a California common—a beer fermented with a lager yeast, but at temperatures normally better suited for ales. Today's Palmetto Brewing Company brewed a dry-hopped California common in 2011 for the 125th anniversary of the earthquake. The beer and the concept itself were so popular, that the brewery now brings it back each year. It exhibits a malty sweetness and some citrus notes from Columbus hops (Zythos and Northern Brewer are used as well).

WESTBROOK BREWING CO.

510 Ridge Rd., Mount Pleasant, SC 29464; (843) 654-9112; WestbrookBrewing.com; @WestbrookBeer

Founded: 2011 **Founders:** Edward and Morgan Westbrook **Brewers:** Edward Westbrook, Scott Koon, Shane Cummings **Flagship Beer:** India Pale Ale **Year-Round Beers:** India Pale Ale, White Thai, One Claw Rye Pale Ale **Seasonals/Special Releases:** Mexican Cake, Dark Helmet Schwarzbier, Gose, Grätzer, Citrus Ninja Exchange, Weisse Weisse Baby, The Raver, Udderly Milk Stout, Bearded Farmer Series, Old Time Series **Tours:** Usually on the hour **Taproom:** Thur and Fri, 4 to 7 p.m.; Sat, 12 to 4 p.m.

Edward Westbrook was a computer science major at Furman University, but his real passion was brewing beer. After graduating, he pursued an MBA from Clemson University with the intention of opening his own brewery, and he and his wife Morgan made that dream a reality in 2011. An expansive two-story building

with beautiful stonework and brown brick marks Westbrook's brewery in Mount Pleasant, SC. A tan grain silo towers above the well-landscaped area just in front of the brewery.

Through its doors is a clean and modern tasting room with beige wood all around, an oval-shaped bar in the middle and a sign with the brewery's "W" logo hanging above it. Here you can enjoy Westbrook's three year-round beers as well as a variety of seasonals, by the glass or a flight of four. Westbrook's **White Thai** offers an interesting spin on the witbier style, using fresh lemongrass, ginger, and Sorachi Ace hops in lieu of the typical coriander and orange peel. The result is a beer that is refreshing on hot days and friendly with Asian cuisine. It, along with the brewery's **IPA,** have been popular since day one, and you can find these two in cans across South Carolina (the **One Claw Rye Pale Ale** later joined these two in cans as a year-round beer). It is also a certainty that the tasting room will feature a few of the brewery's seasonals. Their **Gose,** a German-style sour wheat beer brewed with

Mexican Cake
Style: Imperial stout
ABV: 10.5 percent
Availability: Seasonal

To celebrate their first year in business, Westbrook brewed a 10.5 percent imperial stout and aged it on vanilla beans, cocoa nibs, cinnamon sticks, and habanero peppers. That may sound like a bit much, but all of those ingredients combine to create a delicious interplay of sweet and spice. The cinnamon and habanero do not overpower, but instead provide just enough kick on the finish to satisfy chile lovers and provide some warmth on a cold winter's night. The beer was so wildly successful when it was released in January of 2012, that it is now a yearly release. If you find it on shelves or on tap, grab it as it doesn't last long. Rarer still are the versions of Mexican Cake that have spent time in whiskey, wine, or brandy barrels.

salt and coriander, has developed a cultlike following among many. It is another one that found its way into aluminum. And speaking of aluminum, you are likely to see cans stacked high in the brewery just past the tasting room, where Edward brews on a 30-barrel system. There is a climate-controlled barrel room that Westbrook uses to house a variety of beers aging in barrels that once held bourbon, whiskey, wine, rum, and brandy. Westbrook also allows the gypsy brewery known as Evil Twin Brewing to brew several beers there, and you can also find these in the tasting room.

Brewpubs

OAK BARREL TAVERN

825B Savannah Hwy., Charleston, SC 29407; (843) 901-7251; @OakBarrelTavern
Founded: 2011 **Founders:** Andy Cope, Gavin Lyons **Brewers:** Akai Antia-obong, Lake High **Flagship Beer:** N/A **Year-Round Beers:** N/A **Seasonals/Special Releases:** Chocolate Milk Oatmeal Stout, Sour Pilsner, Three Sisters Pepper IPA, Sour Pepper Amber Ale, Fire on the Mountain Porter, Kitchen Sink IPA, Downtown Brown, #5 Oak Barrel Porter, Bottle Rocket Brown Pepper, Avondale Amber **Tours:** No **Taproom:** Mon through Sun, 3 p.m. to 2 a.m.

The Oak Barrel Tavern isn't quite a brewery, brewpub or beer bar—the three sections used in this book—and yet it has aspects of all three. There is no real brewhouse, but rather a small homebrew-like setup that the brewers take out back to craft some really unique beers. You can usually find a couple of house beers on, with the rest of the taps often filled with beers from other Charleston or South Carolina breweries. There is no kitchen so it's not technically a brewpub, however a sushi chef can be found rolling at the dimly lit bar several nights a week (when he's not in, you can still purchase fresh, pre-rolled sushi).

The bar is a local favorite in the hip Avondale neighborhood. Oak Barrel Tavern is worth a stop for their small but well-curated taplist and low-key ambience—the occasional house beer is just a bonus. Fans of chile beers might especially enjoy stopping by, as many of Oak Barrel's house beers feature peppers.

SOUTHEND BREWERY & SMOKEHOUSE

161 E. Bay St., Charleston, SC 29401; (843) 853-4677; SouthendBrewery.com; @SouthendBrewery
Founded: 1996 **Founder:** Joe Ryan **Brewers:** Ahren Warf, Matt Zeleniak **Flagship Beer:** Love Me Two Times Blonde **Year-Round Beers:** Love Me Two Times Blonde, Castle Pinckney Pale Ale, Watch It Grow Wheat, Riptide Red, Pict's Stout **Seasonals/Special Releases:** Pumpkin Ale, Juniper Rye IPA

Charleston's Southend Brewery & Smokehouse is the last of a chain of brewpubs that originated in Charlotte, NC's Southend neighborhood. The Charlotte location opened in 1995, and the Charleston brewpub the year following. The historic three-story building it calls home, however, dates back to the 1880s. All three of its stories feature more window than wall, providing a great view of the busy East Bay

Street below. This is especially true of the topmost floor, where the Harborview bar makes for a great vantage point of the city.

The brewhouse is located right in the center of the building, and the glass walls that surround it stretch from the first floor to the third. Beside it, a glass-encased elevator transports patrons to the floor of their choice. The brewery's flag-ship is the **Love Me Two Times Blonde,** a light-bodied beer with hints of honey and sweet malt. **Pict's Stout** is a rich, smooth stout that balances roasted coffee and sweet chocolate flavors well—but if it's not sweet enough, consider the Pict's Stout Brownie, which works that beer into a mixture of peanut brittle, caramel sauce and vanilla ice cream. The **Riptide Red Ale** is a great example of its style, with notes of toffee, caramel and just a bit of roast. Of the brewpub's year-round beers, it's perhaps the most versatile option to pair with the food. Popular menu items include the smoked chicken wings, barbecue, and shrimp 'n grits.

Like so many other old buildings in the Charleston area, many claim that Southend's location is haunted. Check out their website or ask a server about the grisly story—just make sure to do it after you've eaten!

Beer Bars

CLOSED FOR BUSINESS

453 King St., Charleston, SC 29403; (843) 853-8466; Closed4Business.com; @ClosedforBiz
Draft Beers: 42 **Bottled/Canned Beers:** 50

Even if they didn't have such a great selection of craft beer, Closed for Business would be worth stopping in just to get a glimpse of the bar's eclectic and funky decor. The wood-planked walls are covered in framed prints and paintings, and shelves behind the bar are filled with all kinds of quirky knickknacks. Leather chairs surround a fireplace filled with lights that alternate so as to mimic a fire's flicker. A stuffed deer head stands sentinel over all. It's hard to tell if you're in a beer bar or a Wes Anderson movie.

Fortunately, the 42 taps behind the bar are a quick reminder. The draft list is broken down into the following sections: light, white/fruit/farmhouse, pale, amber/brown, and dark. Closed for Business does a good job of working in North and South Carolina beers across all of those categories, with an admirable selection of

some of the nation's best craft beers. You can order any of these beers as 10-ounce, 16-ounce, or liter pours.

The bar has a lunch and dinner menu filled with artfully prepared takes on pub fare and Southern cuisine. Appetizers include popular options like crispy green beans with ranch dressing and fries with gravy and cheese, while sandwiches like the Pork Slap—built with fried pork cutlet, house-smoked ham, swiss cheese, green tomato chutney, and house sauce—offer a little more sustenance. Closed for Business also offers brunch on Sunday.

COLEMAN PUBLIC HOUSE

427 West Coleman Blvd., Mount Pleasant, SC 29464; (843) 416-8833; ColemanPublicHouse .com
Draft Beers: 16 **Bottled/Canned Beers:** 25+

Coleman Public House is a Mount Pleasant institution for many beer lovers. Modeled after a "European public house with a coastal twist," Coleman has a relatively small, glossy wooden bar with two TVs and 16 taps behind it. These taps rotate between Belgian and American craft beers, with plenty of local beers finding their way into the mix as well. A large chalkboard hangs on one of the aquamarine-colored walls and shows which 16 beers are on tap.

Coleman has a really great lunch and dinner menu, and they also do brunch on the weekend. The fish-'n-chips and shrimp-'n-grits are popular options, but the restaurant is really best known for its half-pound, 100-percent Angus beef burgers. The Southern Burger is an excellent choice, and it features pepperjack cheese, fried green tomatoes, and a spicy remoulade. All of the burgers are served with your choice of truffle and Parmesan or garlic french fries.

CRAFTSMEN KITCHEN & TAPHOUSE

12 Cumberland St., Charleston, SC 29401; (843) 577-9699; CraftsmenTaphouse.com; @CraftsmenTap
Draft Beers: 48 **Bottled/Canned Beers:** 25+

A copper-backed bar with a dozen taps greets patrons upon walking into the Craftsmen Kitchen & Taphouse. This first room is "The Pale Room," and it features pale ales and India pale ales on tap almost exclusively. Farther back in the restaurant's "middle room" is another copper-backed bar, this one boasting 36 more taps. Contrasting with the copper is lots of white weathered brick, dark rafters stretching above it all. One of Craftsmen's best spots to enjoy a beer, though, is just

outside that bar in a small, outdoor beer garden, complete with German-style tables and hanging lights.

Their name is appropriate: from the first room to the beer garden in the back, the Craftsmen Kitchen & Taphouse is a beautiful space that is itself crafted with as much care as its beer and food menus. In selecting from the well-curated taplist, you can choose to enjoy pints, half pints, and flights. Often Chef Todd Garrigan will work the Craftsmen's beers into the food menu, which features inventive twists on bar classics and daily features that always offer something new and exciting. The Farmhouse Burger is made from a blend of beer and pork, then topped with beer pickles and Idiazabal cheese. One of the most popular dishes is the Crunchy Dame, a name that calls to mind the *croque madame*. Craftsmen's begins with a pork belly that's been braised in stout and sandwiched between bread with raclette cheese. Spread on top of this is cherry jam and an egg served sunny-side up.

HOMEGROWN BREWHOUSE

117 S. Main St., Summerville, SC 29483; (843) 873-4237; HomegrownBrewhouse.com;
@HGBrewhouse
Draft Beers: 40 **Bottled/Canned Beers:** 30+

Homegrown Brewhouse in Summerville, SC, has a lofty goal: to have every South Carolina brewery represented at their bar. While they are not quite there yet, they aren't far off, either. Perhaps more than any other bar in the state, Homegrown Brewhouse is fiercely dedicated in its support of South Carolina's breweries.

Given that the bar is only half an hour outside of Charleston, it's not surprising to see taps dedicated to breweries like Holy City and Westbrook. Where other bars might be tempted to just have one tap for each brewery, though, Homegrown usually provides several. You can purchase beer by the 4-ounce sample, the 12-ounce pour or the 64-ounce growler. If you want to try a wide variety of SC beer in one spot, this is your bar.

HOUSE OF BREWS
1537-C Ben Sawyer Blvd., Mount Pleasant, SC 29464; (843) 416-8094
Draft Beers: 8 **Bottled/Canned Beers:** 600+

House of Brews is nothing if not aptly named: This is a house filled with beer. In rooms that at one point must have held furniture, shelves upon shelves of beer now stand. One room is devoted to new-world beers (mostly American), while another is devoted to old world (think Belgians). Since they are stored warm, these are often purchased to take home; however they will gladly chill them for you if you wish to hang around the house, as so many do. You can also drink in the fenced-in yard, where House of Brews hosts open mic nights every Friday and Saturday. There are plenty of tables and chairs outside.

There is a cooler full of cold beers for those who wish to have a beer there, and there are also eight taps that change pretty frequently. To the delight of beer geeks, limited beers often pop up on tap and in bottles. You would never know it looking at it from the outside, but House of Brews is one of the best craft beer bars in the Mount Pleasant area.

Pub Crawl

Charleston

This pub crawl has one less stop than the others in this book, but if ever there was a city in which to adopt a more leisurely pace it is Charleston. Take your time, enjoy some great beers and admire the old architecture as you crawl through a city rich with history. And if you do end up needing one more bar after this crawl is over, you won't have to look very far in the Holy City.

Craftsmen Kitchen & Taphouse, 12 Cumberland St., Charleston, SC 29401; (843) 577-9699; CraftsmenTaphouse.com. Craftsmen Kitchen & Taphouse is one of Charleston's newest beer bars. The small room you enter first is known as "The Pale Room," and here pale ales and India pale ales are served exclusively. If that's your thing, you have reached your destination (for now). If not, move into the next room, which is larger and home to 36 more taps. Craftsmen is a gastropub in the truest sense of the word, and if you are hungry you should check out the daily features menu. The bar has a small beer garden with authentic German-style tables in the back, which makes a great spot to have a beer.

Leave Craftsmen and take a right on East Bay Street. After about a tenth of a mile, you will see Southend Brewery & Smokehouse on your right.

Southend Brewery & Smokehouse, 161 East Bay St., Charleston, SC 29401; (843) 853-4677; SouthendBrewery.com. Charleston's Southend Brewery and Smokehouse is a great spot to try a flight of beers and have some food if you didn't eat at Craftsmen Kitchen & Taphouse. Upon walking in, head to the glass-encased elevator and ride up to the brewery's Harborview bar, where you can take in a nice view of Charleston. There is a bar on the first floor as well, and of course plenty of places at which to sit and eat.

Walk out of Southend Brewery & Smokehouse and keep straight so as to get on Vendue Range Street. Take this about 300 feet until you see The Griffon on your left.

The Griffon, 18 Vendue Range St., Charleston, SC 29401; (843) 723-1700; GriffonCharleston.com. The Griffon is an English-style pub located on Vendue Range Street just off Charleston Harbor. Thousands of dollars went into decorating this dive-ish bar—no seriously, thousands of dollars blanket the walls, most of which have notes scrawled on them in marker. Ask the bartender for a marker to add your own, and choose from 16 drafts that usually include lots of North and South Carolina options.

Here is where the book's Charleston pub crawl ends, but the Holy City has a vibrant nightlife. The three bars listed above are the best craft options in the immediate area, but there is no shortage of other bars around them. The Griffon is right by Charleston Harbor, so don't miss a walk out on the pier afterwards.

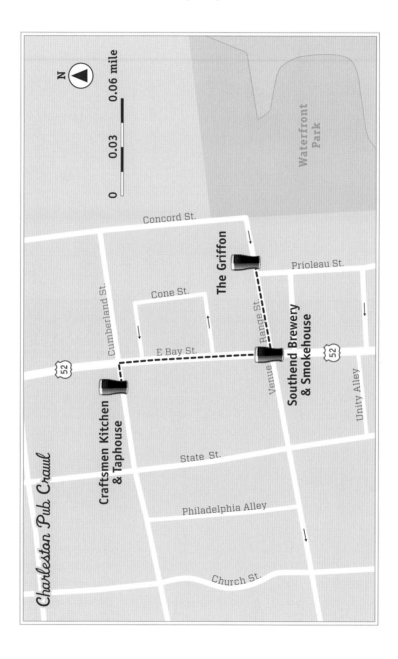

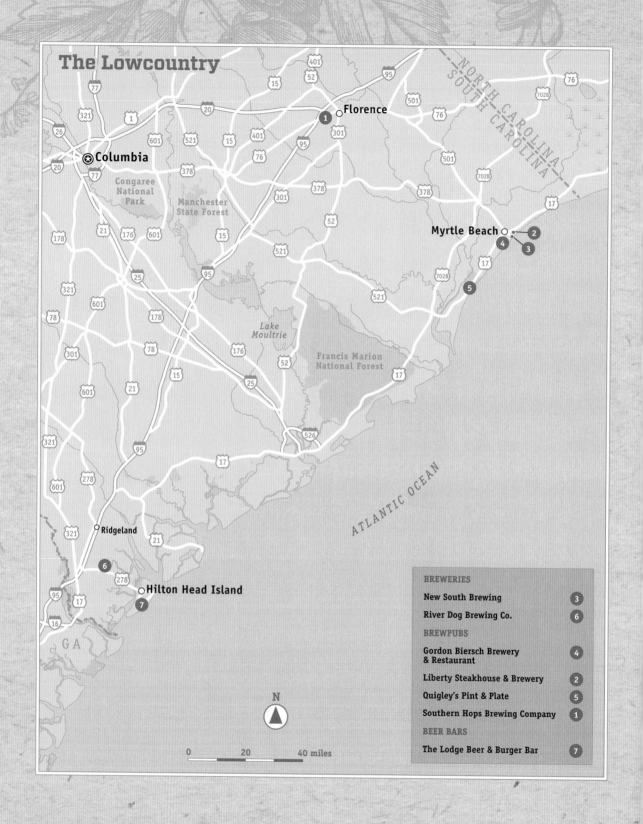

The Lowcountry

NORTH CAROLINA
SOUTH CAROLINA

Florence ● 1

Columbia ◎

Congaree
National
Park

Manchester
State Forest

Myrtle Beach ○ ● 2
● 4
● 3

● 5

Lake
Moultrie

Francis Marion
National Forest

ATLANTIC OCEAN

Ridgeland ○

● 6

GA

Hilton Head Island ●
● 7

N

0   20   40 miles

The Lowcountry

While Charleston gets some much-deserved attention for its beer scene, there is more beer to be found throughout the rest of South Carolina's Lowcountry. To the north there is Myrtle Beach, a longtime vacation spot for many that is also home to New South Brewing and two brewpubs in Gordon Biersch and Liberty Steakhouse & Brewery. Pawleys Island is another coastal town with a wonderful brewpub in Quigley's Pint & Plate, and you have only to go inland a bit to find breweries in Ridgeland and Florence.

Breweries

NEW SOUTH BREWING

1109 Campbell St., Myrtle Beach, SC 29577; (843) 916-2337; NewSouthBrewing.com; @NewSouthBrewing

Founded: 1998 **Founder:** David Epstein **Brewers:** David Epstein, Brock Kurtzman **Flagship Beer:** White Ale **Year-Round Beers:** White Ale, Nut Brown Ale **Seasonals/Special Releases:** Lager, Dry-Hopped Lager, India Pale Ale, Oktoberfest, Dark Star Porter, Stout, Lily the Great **Tours:** Tues and Thurs, 3 p.m. **Taproom:** Tues, Thurs, and Fri, 4:30 to 7 p.m.

South Carolina beer lovers—especially those on the coast—were no doubt thankful when David Epstein opened New South Brewing in Myrtle Beach on Thanksgiving Day in 1998. One of the state's oldest breweries, New South distributed its beers in area restaurants and bars for the first ten years of its existence. In 2009, they began canning their flagship **White Ale.** The **Nut Brown Ale,** an English-style brown with notes of dark malt and toffee, found its way into aluminum shortly thereafter.

New South White Ale

Style: White ale

ABV: 4.6 percent

Availability: Year-round on tap and in cans

New South's White Ale is an American take on the Belgian witbier style. It is brewed with coriander and orange peel, yet fermented with a cleaner American yeast instead of the fruitier Belgian strain. Though the Belgian yeast is a natural complement to those spices, its absence allows them to shine through all the more. New South's White Ale is available in cans and comes in at only 4.6 percent ABV, making it an ideal beach beer.

As more brewery-friendly legislation has passed over the years, New South has responded in turn. When the pint bill passed in 2013 and turned breweries into the destinations they deserve to be, the brewery started to get a little more inventive with their styles and renovated the taproom. Prior to its passage, you could only visit the brewery for tours and samples, but you couldn't enjoy a full pint. Fortunately the tours are highly entertaining and educational—so much so that TripAdvisor named them one of the top 10 brewery tours in America. It is an interactive tour, where visitors are invited up the brewhouse's steps to smell the kettle and see how the entire process would work, from grain to glass.

While the White Ale and Nut Brown Ale are usually the only beers you will find out in the market, you can try a host of beers at the brewery, which is located in an industrial area. The **Dark Star Porter** has minimal roast and a nice espresso-like quality to it. Oftentimes the brewery will age this one in bourbon barrels, adding another layer of decadence to an already great beer. One of the brewery's most popular seasonals is their **Oktoberfest,** which lands in the maltier range of Märzens.

Lily the Great, a big, boozy imperial stout that clocks in at 11.3 percent ABV, was brewed to celebrate the first birthday of head brewer Brock Kurtzman's daughter. The brewery also contract brews a **Red Ale** for the Tbonz Gill & Grill steakhouse chain, which can only be found at those locations and at the brewery.

New South's taproom has been a Myrtle Beach destination for many years, with David Epstein serving as head brewer since day one. Whether you're staying at the beach while on vacation or you're a Myrtle resident, you owe it to yourself to stray a few miles from the beach for a well-crafted pint.

RIVER DOG BREWING CO.

591 Browns Cove Rd., Ste. H, Ridgeland, SC 29936; RiverDogBrewing.com; @RiverDogBrew **Founded:** 2013 **Founders:** James Brown, Josh Luman **Brewers:** James Brown, Dan Baker **Flagship Beer:** River Dog IPA **Year-Round Beers:** River Dog IPA, Carolina Gold, Chocolate Rye Porter, Coastal Wit, American Pale Ale, Galaxy Quest **Seasonals/Special Releases:** Juniper Ale, Cascadian IPA, Belgian Quad, Kölsch, Maker's Mark Barrel-Aged Red Ale, Sinister Stache **Tours:** No **Taproom:** Weds through Fri, 3 to 8 p.m.; Sat, 12 to 8 p.m.

Josh Luman's entry into the beer world came through wine. He and his wife founded the Corks wine bars in Hilton Head and Bluffton where, in addition to wine, one can also find a good selection of craft beers. A local homebrew club called Lowcountry MALTS started holding meetings at Corks, and it wasn't long before James Brown—one of the club's founders—impressed Josh with his knowledge of beer as well as his ability to brew it. They soon decided to become partners in starting a brewery.

While they initially looked at some high traffic areas in Bluffton, they ultimately ended up moving into the Riverwalk Business Park in Ridgeland, just off SC 170. They have ambitious plans of getting their beer in many other markets, and location itself wasn't as important to them as space. Their 10,000-square-foot warehouse has plenty of it. They do have a small taproom overlooking the 15-barrel brewhouse and the many fermenting tanks, though, and this space is becoming more and more popular with locals as well as those passing through. In its short history, the brewery has already brought in additional fermenting tanks to keep up with demand.

You can find River Dog Brewing's beers all across South Carolina and in some Georgia bars (they are located only half an hour north of Savannah). The brewery puts out five year-round beers and brews a host of seasonals as well. Many of their beers are inspired by the Lowcountry, such as the **Coastal Wit,** an ideal beer for those sultry summer days. It is an American take on the Belgian witbier style, combining chamomile and rose petals with the more standard coriander and orange peel. The **Carolina Gold,** inspired by the rice of the same name, offers a fresh and

decidedly Southern take on the cream ale style, which is often brewed with adjuncts like rice and grits. As the brewery grows, keep an eye out for its barrel-aging program and look for them to continue spreading throughout South Carolina.

Beer Lover's Pick

Chocolate Rye Porter
Style: Porter
ABV: 6.5 percent
Availability: On tap year-round
River Dog's Chocolate Rye Porter is a robust beer filled with roasted coffee and bitter dark chocolate notes. The rye half of the beer is far more subtle when compared to those bold flavors, contributing just a bit of pepper.

Brewpubs

GORDON BIERSCH BREWERY & RESTAURANT

3060 Howard Ave., Myrtle Beach, SC 29577; (843) 839-0249; GordonBiersch.com
Founded: 2008 **Founders:** Dan Gordon, Dean Biersch **Brewer:** Michael Grossman
Flagship Beer: Märzen **Year-Round Beers:** Märzen, Golden Export, Czech Pilsner, Hefeweizen, Schwarzbier **Seasonals/Special Releases:** Blonde Bock, Maibock, Summerbrau, Festbier, WinterBock

Gordon Biersch Brewery & Restaurant is the brainchild of Dan Gordon and Dean Biersch, who opened the first of their brewpubs in 1988. More than 30 additional brewpubs would open in the years since, with the Myrtle Beach location opening in the Market Common shopping center in 2008. The look of the brewpub is decidedly modern and clean, a large space filled with booths and tables. A long bar stretches along one of the perimeters, and behind it roll-up windows open to the outside patio, which is a great spot to sit and have beers and food when the weather is nice (and it quite often is at Myrtle Beach).

The brewpub's 15-barrel brewhouse and 30-barrel fermenters are located in a far corner, surrounded by glass. It is here that head brewer Michael Grossman crafts the year-round German styles that are so popular, as well as a host of seasonal and "Brewer's Select" offerings. All of these beers are brewed in adherence with the German Purity Law or *Reinheitsgebot,* which states that beer must be brewed with four ingredients and only four ingredients: malted barley, hops, water, and yeast. The brewpub's **Märzen** is the Myrtle Beach location's most popular beer, followed closely by the lighter **Golden Export**. The **Schwarzbier** is a black lager that is both their darkest beer and yet lightest in alcohol, defying the myth that all dark beers must be heavy and thick. It drinks dryly, with subtle notes of coffee and dark bread.

Almost all of the brewpub's beers are lagered as well, resulting in a crisp, clean character that leaves you craving another sip. Even the **Summerbrau,** which is a kölsch-style beer brewed with an ale yeast, spends weeks lagering in the cold. It's a popular seasonal, as is the **Festbier,** an amber lager with a malty sweetness that's perfect for the fall. All of the beers are food-friendly and pair well with many menu items. Burgers, nachos, and tacos are all popular choices—just make sure you have the legendary garlic fries.

LIBERTY STEAKHOUSE & BREWERY

1321 Celebrity Circle, Myrtle Beach, SC 29577; (843) 626-4677;
LibertySteakhouseandBrewery.com
Founded: 1995 **Founder:** Homegrown Hospitality Group **Brewer:** Mike Silvernale
Flagship Beer: Liberty Lager **Year-Round Beers:** Liberty Lager, White Ale, Raspberry Wheat, Honest I.P.Abe, Broadway Brown Ale **Seasonals/Special Releases:** Golden Ale, Rocket's Red Ale, Coffee Porter, Irish Stout, Hefeweizen, Santa's Little Helper

Broadway at the Beach is a sprawling center of restaurants, bars, shops, and other tourist attractions, most of them done up in the same over-the-top cheesiness one would expect at Myrtle Beach. There is much to see, including Ripley's Aquarium, Hard Rock Cafe's pyramid, Planet Hollywood's big blue globe and the upside-down WonderWorks building. Most restaurants and shops have a theme here, and such is the case with the Liberty Steakhouse & Brewery.

The decor of Liberty is mild and more restrained when compared with the rest of Broadway at the Beach. Lady Liberty herself sits atop the entrance, beckoning

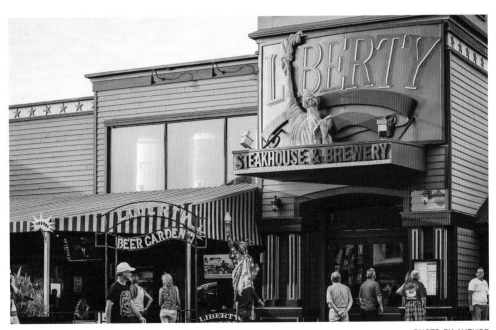

PHOTO BY AUTHOR

the poor, tired and huddled masses, yearning for a beer and some food. Underneath her and beside the tourist-filled streets is a covered beer garden. The back of the restaurant provides a great view of Lake Broadway.

The brewhouse is visible from behind glass as soon as you walk in. It is here that head brewer Mike Silvernale crafts a variety of styles for the brewpub. Given the area, it is not surprising that the approachable **Liberty Lager** is the most popular option. It is light bodied with the mildest bit of sweetness from the malt, and very little perceived bitterness. The **Raspberry Wheat,** brewed with over 80 pounds of fresh raspberries, is a tart and refreshing wheat beer that hits the spot on hot Myrtle Beach days. In addition to those (and other) year-round beers, Liberty taps a variety of seasonal and brewmaster special offerings. The food is what you might expect for a combination steakhouse and brewery, with several specialty steaks as well as burgers, pizzas, sandwiches and wraps, and the restaurant's happy hour offers great deals on food and beer alike.

QUIGLEY'S PINT & PLATE

257 County Rd. S-22-362, Pawleys Island, SC 29585; (843) 237-7010; PintandPlate.com
Founded: 2007 **Founders:** Josh Quigley, Michael Benson **Brewer:** Josh Quigley
Flagship Beer: Longboard Lager **Year-Round Beers:** Longboard Lager, Shakedown
Wheat, Peach Wheat, Neck Red Ale, Swamp Fox IPA, Nut Brown Ale **Seasonals/Special
Releases:** Billy Bock, Summer Pilsner, Rye Ale, Irish Stout

Chipping distance from a golf course, in a center of businesses all topped with the tin roofs usually reserved for beach houses, sits Quigley's Pint and Plate. Behind Quigley's is a patio that overlooks a pond and fountain, making for a scenic spot in which to have a beer.

The brewpub's founder and namesake, Josh Quigley, opened the Pawleys Island establishment in 2007. He is a veteran of the South Carolina beer scene, having worked at the now-closed Vista Brewing in Columbia, as well as Aiken Brewing and Liberty Steakhouse and Brewery in Myrtle Beach. At Quigley's, he serves a variety of styles, most of which are lighter beers that fit the coastal climate. The **Longboard Lager** is such a beer, having a soft touch of maltiness and a clean, crisp finish. Josh brews a handful of wheat beers, especially in the summer months. There's the standard **Shakedown Wheat,** a refreshing American take on the style. Fans of fruit beers will appreciate the **Peach Wheat,** which features one of South Carolina's most popular fruits in abundance.

The brewpub's food menu is substantial, with a range of sandwiches and inventive takes on Southern classics. Take the fried green tomatoes, for instance. Yes,

they are indeed battered and fried like most, but then they are topped with goat cheese, blackened shrimp, and a Thai chile glaze. If you want a smattering of things that would go well with a flight of the brewpub's beers, opt for the Plowman's Platter, which includes a variety of meats, cheeses, pickled okra, apple wedges, a hard-boiled egg, and a pretzel served with a beer mustard. No visit to Quigley's would be complete, however, without an order of fries and gravies. Hot, fresh fries come out with both redeye and mushroom gravy, and both are so good you'll start rethinking ketchup as the obligatory fry condiment of choice.

SOUTHERN HOPS BREWING COMPANY

911 S. Sunset Acres Dr., Florence, SC 29501; (843) 667-1900; SouthernHops.com
Founded: 2010 **Founders:** Jimmy Deaton, Christian Gibson **Brewer:** Jimmy Deaton
Flagship Beer: Goldilocks Golden Ale **Year-Round Beers:** Goldilocks Golden Ale, Pop's Pilsner, Leeroy Brown, Five Points IPA, Blackwater Porter **Seasonals/Special Releases:** Pecan Porter, Vanilla Porter

From the outside, Southern Hops Brewing Company looks like a Southern-style restaurant or steakhouse. The silo at the road and hop bines by the side of the building, however, should alert passersby that good beer is produced inside.

Founders Jimmy Deaton and Christian Gibson built Southern Hops Brewing Company on land that had been in Jimmy's family since the 1940s.

Wood and tin from an old barn were used to construct the porch out front. Hanging inside is a variety of lights, some from an old church, some from an old Thunderbird motel. Doorknobs from old country homes were installed underneath the bar, where they are now used as convenient purse hooks. Hanging from the ceiling are four door-sized sheets of wood, each painted with a scene representative of beer's four primary ingredients: barley, hops, water, and yeast. More than just pretty paintings, these also serve as acoustic aids for the bands that take the stage. Outside,

there is a beer garden of sorts with plenty of space to let kids roam around. Movies and football games are projected onto a fence, which makes for a fun experience.

On a seven-barrel system behind the bar, Jimmy—who worked at New South Brewing in Myrtle Beach and graduated from the American Brewers Guild in 2006—brews a handful of beers that make up the regular rotation. The most popular of the brewpub's beers is the **Goldilocks,** a light-bodied and slightly sweet golden ale that Jimmy uses as a gateway for those new to craft beer. The **Leeroy Brown** has the nutty and toffee flavors you expect from the style, with a bit more roast than is usual—but it works well with this beer.

The brewpub sources as much meat and produce from local farms as it can. They have even held beer dinners where farmers stand alongside the brewers and elaborate on their pairings. Looking at the menu, it might surprise you to know that there is not a single fryer in the building—everything is baked. Instead of sugar, a local honey is used in the dough to make pretzels, calzones, and pizzas. Popular examples of the latter include the Carolina BBQ Pizza and the Loaded Hoppin' Nacho Pizza.

Beer Bar

THE LODGE BEER & BURGER BAR

7B Greenwood Dr., #4, Hilton Head Island, SC 29928; (843) 842-8966; HiltonHeadLodge
.com; @LodgeHiltonHead
Draft Beers: 36 **Bottled/Canned Beers:** 100+

Hilton Head Island is one of South Carolina's most visited coastal towns, yet when you step into The Lodge Beer & Burger Bar you feel as if you are hundreds of miles west in the Appalachian mountains. The floors, walls, and ceiling are all covered in wood, and a thick slab of rough-cut lumber serves as the bar. Behind that bar are 36 taps fed through a beautiful wall of granite. The bar rotates its taps frequently, showing much love to South Carolina breweries like RJ Rockers, Westbrook Brewing, and River Dog Brewing, which is located about half an hour west in Ridgeland.

Chandeliers made from antlers cast their light from above. There are plenty of booths and tables (even of the shuffleboard and pool varieties). The menu at The Lodge is filled with sandwiches and burgers, and several of the dishes incorporate craft beer. The Stone'd Double Burger is topped with cheddar cheese, BBQ ranch, and onions that have been cooked with Stone Smoked Porter. The baby back ribs are also a popular option, and you can get them slathered with a Chocolate Stout BBQ sauce.

Beer Festivals

Short of visiting all of the breweries in this book—which I can assure you is a worthy yet daunting endeavor—the best way to try a wide variety of Carolina-brewed beer is to attend a beer festival. Winter, spring, summer, or fall, mountains, coast, or somewhere in between, there are plenty of beer festivals across the Carolinas.

January

ASHEVILLE WINTER WARMER BEER FESTIVAL

Asheville Civic Center, 87 Haywood St., Asheville, NC 28801; AshevilleBeerFest.com

The origins of Asheville's Winter Warmer Beer Festival date back to 2008, when Mark and Trish Lyons, owners of the Asheville Brews Cruise, decided the city needed a good winter festival to "shake off the winter blahs." The festival continues to grow, with more breweries and beer lovers attending every year. And each year, the festival features live music and donates a portion of its proceeds to charity. The brewery list primarily consists of local and regional breweries, though guest breweries like Founders Brewing or Cigar City have been featured in the past.

THE BIGGEST LITTLE BEER FEST

25 W. Washington St., Greenville, SC 29601; BarleysGville.com/Beerfest

The Biggest Little Beer Fest boasts more than 40 breweries pouring more than 100 beers between the three floors of The Trappe Door and Barley's Taproom. Local and national breweries are represented, with most bringing their more special or limited beers. Some beers are run through Randalls or served from a cask. And like many festivals, there is a VIP option that grants earlier entry and access to exclusive beers.

RALEIGH RARE AND VINTAGE BEER TASTING

Tyler's Taproom, 18 Seaboard Ave., Ste. 150, Raleigh, NC 27604; RaleighRareBeerTasting.com

The Raleigh Rare and Vintage Beer Tasting is an event you can feel good about attending. Not only can you enjoy close to 50 rare and vintage offerings from a variety of breweries in an intimate setting, but 100 percent of the event's proceeds go to non-profits. In 2013, the event raised almost $13,000 for Toxic Free NC and Pints for Prostates. There really isn't another festival like this in all of NC, and as a result tickets sell very quickly. Make sure to purchase yours as soon as they go on sale.

WORLD BEER FESTIVAL COLUMBIA

Columbia Convention Center, 1101 Lincoln St., Columbia, SC 29201; AllAboutBeer.com; @WorldBeerFest

Every January, beer lovers flock to the Columbia Convention Center to enjoy unlimited samples of local and national breweries. *All About Beer* magazine has been putting on the World Beer Festival for decades, and in addition to this event they also host festivals in Durham and Raleigh.

The chance to try hundreds of beers in a single venue is the main draw, of course, but the festival also features educational seminars and classes. The VIP ticket option grants attendees more limited beers, an exclusive buffet, and access to a private bathroom.

February

CHARLESTON BREWVIVAL

COAST Brewing, 1250 N. 2nd St., North Charleston, SC 29405; Brewvival.com; @Brewvival

Started in 2010 by COAST Brewing Company and The Charleston Beer Exchange, Brewvival is one of the southeast's premier beer festivals. So many rare and limited beers are poured at this event that you would think the brewers are trying to outdo one another (and perhaps they are!).

How do COAST and Charleston Beer Exchange get such limited offerings? They pay for them. That might seem like an obvious approach, but many festivals get kegs donated for free. Naturally, a brewery probably won't send their really limited beers in cases like this. But by paying for the best, the folks at Brewvival get to cherry-pick exactly what they want.

It wouldn't be a beer festival without some live music and food, the latter often supplied by area food trucks or bars. This festival attracts some of the region's most die-hard beer geeks, so make sure to purchase your ticket well in advance.

QUEEN CITY BREWERS FESTIVAL

NC Music Factory, 1000 NC Music Factory Blvd., Charlotte, NC 28206; QCBrewFest.com; @QCBrewFest

In its young history, the Queen City Brewers Festival has developed a reputation as an intimate, hyperlocal festival that includes not just Charlotte breweries, but also local artists, restaurants, and bottle shops. Because the event always takes place the day before the NFL's big game, each brewery is encouraged to bring one "super" beer that might be a one-off or more limited option. It is truly a celebration of all that Charlotte's beer scene has to offer. The festival also raises funds each year for its nonprofit partners.

March

BEERTOPIA
1012 Market St., #105, Fort Mill, SC 29708; MyGrapevineOnline.com; @GrapevineWine

Every year, Grapevine Wine hosts the Beertopia festival in its parking lot on the Saturday before St. Patrick's Day weekend. This wine and craft beer bar is in South Carolina but just miles from Charlotte, NC, and the festival's lineup includes breweries from both Carolinas (as well as other regional and national breweries). Homebrewers also attend the festival to pour their beers and compete for top honors.

BRAWLEY'S BLACK & BLUE
The Visulite Theater, 1615 Elizabeth Ave., Charlotte, NC 28204; Visulite.com; @BlackandBlueCLT

Michael Brawley worked as a bartender at The Visulite Theater long before he owned Brawley's Beverage on Park Road. It is fitting, then, that he should return to the venue to host his Brawley's Black & Blue festival every year. The event mostly focuses on NC brewers, who bring their best for one of the Charlotte beer scene's earliest advocates. The vast majority of the beers poured are high gravity, one-offs, and/or barrel-aged. And as the name suggests, most are also dark beers that can be consumed while listening to live bluegrass. Usually only a few hundred tickets are sold, which can be purchased at Brawley's Beverage.

April

HICKORY HOPS
Union Square, Hickory, NC 28601; HickoryHops.com

For over a decade, brewers and beer lovers have flocked to downtown Hickory for Hickory Hops. The large number of Carolina breweries present is reason enough for beer drinkers to attend, and brewers have their own incentive as all attending breweries are invited to enter into the Carolinas Championship of Beer, which announces its winners at the festival (judging takes place weeks earlier). Certified beer judges award gold, silver, and bronze medals in as many as 75 categories, including Best of Show.

WORLD BEER FESTIVAL RALEIGH
Moore Square, 300 S. Blount St., Raleigh, NC 27603; AllAboutBeer.com; @WorldBeerFest

Like its sister events in Columbia and Durham, World Beer Festival Raleigh is put on by *All About Beer* magazine. Local, regional, and national breweries attend this festival in downtown Raleigh. In addition to hundreds of beers available for sampling, the festival also offers attendees the chance to attend classes and seminars about beer. The VIP ticket option grants attendees more limited beers, an exclusive buffet, and access to a private bathroom.

May

CHARLOTTE BREWERS FESTIVAL

The Olde Mecklenburg Brewery, 4150 Yancey Rd., Charlotte, NC 28217; CharlotteBrewersFestival.com; @CLTBrewersFest

The Charlotte Brewers Festival is an event "for the brewers, by the brewers." All of Charlotte's breweries attend the event, and afterward they all split the proceeds. In keeping with the local theme, local food trucks are also parked and ready to serve, and a lineup of bands play throughout the day. With so many breweries now calling the Queen City home, this is the perfect venue to sample Charlotte classics and new favorites alike.

GASTONIA GRIZZLIES BALLPARK BEER FEST

Sims Legion Park, 1001 N. Marietta St., Gastonia, NC 28054; GastoniaGrizzlies.com; @GastoniaGrizz

Just south of Charlotte, the Gastonia Grizzlies play under the lights of Sims Legion Park in a summer collegiate baseball league. Every May, you get to play under those lights, too. The Gastonia Grizzlies Ballpark Beer Fest invites beer lovers out to center field to enjoy a variety of beers from local and national breweries. VIP tickets grant holders early entrance, a food voucher, and access to specialty beers.

NORTH CAROLINA BREWERS & MUSIC FESTIVAL

Rural Hill, 4431 Neck Rd., Huntersville, NC 28078; NCBrewsMusic.com; @NCBrewsMusic

The North Carolina Brewers & Music Festival takes place at Rural Hill, a historic site and nature preserve in Huntersville. The festival features a variety of bands and breweries and lasts virtually the entire day (though the beer tasting portion lasts only a few hours, after which you will have the option to purchase additional beers if you like). Bring a tent or pop-up and plan to camp out at the site's campground afterward if you want to make a weekend of it.

June

BREW BERN BEER FEST

New Bern Riverfront Convention Center, 203 S. Front St., New Bern, NC 28563; BeerArmy .com/BrewBern

Before they opened a bottle shop in New Bern and a brewery in Trenton, the Beer Army was organizing beer festivals to raise awareness for craft beer in the area and funds for a variety of nonprofits. The Brew Bern Beer Fest takes place in the New Bern Riverfront Convention Center, which is located on the Trent River waterfront. Attending the festival are more than 50 breweries, a mix of local and national. Make sure to stop by the Beer Army booth to learn more about how they are growing the craft beer culture in Eastern NC.

September

BREWGRASS FESTIVAL

Martin Luther King Jr. Park, 50 Martin Luther King Jr. Dr., Asheville, NC 28801; BrewgrassFestival.com; @Brewgrass

Asheville is home to some of North Carolina's best-known breweries, and they—along with other breweries across the state and region—come together every year at the highly anticipated Brewgrass Festival. The festival is so popular, in fact, that servers have been known to crash when tickets go on sale online. They are usually easier to come by if you buy them locally in Asheville.

If you get a ticket, you're in for a treat. In the past, the festival has been held in Asheville's Martin Luther King Jr. Park—but look for a new venue starting in 2014. Wherever it will be held, expect some of the state's best breweries to be in attendance, with bluegrass being picked nearby.

CHARLOTTE OKTOBERFEST

NC Music Factory, 1000 NC Music Factory Blvd., Charlotte, NC 28206; CharlotteOktoberfest .com; @CltOktFst

Charlotte's beer scene was quite different when the first Charlotte Oktoberfest was held in 1999. A handful of Charlotte's first wave of craft breweries—including co-organizers from Johnson Beer Co.—called the Queen City home, though most would close their doors a year or two thereafter. Even in Charlotte's dark days, though, beer lovers could always count on Charlotte Oktoberfest to deliver some of the region's best breweries to Charlotte beer lovers.

The Carolina BrewMasters homebrew club has organized the festival since its humble beginnings, and every year they devote a portion of the proceeds to area charities. One of the most unusual aspects of the festival is the hundreds of home-brews, brought from clubs across the Carolinas. The festival is one of the largest in the Southeast, and one of the largest Oktoberfest celebrations in the United States, for that matter. If you want in before everyone else, consider splurging for the VIP ticket.

October

ASHEVILLE OKTOBERFEST
Coxe Avenue, Asheville, NC 28801; AshevilleDowntown.org; @AVLDowntown

Asheville is no stranger to beer festivals, and the Asheville Oktoberfest just continues to gain in popularity year after year. The festival is put on by the Asheville Downtown Association, and it takes place in the city's "south slope" neighborhood. As should be expected, local breweries are heavily represented, but there are usually a couple German offerings, too. A polka band only adds to the feeling that Beer City has turned into Bavaria, if only for a day.

CASKTOBERFEST
1249 Wicker Dr., Raleigh, NC 27604; Casktoberfest.com; @BigBossBeer

Each year, the folks at Big Boss Brewing Company host Casktoberfest to recognize two beer events: Real Ale Week in the United Kingdom, and Oktoberfest in Munich. Those are two very different beer cultures, as is ours here in the United States. As a result, don't expect to find a lot of milds and bitters or festbiers. Instead, most of the casks on hand have been filled not just with beer, but with a range of ingredients. Some are simply dry-hopped, but most are a little more creative—and distinctly American—in their approach to the cask. Take, for example, the cask that was filled with Big Boss Blanco Diablo and Sour Patch Kids. The "Firkin Meister" package gets you a T-shirt, a Casktoberfest mug, two tickets, a food voucher, magnet, bottle opener, and bumper stickers.

LIGHTHOUSE BEER FESTIVAL
3400 Randall Pkwy., Wilmington, NC 28403; LighthouseBeerFestival.com

Lighthouse Beer and Wine, a bottle shop located in Wrightsville Beach, has been organizing the popular Lighthouse Beer Festival since 2001. It has grown with each passing year, attracting more and more breweries and fast becoming one of the best beer events in the area. At the most recent festival, attendees could enjoy more than 300 different beers in the tree-dotted field of a business park. Like many festivals, there is a VIP option that grants the ticket holder earlier entry and access to more limited beers. Each year, a portion of the festival's proceeds benefit The Carousel Center, a nonprofit that assists victims of child abuse throughout southeastern North Carolina. In an effort to make sure everyone goes home safely, the festival organizers also provide free taxi and shuttle service to the greater Wilmington area.

RELEASE THE FUNK SOURFEST

Neighborhood Theater, 511 E. 36th St., Charlotte, NC 28205; SaludBeerShop.com; @SaludNoDa

Salud Beer Shop's founder Jason Glunt is a big fan of sour beers, so much so that in addition to stocking a good selection in his NoDa beer store, he also organized the first Release the Funk SourFest in 2013 (with the help of New Belgium). The festival is a sour beer lover's paradise, with sour, wild, and/or funky beers hailing from all over the globe, and a good portion of them from North Carolina breweries. If you love sour beers, this is one you have to attend.

WORLD BEER FESTIVAL DURHAM

428 Morris St., Durham, NC 27701; AllAboutBeer.com; @WorldBeerFest

The World Beer Festival Durham is held in the Durham Athletic Park, the minor league ballpark made famous thanks to the film *Bull Durham*. Like the park, the festival has some history—it is the longest standing of *All About Beer* magazine's World Beer Festivals, which are also hosted in Raleigh, Columbia, SC, and Cleveland, OH. Like those sister events, the World Beer Festival Durham is a great way to sample hundreds of breweries in a single setting. There are two sessions, and during each attendees also have the chance to attend classes and seminars to learn more about beer. The VIP ticket option gets you more limited beers, a buffet, and access to a private hospitality area and bathroom.

November

BLACK FRIDAY CASK FESTIVAL

Triangle Brewing Company, 918 Pearl St., Durham, NC 27701; TriangleBrewing.com/Black-Friday

The day after Thanksgiving, many Americans—their turkey dinners not yet digested—rise late at night or early in the morning and head to the dark and crowded parking lot of their choice, hoping for a chance to snatch the deal-of-the-day before racing to the big-box behemoth to do it all over again.

If that is not your cup of tea, you might want to instead consider heading out to the Black Friday Cask Festival, which is held annually at the Triangle Brewing Company on the day after Thanksgiving. The festival includes more than 20 casks from NC breweries, most of which have been dry-hopped or filled with other unique ingredients. And you don't even have to get up at the crack of dawn.

HOMEBREW FOR HUNGER

West End Public, 462 W. Franklin St., Chapel Hill, NC 27516; HombrewforHunger.com; @Homebrew4Hunger

Chapel Hill's Homebrew for Hunger festival, presented by Fifth Season Gardening Co., is one of the most unusual and philanthropic beer festivals out there. The festival features beer from local breweries as well as homebrewers, which means attendees get to sample beers they have likely never tried before and may never try again. More importantly, all of the money goes to a local charity. The event sold out in its first two years, so be sure to keep your eye out whether you want to pour your homebrew or simply sample someone else's.

You can read entire collections of books about beer, but nothing will teach you more about it than brewing it yourself. By homebrewing, you learn firsthand the differences between so many varieties of hops, grains, and yeast strains. More importantly, you learn how to manipulate and control these ingredients to produce beer that might even rival some of the beers listed in this very book. Whether you want to get your feet wet with some extract brewing or are looking to make the move to all-grain, the Carolinas are home to several homebrew shops that can help you on your journey.

Homebrew Shops—North Carolina

ALTERNATIVE BEVERAGE (MULTIPLE LOCATIONS)
1500 River Dr., Belmont, NC 28012; (800) 365-2739; Ebrew.com

Alternative Beverage has been supplying Charlotte-area homebrewers with everything they need to brew for decades. They have several locations around Charlotte: the large warehouse in Belmont; the popular Charlotte store on South Boulevard; The Beer and Wine Hobbies, Int'l. in Mooresville; and the Beer and Wine Hobbies, Int'l. in Monroe. At all of these locations, you can find a good selection of prepackaged Brewmasters Select kits, as well as grains, hops, and yeast by themselves. Alternative Beverage keeps a few different starter setups in stock and carries brew kettles and kegging equipment as well.

This homebrew shop hosts a variety of homebrewing events throughout the year, including their Big Brew for National Homebrewing Day every May. That one takes place at the Belmont location, right by the edge of the Catawba River.

AMERICAN BREWMASTER
3021-5 Stoneybrook Dr., Raleigh, NC 27604; (919) 850-0095; AmericanBrewmaster.com

Raleigh's American Brewmaster was established in 1983, when if you wanted a craft beer you likely had to brew it yourself. Homebrewing equipment and ingredients have changed over the last thirty years, but American Brewmaster has kept pace with the industry every step of the way. They carry a wide selection of ingredients, prepackaged recipes, homebrew starter kits, brew kettles, fermenters, and kegging equipment. American Brewmaster carries kits for just about any style of beer, as well as a selection of clone recipes for those interested in trying to replicate popular commercial beers.

ASHEVILLE BREWERS SUPPLY

712 Merrimon Ave., Asheville, NC 28804; (828) 285-0515; AshevilleBrewers.com

Asheville Brewers Supply came to Asheville in 1994, the same year Highland Brewing Company started brewing in the basement of Barley's Taproom. For two decades, they have supplied the residents of Asheville with everything they need to make their own beer. They have a decent line of "Our Own" kits that are perfect for novices, and they also carry a line of malt extracts, grains, hops, and yeast. They are happy to help with recipe suggestions or troubleshooting, and they occasionally host brewing demonstrations on the weekends.

ATLANTIC BREW SUPPLY

3709 Neil St., Raleigh, NC 27607; (919) 400-9087; AtlanticBrewSupply.com

When Kristie and Patrik Nystedt were looking for equipment to start Raleigh Brewing Company, they noticed that most new equipment took many months to procure, and as a result used equipment prices were through the roof. They wanted to be able to supply breweries with new equipment without them having to wait so long, and as a result they opened Atlantic Brew Supply in the same building as their brewery. They cater not just to commercial breweries, but to homebrewers as well. From equipment to ingredients, they really have everything you need, no matter what your experience level with homebrewing. They hold ABS University classes every month, where for just $25 you are walked through the entire brewing process of an extract beer and provided with that extract kit so you can go home and brew it again yourself. The homebrew shop and Raleigh Brewing also host a homebrew competition, Carolina Quarterly Brew Off, four times a year.

BIG DAN'S BREW SHED

602 Hickory Ridge Dr., Ste. 104, Greensboro, NC 27409; (226) 812-3756; BigDansBrewShed.com

The "Big Dan" in question is none other than Dan Morgan, the 2010 Carolinas Master Brewer and Brewer of the Year. In 2011, he opened his Greensboro brew shed, which is stocked with fresh grains, hops, and yeast, as well as everything you need to brew, from starter kits to all-grain setups. He also exchanges out CO2 cylinders and sells parts for kegerators and home draft systems. Dan is happy to share the knowledge he's amassed as an award-winning homebrewer, so feel free to stop in and pick his brain about your next brew.

BULL CITY HOMEBREW

1906 NC Hwy. 54, Ste. 200-B, Durham, NC 27713; (919) 682-0300; BrewmasterStore.com

Bull City Homebrew stocks all the extracts, grains, hops (pellets), fresh yeast, and assorted equipment you need to brew beer. They also have put together their own extract, partial mash and all-grain recipes of certain styles, and they even have a few 1-gallon recipes that can be made easily on the stove.

Bull City Homebrew offers an abbreviated beer brewing class, from brewing to bottling, that takes only 45 minutes. It is a small batch process that essentially cuts out the times usually spent waiting. They also offer more advanced courses for those looking to get into kegging.

In what is sure to gain them the business of all homebrewing parents in the vicinity, Bull City Homebrew keeps a treasure chest full of toys behind the counter. If kids who come in behave well while their parents are shopping, they get to pick something out upon checkout.

THE FERMENTATION STATION

216 Henderson Dr., Jacksonville, NC 28540; (910) 455-7309; Fermentation-Station.com

The Fermentation Station offers a wide variety of malts, hops, and yeast, as well as starter equipment, kettles, kegging equipment, and lots of accessories. They stock over 20 different styles of extract kits and 30 partial mash kits, but are able to order from the full catalog of Brewers Best kits.

FIFTH SEASON–CARRBORO

106 S. Greensboro St., Carrboro, NC 27510; (919) 932-7600; FifthSeasonGardening.com/Homebrew

FIFTH SEASON–RALEIGH

5619 Hillsborough St., Raleigh, NC 27606; (919) 852-4747; FifthSeasonGardening.com/Homebrew

Fifth Season Gardening Company caters not simply to people who enjoy the finer things in life, but to people who enjoy *making* the finer things in life. They sell the supplies and equipment needed to produce your own garden, cheeses, vinegars, wine, and beer. When it comes to the latter, they carry more than 30 types of grains and hops, plus a nice selection of fresh yeast from Wyeast and White Labs. For beginners, they offer prepackaged kits from Brewers Best. They also offer all of the equipment needed to brew beer, from starter kits to larger brew kettles and fermenters.

HOPS & VINES

797 Haywood Rd., Ste. 100, West Asheville, NC 28806; (828) 252-5275; HopsandVines.net

Alex Buerckholtz has won many awards for his homebrews, including a gold medal at the National Homebrews Conference, the largest homebrew competition in the world. He won Highland Brewing's Highland Cup in 2008, and as a result they brewed and bottled his smoked porter. Olde Hickory's popular Death by Hops was fashioned from Alex's winning entry in the 2010 Olde Hickory Pro-Am Brewing Competition. To say he knows a thing or two about homebrewing is an understatement.

Alex's passion led him and his wife, Melissa, to open Hops & Vines in West Asheville, where he carries a great selection of fresh ingredients and homebrewing equipment. He leads several different classes for beginners and experts. As an added bonus, Alex carries over 300 different kinds of beer as well.

NASH STREET HOMEBREW

234 S. Nash St., Hillsborough, NC 27278; (919) 241-4051; NashStHomebrew.com

Nash Street Homebrew is a subsidiary of Mystery Brewing, and the two Hillsborough businesses sit next door to each other on—you guessed it—Nash Street. Here you can find a handful of their own homebrew extract kits with names inspired by the area, like Nash Street Pale Ale and Eno River IPA. The Hillsborough homebrew club often meets at Mystery Brewing, so stay tuned to their Facebook page for meeting announcements.

TRIAD HOMEBREW SUPPLY

105A Guilford College Rd., Greensboro, NC 27409; (336) 294-1550; Homebrew-Supply.com

Since 2004, Triad Homebrew Supply has been a go-to shop for area homebrewers. They stock a variety of ingredients, kits, and equipment. On select Saturdays, they host all-grain homebrewing classes, and it's not uncommon for them to grill brats or burgers in addition to brewing beer. The food's not included with the $25 tuition fee for the class, but they do invite you to make a donation. They will even do their best to open up the store for you if you have a brewing emergency while they are closed—just give them a call first.

WILMINGTON HOMEBREW SUPPLY

4405 Wrightsville Ave., Wilmington, NC 28403; (910) 302-3315; WilmingtonHomebrew .com

Wilmington Homebrew Supply owners John Savard and Michelle Peck carry a wide variety of homebrewing equipment and ingredients. They sell their own house recipe kits for a variety of styles, all of which are made fresh to order. They will mill your grain in the store or sell it unmilled.

Wilmington Homebrew Supply offers a free beer tasting from 4 to 7 p.m. every Friday, as well as a free brewing demonstration at 1:30 p.m. every Saturday. In early 2014, they will be opening a larger homebrew shop and brewery at 824 South Kerr Avenue in Wilmington.

Homebrew Shops—South Carolina

ANDERSON BINE AND VINE
130 N. Main St., Anderson, SC, 29621; (864) 367-0991

Anderson Bine and Vine (abbreviated ABV—get it?) is one of SC's newest homebrew shops. In addition to selling homebrew supplies, ABV is also part bar and part bottle shop. Check their Facebook page for specials and news on events and homebrewing demonstrations.

BET-MAR LIQUID HOBBY SHOP
736 Saint Andrews Rd., Columbia, SC, 29210; (803) 798-2033; LiquidHobby.com

Bet-Mar Liquid Hobby Shop has been in business since 1968, long before the rise in homebrewing or craft beer in general. They sell a couple basic equipment kits, specialty grains, dry and liquid malt extract, dry and liquid yeast, pellet and whole leaf hops, a few prepackaged kits and just about anything else you would need to brew. In addition to their storefront in Columbia, they also have a shop online.

GRAPE & GRAINS
104 Mauldin Rd., Ste. A, Greenville, SC 29605; (864) 940-2938; GrapeandGrains.com

Greenville's Grape & Grains carries all of the ingredients, equipment, and accessories needed to brew beer. As of the time of this writing, they are the only retailer of local wild yeast from SouthYeast Labs in Clemson, SC. They offer homebrewing classes every week and are active with the Upstate Brew Crew. On the Grape & Grains website, you can purchase "recipe deposits" and have your recipe prepared in advance.

GREENVILLE HOP HOUSE
1619 E. North St., Greenville, SC 29607; (864) 621-8179; Facebook.com/GreenvilleHopHouse

"Greenville Hop House" isn't just a cute name—the business is actually located in a house that was built in the 1930s. It is part bottle shop and part homebrew supply shop, so you can get your growler filled and pick up some home-brewing supplies in the same place. Follow them on Facebook to keep up with their brewing demonstrations.

KEG COWBOY
108 E. Main St., Lexington, SC 29072; (803) 520-0404; KegCowboy.com

Just down the road from Lexington's Old Mill Brewpub is Keg Cowboy, part home-brew shop and part bar. They carry an extensive selection of homebrewing ingre-dients as well as equipment, and they also host brewing demonstrations and classes. If they don't have what you are looking for in the store, chances are they can get it—their online store has hundreds of products.

THOMAS CREEK BREWERY
2054 Piedmont Hwy., Greenville, SC 29605; (864) 605-1166; ThomasCreekBeer.com

Thomas Creek Brewery has been around since 1998, long before many of the Greenville-Spartanburg area's homebrew shops opened up. Because they had access to grain, hops, and yeast, homebrewers started asking if they could buy a little here and there. That led to Thomas Creek stocking a full-service homebrew shop, selling not just the ingredients but much of the equipment needed to brew as well. They are committed to their local homebrew community, and happy to help answer questions when they can.

Clone Beer Recipes

WICKED WEED SAISON III—APPALACHIAN SAISON

Since they opened their doors, Wicked Weed has brewed several saisons, with ingredients ranging from nutmeg and apple peel to tamarind. While saisons are a Belgian style, they were often brewed with whatever herbs or other ingredients farmhands had available. For Saison III, Wicked Weed brewed a distinctly southern saison that incorporates honey, sweet potatoes and grits.

OG 1.056   FG 1.005   IBU 21   SRM 13.5

3 pounds Pilsner dry malt extract
3 pounds Golden dry malt extract
2 pounds Riverbend six-row pale malt
0.25 pound CaraPils
0.60 pound Crystal 120
0.25 pound Munich malt
0.65 pound honey
1 pound grilled sweet potatoes
0.25 pound corn grits
0.33 ounce Warrior (pellets, 16.00 %AA), boiled 90 minutes
0.25 ounce Northern Brewer (pellets, 8.00 %AA), boiled 1 minute
0.25 ounce Saaz (whole, 5.00 %AA) boiled 1 minute
Yeast 3724 Belgian Saison yeast

While steeping your specialty grains, add a pound of grilled sweet potatoes that have been well-charred. After this, add the 0.25 pounds of corn grits. Follow the hop schedule as listed above, with Warrior at the 90-minute mark and the Northern Brewer and Saaz hops at the end of the boil. Cool the wort and aerate it before pitching the saison yeast, and ferment at 73–80°F.

COURTESY OF WICKED WEED BREWING IN ASHEVILLE, NC (P. 22)

HIGHLAND GAELIC ALE

There are hundreds of beers brewed in Asheville, but none so iconic and widely distributed as the Highland Gaelic Ale. First brewed in the basement of Barley's Taproom under the name Celtic Ale, this amber ale strikes a nice balance between its caramel malt backbone and piney, earthy hops. This recipe originally appeared in *Brew Your Own* magazine and on www.byo.com, and according to the folks at Highland it is as close as you'll get to brewing Gaelic yourself. It is reused here with permission of the publisher.

OG 1.056 (1.052–1.060)   FG 1.013 (1.010–1.016)   IBU 30-32   SRM 15

1.5 pounds Munich malt (10L)
0.5 pound Crystal (60L)
1 pound Crystal (40L)
0.25 pound Briess Extra Special malt (or substitute Special B)
3.3 pounds light liquid malt extract
2 pounds light dry malt extract
8 AAU Chinook bittering hops (0.75 ounce 12.0 % alpha)
1 teaspoon Irish moss (15 minutes)
2.5 AAU Willamette aroma hops (0.5 ounce 5.0% alpha)
2.9 AAU Cascade aroma hops (0.5 ounce 5.8% alpha)
White Labs WLP001 California Ale or Wyeast 1056 American Ale yeast

Steep the specialty grains in 3 gallons of water at 150°F for 30 minutes. Remove the grain from the wort. Add the liquid malt extract and dry malt extract and bring to a boil. Add Chinook hops and boil for 60 minutes. Add Irish moss for the final 15 minutes of the boil. At the end of the boil, add Willamette and Cascade hops and steep for two minutes. Strain out the hops and add the wort to a sanitary fermenter holding two gallons of cool water. Add more cool water to top off to 5.5 gallons and cool the wort to 64–66°F. Aerate the beer and pitch the yeast.

COURTESY OF *BREW YOUR OWN* MAGAZINE

NODA BREWING JAM SESSION

A shift has occurred in recent years away from some of the high-ABV styles in favor of more sessionable pale ales and IPAs. NoDa Brewing's example of this is Jam Session, a pale ale with an assertive hop profile and just a bit of sweet biscuity malt behind it. The beer proved so popular at the taproom that they started canning it in 2013.

OG 1.052   FG 1.014   IBU 30   SRM 7.4

5.75 pounds light DME
4 ounces Vienna malt
3 ounces CaraMunich malt
2.75 ounces CaraPils malt
1.25 ounces Centennial hops
1.75 ounces Simcoe hops
1.50 ounces Citra hops
White Labs WLP001 California Ale Yeast

Heat 2.5 gallons of water to 160°F and steep the grains in a mesh bag for 30 minutes. Remove the grain and allow the bag to drain. Bring the wort to a boil for 60 minutes, with the following hop schedule: add 0.75 ounce of Centennial at 60 minutes; 1.00 ounce of Simcoe at 10 minutes; 0.50 ounces of Citra at 5 minutes.

Chill your wort to 70°F and oxygenate. Add the wort to your fermenter with the White Labs WLP001 California ale yeast, then top with sanitized water to 5.5 gallons. Top your fermenter with an airlock and allow the beer to ferment at 68°F. When fermentation is complete, rack the beer to secondary and dry hop with 0.50 ounce of Centennial, 0.75 ounce of Simcoe, and 1.0 ounce of Citra.

Allow the beer to sit with the dry hops for 5 days before adding your fining agent of preference (i.e., Polyclar or gelatin).

COURTESY OF NODA BREWING COMPANY IN CHARLOTTE, NC. (P. 113)

THOMAS CREEK RIVER FALLS RED ALE

A 2010 Great American Beer Festival Silver Medal winner, Thomas Creek's River Falls Red Ale is a medium-bodied, extremely smooth Irish-style red ale with an evenly roasted malt character from start to finish. As their flagship, this beer continues to win over the taste buds of craft beer aficionados and novices alike.

OG 1.055   FG 1.013   IBU 24.8   SRM 9.2

> 7.8 pounds 2-Row
> 1.9 pounds C30
> 1.8 pounds Carapils
> 0.23 ounce Fuggles (60 minutes)
> 0.30 ounce Goldings (35 minutes)
> 0.17 ounce Willamette (15 minutes)
> 0.17 ounce Tettnanger (15 minutes)
> 0.32 ounce Goldings (0 minutes)
> Wyeast 1272 American Ale II Yeast

Clean and assemble your mash tun. Add 1 quart of 170°F water for every pound of grain to be mashed. Next, add your crushed grains to the cooler. Gently dough grains in until all grain is covered by water. Place a lid on the mash tun.

After 10 minutes you can check your temperature. You should be between 152–154°F. Replace lid and "mash" for one hour. Start to heat your sparge water at this point. You will need enough 200°F water for your expected final volume.

Slowly drain half a gallon of wort and pour it back on top of your mash. This process is used to clear your wort. Once the wort is clear, it's time to move on to sparging. Sparging is no more than rinsing the sweet wort from the grains in your mash tun. You will want to pour 175°F water over your grains and slowly collect your wort from the spigot at the bottom of your mash tun. This process should take one hour. If this is rushed, your gravity will be low. Take your time.

After you have collected enough wort, it is time to start your boil. Keep in mind you will lose approximately 15 percent of your boil due to evaporation. If you want five gallons of beer, start with six gallons of wort. Add your hops as scheduled in the recipe above.

Chill your wort as quickly as possible. Add your wort to a clean, sanitized fermenter. Aerate your wort aggressively and pitch your yeast.

COURTESY OF THOMAS CREEK BREWERY IN GREENVILLE, SC. (P. 226)

In the Kitchen

For many professional brewers across the Carolinas, the beer they brew is simply an extension of the South's great culinary tradition. Like the best chefs, brewers use fresh and often local ingredients to bring time-honored classics and new creations to life. Beer can be served alongside these dishes to complement or contrast, or it can be used *inside* recipes to enhance the end result in different ways.

In this chapter, you'll find recipes from breweries and brewpubs that use their beers to do just that. If you're near these establishments, grab the beers called for in the recipes and try your own hand at re-creating them. If you don't have access to these beers, do your best to substitute a similar beer in the same style.

Food Recipes

ESB PIMENTO CHEESE SPREAD

It seems everyone has a different take on pimento cheese, that spreadable edible consumed throughout both North and South Carolina alike. Hunter-Gatherer Brewery in Columbia, SC, for example, forgoes the very pimento peppers themselves in favor of sweet Peppadew peppers. The addition of smoked Gouda and Tabasco sauce makes this a more modern take on the classic. At the brewpub, you'll find it spread across pieces of grilled ciabatta bread, a grown-up's grilled cheese if ever there were one. Don't feel limited to bread alone, though, as there are myriad ways to use pimento cheese (try melting it on a fresh-from-the-grill burger if you don't believe me).

YIELDS ABOUT 3 CUPS

> 8 ounces smoked Gouda, skin off
> 8 ounces grated sharp cheddar cheese
> 4 ounces diced Peppadew peppers
> $\frac{1}{2}$ cup Hunter-Gatherer ESB
> 1 teaspoon Tabasco sauce
> 1 clove garlic, minced

Remove the skin from the smoked Gouda and either grate the cheese or cut it into small cubes. Do the same for the cheddar.

Dice the Peppadew peppers into small pieces, and then throw all of the ingredients into a food processor and blend until it has a spreadable consistency.

COURTESY OF KEVIN VARNER, FOUNDER OF HUNTER-GATHERER BREWERY IN COLUMBIA, SC (P. 241)

SHRIMP & GRITS

Shrimp and grits are a classic Southern recipe, and a handful of Carolina brewpubs serve them on their menus. Wilmington's Front Street Brewery prepares theirs with white wine, but you can replace it with their Coastal Kölsch or other beers that are not too hoppy (the bitterness is intensified when used in cooking).

SERVES 2

> 4 slices bacon (cooked and chopped, save the grease)
> 1 cup instant grits
> ½ pound of shrimp (41–50 size recommended)
> ½ white onion, finely diced
> 2 teaspoons blackened seasoning
> 1 teaspoon black pepper
> 1 teaspoon garlic powder
> ¼ cup Coastal Kölsch
> 1½ cups heavy cream
> ¼ cup grated Parmesan cheese
> 1 bunch of green onions

Over medium heat, cook the bacon slices until brown and crisp (about 4 minutes). Transfer the bacon to a paper towel–lined plate to cool, reserving any bacon grease in the skillet. Roughly chop the bacon and set it aside.

Prepare the grits in a small saucepan according to the package instructions (for a richer version, use chicken broth and milk in place of water). Remove the saucepan from the heat and cover it to keep warm.

Add the shrimp, onion, spice mixture, black pepper, and garlic powder to the bacon grease in the skillet and cook over high heat, stirring occasionally, until the shrimp are cooked through (about 2–3 minutes). Transfer the shrimp mixture to a medium bowl, cover, and set aside. Deglaze the pan with the Kölsch and let reduce for 1 minute, taking care to stir and scrape up the flavorful bits from the bottom of the pan.

Add the cream and Parmesan cheese; bring to a boil, and then simmer until the sauce starts to thicken (about 5–6 minutes). Stir occasionally.

Pour the grits into two serving bowls and pour the shrimp and sauce mixture over top of the grits and serve. Sprinkle chopped bacon on top and garnish with chopped green onion.

COURTESY OF FRONT STREET BREWERY, WILMINGTON, N.C. (P. 212)

PEAR & ARUGULA SALAD WITH CANDIED PECANS & STOUT CRANBERRIES

Leave it to the brewers of Sexual Chocolate to actually create a decadent salad. This one is made not with the brewery's highly coveted imperial stout, however, but with their Foothills Stout. The beer's chocolate and coffee characteristics are a perfect match for the cranberries. Candied pecans, sharp blue cheese, and pear wedges are also piled atop a bed of arugula, making for a complex salad full of sweetness.

SERVES 4

> 1 pint Foothills Stout
> ½ cup water
> ½ cup sugar
> 1 pound dried cranberries
> 4 ounces pecan halves
> ¼ cup powdered sugar
> 1 large bunch fresh arugula
> 4 ounces blue cheese crumbles
> 1 Anjou pear

Place beer, water, and sugar into a heavy-bottom pot. Stir until sugar dissolves. Add cranberries. Heat on medium heat, stirring frequently, until cranberries have plumped, about 15 minutes.

In the meantime, preheat oven to 350°F. Place the pecans in a shallow roasting pan and toast them in the oven, checking every few minutes until they are golden brown. Remove the pecans from the oven and toss in a large mixing bowl with powdered sugar. Spread the pecans on a baking sheet to cool.

Divide arugula over four separate salad bowls. Top with blue cheese. Slice the pear into four equal portions and arrange in a fan on top of the blue cheese. Garnish with candied pecans and stout cranberries.

Balsamic Vinaigrette:

YIELD ABOUT 1 CUP

> 2 ounces balsamic vinegar
> 1.5 ounces Dijon mustard
> 1 ounce shallots, minced
> 1 teaspoon dried thyme
> Salt and pepper to taste
> 5.5 ounces oil blend
> $^{1}/_{2}$ teaspoon dried thyme

In a stainless steel bowl, whisk together vinegar, mustard, shallots, thyme, and salt and pepper. Slowly whisk the oil into the vinegar and mustard mixture to form an emulsified dressing.

COURTESY OF SHANE MOORE, EXECUTIVE CHEF AT FOOTHILLS BREWING IN WINSTON-SALEM, NC (P. 94)

SOFT RYE PRETZELS WITH BEER CHEESE SPREAD

Beer and pretzels have long been a popular combination, and this is especially true at Bull City Burger & Brewery in Durham, NC. They make nine orders of these pretzels at a time and bake them throughout the day to keep them fresh and warm, and that's the way these soft, dense, and chewy pretzels are best enjoyed. The addition of rye adds a bit of spiciness to the pretzel dough, which also incorporates a cup of spent brewer's grain. You can save some of your own spent grain if you homebrew, and if not, breweries have plenty of spent grain they're usually happy to share.

This beer cheese spread has some spiciness, too, thanks to horseradish and a touch of cayenne. It can be used as a dip or spread it onto the warm twisted knots. The recipe here has been scaled down to make about 12 to 14 pretzels. While Bull City uses metric measurements, the US measurements are listed below as well.

YIELDS 12–14 PRETZELS

Soft Rye Pretzels:

530 grams (4¼ cups) bread flour
90 grams (¾ cup) rye flour
1 cup spent brewer's grain (barley still moist, but not super wet), packed tightly
15 grams (½ ounce) kosher salt
350 ml (1½ cups) water at 85–90°F
15 grams (½ ounce) granulated sugar
20 grams (2 tablespoons) instant dry yeast
65 grams (4½ tablespoons) melted butter
12 cups water
⅔ cup baking soda (or real lye if you want more authentic color and flavor)
1 egg yolk with 1 tablespoon of water mixed together for an egg wash (optional)
Pretzel salt or sea salt

In a mixing bowl with a dough hook combine the flours, spent grain and salt. In another bowl, combine the water, sugar and yeast. When yeast mixture is foamy, slowly add it to the flour along with the melted butter, with the mixer on slow speed, until it is loosely combined, maybe 20 seconds. Stop the mixer and let the flours hydrate for 20 minutes. After hydration, mix on speed 2 for 1 minute, then speed 1 for 2 minutes, until the dough forms a ball and pulls cleanly from the sides of the bowl. Remove from the bowl and hand knead for 2 minutes. Put into an oiled bowl, cover with a moist towel, and let rise in a warm place until doubled in size (about 90 minutes).

Preheat oven to 400°F. Portion the dough into about 12–14 pieces (this should work out to 65 grams or 2¼ ounces a piece). Roll out each piece into a 20-inch-long rope about the diameter of an adult middle finger. Fold into the pretzel knot shape, press the places of dough intersection together firmly at the twist and the ends. Bring the 12 cups water and baking soda to boil. Slowly lower each pretzel into the boiling water and cook 30–45 seconds each, pushing down and resubmerging with a slotted spoon. Remove from water to a wire rack to drip dry. When all pretzels are boiled, place on a wax papered baking sheet. Bake for 6 minutes. Remove and brush with egg wash, sprinkle with pretzel salt or sea salt. Bake for 6–8 more minutes until dark brown.

Pretzel Beer Cream Cheese Spread:

YIELDS ABOUT 4 CUPS

> 24 ounces cream cheese, room temperature
>
> 3 tablespoons fresh horseradish, drained
>
> 1 tablespoon roasted garlic, minced
>
> 1 tablespoon shallot, minced
>
> 1½ teaspoons cayenne powder
>
> 1½ teaspoons caraway seed, toasted
>
> 1 tablespoon dry yellow mustard powder
>
> 1½ teaspoons kosher salt
>
> 1 tablespoon black pepper
>
> 3 ounces fresh-squeezed lemon juice
>
> 1 tablespoon plus 1 teaspoon granulated white sugar
>
> 6 ounces beer (Bull City recommends an IPA or hoppier beer)
>
> 6 tablespoons chives, chopped

In a mixer with a paddle, beat all of the ingredients except the beer and chives until well mixed and soft. Slowly add in the beer with the mixer on low speed until smooth, then add the chives and beat just until evenly incorporated (stop so as not to beat them up). Use at room temperature or chill for a few hours and the spread will firm up.

COURTESY OF SETH GROSS, FOUNDER OF BULL CITY BURGER & BREWERY IN DURHAM, NC (P. 189)

HEINZELMÄNNCHEN BREWERY GERMAN POTATO SALAD WITH BEER DRESSING

Heinzelmännchen Brewery's slogan is "The Beer Brewed for Food," and to prove it, founders Dieter Kuhn and Sheryl Rudd wrote *Your Gnometown Cookbook: Heinzelmännchen Brewery's Favorite Recipes*. In it are recipes for appetizers, breads, soups, salads, pastas, sauces, marinades, entrees, and desserts. This German potato salad recipe is a classic dish prepared with a beer dressing. Dieter and Sheryl use their Ancient Days Honey Blonde or Gopher Ale for this recipe, but any milder, non-hoppy beers should work well.

SERVES 4

Potato Salad:

2½ pounds of red potatoes
½ cup of finely chopped mild red or yellow onions
¼ cup finely chopped fresh parsley
4–5 strips bacon, cooked and crumbled (optional)
2 tablespoons finely chopped fresh chives

Beer Dressing:

6 tablespoons olive oil, divided
½ cup finely chopped onion
6 ounces (¾ cup) Ancient Days Honey Blonde or Gopher Ale
3 tablespoons malt or cider vinegar
½ teaspoon sugar
1 tablespoon Dijon-style mustard
Salt and pepper

Cook the potatoes in boiling, salted water until a knife point can be easily inserted, about 20–25 minutes. While potatoes are cooking, make the beer dressing.

Heat 2 tablespoons of the olive oil in a small frying pan over medium heat. Add the onions and cook until just soft, about five minutes. Add the beer, vinegar, and sugar, then boil for five minutes.

Put the dressing mixture and mustard into a food processor. With the motor running, very slowly pour in the remaining 4 tablespoons of olive oil. Add salt and pepper to taste.

As soon as you can handle the potatoes, slice them into ¼-inch rounds, leaving unpeeled. While the potatoes are still warm, gently mix them with the onions, parsley, bacon (if using), and beer dressing. Do not overmix or the potatoes may break into pieces. Taste again for salt and pepper.

Garnish with chopped chives. Serve warm or at room temperature.

COURTESY OF DIETER KUHN AND SHERYL RUDD, FOUNDERS OF HEINZELMÄNNCHEN BREWERY IN SYLVA, NC (P. 40)

BROWN SUGAR & SON OF A PEACH SALMON

The complementary flavors of peach and brown sugar come together in this sweet approach to salmon. Serve with vegetables and rice or your choice of side.

SERVES 2

2 salmon fillets
1 cup of RJ Rockers Son of a Peach Ale
1 clove pressed garlic
1 tablespoon packed light brown sugar
1 tablespoon Bad Byron's Butt Rub or other rub
2 tablespoons melted butter

Place salmon skin-side up in a shallow dish and pour a cup of RJ Rockers Son of a Peach Ale over the fillets, letting them marinate for at least an hour. Preheat the oven to 350°F (or, better yet, the grill). Mix together garlic, brown sugar, and Bad Byron's Butt Rub. Remove the salmon from the beer marinade and rub it with the seasoning mixture. Drizzle just a bit of melted butter over the salmon fillets and cook them skin-side down for 10–12 minutes at 350°F.

COURTESY OF RJ ROCKERS BREWING'S JOHN E. BAUKNIGHT IV (P. 224)

Appendix A:

Deviant Dale's, Oskar Blues Brewery–Brevard, American India Pale Ale, 49

DUH!, Starpoint Brewing Company, Double India Pale Ale, 180

The Dweller, Green Man Brewery, Imperial Stout, 8

English Ale, Fortnight Brewing Company, Bitter, 172

English Table Beer, Fonta Flora Brewery, English Mild, 68

The Event Horizon, Olde Hickory Brewery, Imperial Stout, 73

Hidden Pipe Porter, Raleigh Brewing Company, Porter, 143

Hi-yo, Saison!, Sub Noir Brewing Company, Saison, 146

Hop Drop 'n Roll, NoDa Brewing Company, American India Pale Ale, 114

i77 IPA, Four Friends Brewing, India Pale Ale, 110

India Pale Ale, Altamont Brewing Company, India Pale Ale, 3

Iron Rail IPA, Wedge Brewing Company, English India Pale Ale, 15

Jalapeño Pale Ale, Birdsong Brewing Company, Chile Beer, 107

Kaldi Coffee Imperial Stout, Quest Brewing Co., Imperial Stout, 223

King Don's Pumpkin Ale, Catawba Brewing Company, Pumpkin Ale, 66

Leiser's Evening Stout, Hoots Roller Bar & Beer Co., American Stout, 85

Limónhead IPA, Small Batch Beer Company, India Pale Ale, 91

Long Leaf IPA, Appalachian Mountain Brewery, India Pale Ale, 34

Lost My Way IPA, Bombshell Beer Company, India Pale Ale, 164

Mastiff Oatmeal Stout, Railhouse Brewery, Oatmeal Stout, 208

Mecktoberfest, The Olde Mecklenburg Brewery, Märzen, 116

Mexican Cake, Westbrook Brewing Co., Imperial Stout, 262

Milk Stout, The Duck-Rabbit Craft Brewery, Milk Stout, 201

Munich Dunkel, Brevard Brewing Company, Dunkel, 38

New South White Ale, New South Brewing, White Ale, 275

Noon Day IPA, Nantahala Brewing Company, India Pale Ale, 47

Oatmeal Stout, Hosanna Brewing Company, Oatmeal Stout, 176

O'SOO Oyster Stout, Benford Brewing Company, Oyster Stout, 235

Outpost Tea Ale, D9 Brewing Company, Pale Ale, 108

Over the Edge USPA, The Unknown Brewing Company, India Pale Ale, 121

Palisade Wasp IPA, Gizmo Brew Works, American India Pale Ale, 140

Pluff Mud Porter, Holy City Brewing, American Porter, 257

Pontoon Pale Ale, Lake Norman Brewing Company, American Pale Ale, 112

Queen Anne's Revenge, Mystery Brewing Company, Carolinian Dark, 178

Raspberry Jalapeño Stout, Ass Clown Brewing Company, American Stout, 105

Red Oak Amber Lager, Red Oak Brewery, Amber Lager, 89

Rickshaw Rye IPA, Crank Arm Brewing, Rye IPA, 139

Ringmaster Red Rye, Hi-Wire Brewing Company, Rye Beer, 13

Rubber Room Session Ale, Steel String Brewery, American Pale Ale, 182

Scottish Ale, White Street Brewing Company, Scottish Ale, 188

Silent Night, Mother Earth Brewing, Imperial Stout, 203

Son of a Peach, RJ Rockers Brewing Company, Fruit Beer, 225

Tadpole Porter, Frog Level Brewing Company, English Porter, 40

Tea Party Vanilla Bourbon Porter, White Rabbit Brewing Company, Porter, 186

Up All Night Breakfast Porter, Triple C Brewing, Imperial Porter, 119

Upper Falls Double IPA, BearWaters Brewing Company, Double IPA, 36

Vortex I, Pisgah Brewing Company, Double IPA, 51

Warrior Heart IPA, Conquest Brewing Company, India Pale Ale, 238

Westbend Stout, Westbend Brewhouse, Stout, 93

Wilma's Wandering EyePA, Double Barley Brewing, Double IPA, 171

Zingiber Pale Ale, The Frothy Beard Brewing Company, Pale Ale, 255

Appendix B:

Up & Coming Breweries

Breweries are popping up at a record pace in both North and South Carolina. While that is undoubtedly a good thing for beer lovers, it also means that the breweries listed below did not make it into the manuscript. These businesses have secured their locations and are on their way to bringing you more good beer. Most will open shortly after this book is printed, and some may even open between the time this book was sent to the publisher and when it goes to print. I regret that I was not able to include this newest crop of breweries, but hope you will keep your eye out for their opening announcements and visit them once they are open.

North Carolina

Beech Mountain Brewing Company
1007 Beech Mountain Pkwy.
Beech Mountain, NC 28604

Broomtail Craft Brewery
6404 Amsterdam Way, Ste. 100
Wilmington, NC 28405

Catawba Brewing Company–
Asheville
2 Fairview Rd.
Asheville, NC 28803

Flat Top Brewing Company
567 Main St. East
Banner Elk, NC 28604

Flytrap Brewing
319 Walnut St.
Wilmington, NC 28401

Four Saints Brewing Company
218 S. Fayetteville St.
Asheboro, NC 27203

Free Range Brewing
2320 N. Davidson St.
Charlotte, NC 28205

Gibb's Hundred Brewing Company
117 W. Lewis St.
Greensboro, NC 27406

Good Hops Brewing
811 Harper Ave.
Carolina Beach, NC 28428

Haw River Farmhouse Ales
1713 Sax-Beth Church Rd.
Saxapahaw, NC 27340

Lost Province Brewing Company
130 N. Depot St.
Boone, NC 28607

Medieval Brewing Company
479 S. Broad St.
Mooresville, NC 28115

New Belgium
55 Craven St.
Asheville, NC 28806

One Word Brewing
10 Patton Ave.
Asheville, NC 28801

Pig Pounder Brewery
1107 Grecade St.
Greensboro, NC 27408

Ponysaurus Brewing
The Cookery
1101 W. Chapel Hill St.
Durham, NC 27701

Sierra Nevada Brewing Company
111 Westfeldt Rd.
Mills River, NC 28759

Skull Camp Brewing
200 N. Bridge St.
Elkin, NC 28621

Sycamore Brewing
2161 Hawkins St.
Charlotte, NC 28203

Twin Leaf Brewery
144 Coxe Ave.
Asheville, NC 28801

Union Square Brewery
506 Pershing Rd.
Raleigh, NC 27608

Wilmington Brewing Company
824 S. Kerr Ave.
Wilmington, NC 28403

South Carolina

Brewery 85
6 Whitlee Ct.
Greenville, SC 29607

Edmund's Oast
1081 Morrison Dr.
Charleston, SC 29403

River Rat Brewery
1231 Shop Rd.
Columbia, SC 29201

Seminar Brewing
1903 W. Palmetto St.
Florence, SC 29501

Swamp Cabbage Brewing
801 Brookwood Dr.
Columbia, SC 29201

Swamp Rabbit Brewery
26 S. Main St.
Travelers Rest, SC 29690

Tradesman Brewing Company
1639 Tatum St.
Charleston, SC 29412

Wooden Skiff Brewing Company
141 Island Dr. Ste. 16
Hilton Head Island, SC 29926

Index